CORPORAL COMPASSION

CORPORAL COMPASSION

Animal Ethics and Philosophy of Body

RALPH R. ACAMPORA

UNIVERSITY OF PITTSBURGH PRESS

Published by the University of Pittsburgh Press, Pittsburgh, PA 15260

Copyright © 2006, University of Pittsburgh Press

All rights reserved

Manufactured in the United States of America

Printed on acid-free paper

10 9 8 7 6 5 4 3 2 1

Library of Congress Cataloging-in-Publication Data

Acampora, Ralph R., 1965–

  Corporal compassion : animal ethics and philosophy of body / Ralph R. Acampora.

    p. cm.

  Includes bibliographical references and index.

  ISBN 0-8229-4285-2 (cloth : alk. paper)

  1. Animal rights—Philosophy. 2. Animals (Philosophy) 3. Human-animal relationships
—Philosophy. I. Title.

  HV4708.A24 2006

  179'.3—dc22

                              2006008627

Dedicated

to the memory of Czar and Lucifer

and

for the weal of the nameless.

You only have to let the soft animal of your body
love what it loves.

MARY OLIVER (1986)

Its [love's] luminous delight arises from our visceral recognition
of the mutual self-constitution we share with all sentient beings.

MICHAEL STEINBERG (2005)

. . . foregrounding the vital experience of an encounter with another kind of [animal] being leads us to feel what it might mean
to renounce the authority of the reigning [humanist] social order
altogether.

MARCUS BULLOCK (2002)

CONTENTS

ACKNOWLEDGMENTS

The circumstances under which this book finally came together were trying. First and foremost I want to express deepest gratitude to my spouse and colleague, Christa Davis Acampora, without whose substantial support—on all fronts—I could not have carried out the project successfully. My parents, Gaby and Rudy Acampora, also contributed mightily to the family endeavor, which allowed me the frame of time and mind in which to complete the manuscript —and they should be proud not only of the product but of the process as well. Maxwell, my son, was too young to know why he spent so many nights over at his grandparents' house this past spring—but his growth from baby to toddler during that period was (usually) a pleasure for both households to share. I love you all.

Professionally, the stand-out person to whom I wish to extend the greatest kudos is my editor, Kendra Boileau: she solicited, shepherded, encouraged, and facilitated the project from initial interest to final approval. At the University of Pittsburgh Press, the whole staff treated me well; special mention goes to Deborah Meade, who diligently yet delicately helped me to recast many purple passages from deepest indigo into a lighter shade of violet. On campus, at Hofstra University, I would like to thank Warren Frisina for leaving the door unlocked, Bernie Firestone for opening and clearing the way, and Herman Berliner for welcoming me over the threshold.

Intellectually, my work on this book owes much to the congenial counsel of Ken Shapiro and the kindred sensibility of J. M. Coetzee. Knowing there were others working in different parts of the same vineyard fortified a somewhat risky, yet vital, resolve on my part to follow and cultivate an organic development of thinking.

Finally, there are several friends and associates whose varied forms of assistance (noted here in no particular order of priority) are much appreciated: Anne O'Byrne and Elliot Jurist for courage, Eduardo Duarte for solidarity, Jeanie Elford for morale from afar, Lonnie Stevans and Estelle Gellman for attentive advocacy, John Teehan for empathetic concern, Stanislao Pugliese for princely advice, Lou Kern for collegial camaraderie, Tad Krauze for avuncular reassurance, and Mr. Boogles for innocent mirth. Mention should also be made, last but not least, of several students who buoyed my vocational spirits along the way: Chris Price, Kenny Levin-Epstein, Rob Spinelli, Lauren Brown, Sara Gerard, and Russell Wiener (who also composed the index).

To Stella and Matty: your mother was right, after all!

INTRODUCTION

Somaesthetics and Animal Ethics

My aim in this study is to produce a proto-ethical essay on moral experience involving other animate beings.[1] Reflection proceeding along this line of enquiry cannot hope to become discursively crystalline; rigor here comes in the form of prospecting promising routes for further thought, and the report of its results or progress must be measured "topographically," that is in terms of surveying the terrain perspicuously.

Although I do not claim pure originality of insight, I believe that this book cultivates a comparatively novel synthesis of ideas. Most Anglo-American animal ethicists cannot or do and will not engage with the largely European philosophic traditions of phenomenology, existentialism, and hermeneutics; most Continental philosophers do not and/or are unprepared to deal with transhuman morality. My synthesis seeks to bring the two camps into dialogue.[2] In particular, I want to show that, and how, description and interpretation of phenomenal bodiliness is especially relevant to the experiential navigation of an interspecies ethic or ethos.

That "somatological" demonstration is consummated only in the fourth chapter because it has been my abiding conviction throughout research and writing that any morality presupposes axiological assumptions that in turn raise ontological questions. These presuppositions and interrogations have to be treated first; consequently, chapters two on ontology and three on axiology do just that—with respect, of course, to the specific thematic nexus already identified. Chapter five charts the practical engagement of my bodily bioethic in sample contexts (the laboratory and the zoo). The framing chapters, one and six, conduct a methodological literature survey and lay out comparisons and implications.

My concluding thesis is that it is possible to axiologically thematize the ontology of animate modes of bodily being such that it is sensible—on the levels of both conceptual intelligibility and existential attraction—to incorporate other animals into a transhuman form of morality. Why is this conclusion important? Why might professional philosophers, animal advocates, or generally educated and concerned people care about it? The import of my work for contemporary philosophy and culture lies in its emphasis on the specifically somatic core of cross-species moral experience.[3]

Late modernity is a time of valuational ferment, when it has become widely acknowledged that the reigning modernist ethos of humanism presents us with the problematic situation of environmental crisis and bioethical confusion.[4] Consequently, a number of transhuman moral theories have arisen in opposition to the dominant ideology of anthropocentrism. Typically, however, these ethical systems—for example, the animal rights view—tend to "elevate" non-human beings into our still all-too-humanist sphere of moral concern, often by drawing attention to the "higher" (i.e. humanoid) mental capacities of other organisms.[5] By stressing the somaesthetic mediation of proto-ethical "intuition" or deontic deliverance, we can shed residual homocentrism and place our moral reflection behind the truly post-humanist task of reappreciating bodily animacy as such. In this way, we may expand the range of caring regard through the very gesture of recognizing our own vital status as animate zoomorphs.

Does this mean that our criterion of moral standing ought to include all (and only) animals? It is only fair to warn readers who may be prepossessed by this sort of question that this book does not explicitly contain any straight-forward answer, since that kind of concern is not the focus of the study here engaged. Still, from experience and upon reflection, it seems to me that we draw the line of ethical considerability around those beings that are possible "associates" of compassion.[6] Furthermore, I would contend, my discussion enables us to clarify that claim—for it suggests that compassion becomes plausible on the horizon of somatic constitution, that primary moral experience can and does occur with direct reference to connaturally live bodies (as vulnerable or associable existents).[7]

In the following chapters I use a number of special terms repeatedly and distinctly. It will help the reader to be aware of the precise designations I intend, so that confusion or misapprehension will not result. All of the relevant words and concepts have some reference to, or association with, the central notion of body. Generally, I use *body* in the all-inclusive sense meaning "actually or phenomenally physical entity."[8] When speaking abstractly, I sometimes talk of substantive or phenomenal bodily reality as *bodiment*.[9] More specifically, bodily beings may be merely material objects or also live (living/lived) bodies. In the former case and by that status, they are called *corporeal* (*körper-*

lich in German)—examples include rocks and beds. For the latter condition, Anglophonic philosophy—indeed the English language—has no standardly recognized word or even established idea. Half from deference to Husserl's *Zomatologie* and half out of personal preference (not necessarily conforming to philologically proper etymology), I have chosen *somatic* as the applicable term of art here (*leiblich* is a Germanic cousin).

Part of the book's philosophic burden is to articulate just that: the dimension of bodiment experienced through animate being, that is, animality as alive/aware.[10] The phenomenal horizon of somatic awareness is usually centered upon, but not always coincident with, a particular corporeal body. Within that horizon the corporeal body takes on a subjective, ontologic/existential state different—but not divorced—from its objective, epistemic/scientific aspect; by stipulation, I name this state *corporal(ity)*—not *corporeal(ity)*. *Flesh* is shorn of the reductively erotic and edible connotations that make it the corporeal object of consumptive desire. *Flesh* shows two semantic sides: *carnal* may pertain to corporal boundary—felt most intensively at some surface level (e.g., skin or cornea), but sometimes including relative recesses (veins, e.g., even viscera); or it may pertain to somatic expanse that extends beyond the bounds of corporality—for instance, as in or with Merleau-Ponty's matrix of perceptibility, "flesh-of-the-world." If this lexicon appears to indulge terminology overmuch, the reader would be well advised to heed another contemporary body-thinker's warning that, because "corporeality is inherently difficult to discuss," any worthwhile treatment must "unsettle familiar distinctions and stretch our conceptual vocabulary."[11] *Somaesthetics*, for example, used in the title to this introduction, can refer either to bodily feelings per se or to the discipline that studies them. *Ethos*, as I use it in chapter four's subtitle, indicates a broader, more cultural conception of morality than the strict, narrow sense of discursive system conveyed by 'ethics' as a purely theoretical term.[12]

CORPORAL COMPASSION

ONE

Interspecies Ethics and Phenomenology of Body
Precursors and Pathways

Sometimes we think / that we humans can live / without them, / but we are wrong.

JOSEPH BRUHAC (1992)

THE GUIDING QUESTION of this study is: How can we sensibly describe, explain, and interpret transhuman morality? Note that I did not say justify. That is because I rather doubt that transhuman morality can be justified. This will strike many animal ethicists and advocates, as well as most moral philosophers, as a nonstarter position. However, I am not trying to indicate some special deficiency of so-called animal ethics against more traditional forms of purely human morality. Indeed, I do not see that any form of normative ethics has ever been justified in the classical, hard-core sense of truly objective legitimacy. Though surprising, even shocking to some, this stance is not unprecedented. In adopting it, I tend to agree with such contemporary critics of moralism as John Caputo and Richard Garner.[1]

I am not denying that humans have evolved, naturally and culturally, various practices and discourses that might rightly be called "moral" or "ethical." I do believe, however, that such classifications run the risk of misleading the incautious, because they commonly imply a tone of objective normativity that I want to deny or at least hold in abeyance. A rough analogy with the distinction between science and scientism may help illuminate what I take to be the difference between modest morality and haughty moralism. Just as one may practice and/or defend certain more or less well-established methods of scientific investigation without necessarily adopting the scientistic position that science is the ultimate metaphysical or ontological arbiter of the "really real," so I wish to acknowledge the existence of certain more or less well-established modes of moral or ethical valuing without endorsing any moralistic pretense of metaphysical justification for or axiological objectivity of those modes.[2]

I am not going to rehearse in detail the defenses of metaethical skepticism mounted by Caputo and Garner. I find the skeptical arguments and reflections of these authors compelling,[3] and I am as yet unaware of any convincing refutations of their outlooks. The basic idea they espouse is that there is nothing else "backing up" or "undergirding" our systems of morality other than essentially contingent forces of natural evolution and/or cultural convention (what Husserl would call "lifeworld" and Wittgenstein "form of life").[4] There does not appear to be any metaphysical guarantor of our values—neither the divine dictates of God, nor the transcendental presuppositions of pure or practical reason, nor some putatively foundational normativity threaded into the fabric of the universe. In other words, we can always ask the question *why?* of any given attempt to ground a moral prescription or judgment in some principle of alleged necessity—and such efforts at justification have historically resulted in infinite (or indefinite) regresses that are simply abandoned, or circular argumentation (whether unwitting or mischievous), or an arbitrary terminus. A late-modern example of the last tactic is G. E. Moore's intuitionism, the essentially occult nature of which has led many (including myself) to reject it as a mystification of the conventional.[5]

Rather than impaling myself on any of this trilemma's horns (infinity, circularity, or sheer finality), I prefer to get off the train of thought that seeks necessity in the first place. It does not seem—ultimately—that any of our values "must" be or "had" to be as they in fact are, have come to be, or might become over the course of future evolution or cultural development. This viewpoint, though, does not give up the whole project of moral philosophy and its ancillary pursuit of ethical critique. In the practical zone of applied ethics at least, the relatively ordinary yet potent standards of consistency and coherence can serve as a critical fulcrum sufficient to dislodge ideological construction. Consider, for example, that in animal ethics great mileage has been gotten by exposing speciesism with analogies to racism and/or sexism.[6] We need not get embroiled in metaphysical controversies surrounding intrinsic value or inherent worth to recognize that there is much in our culture's treatment of other species that is wildly out of reflective equilibrium with our denunciations of racial and sexual prejudice.

Moreover, some of the most historically influential moral thinking has occurred in the mode of prophetic illumination or edification rather than in the vein of analytical argumentation or foundational deduction. What made Martin Luther King Jr. both effective and memorable was that he had a dream, not a proof. I am not saying that King's discourse was all heat and no light. The visionary language of metaphor he and others have drawn upon can light up a moral phenomenon where none had previously been seen (or had been obscured for too long). This poetic function of ethics is no less a part of philosophy than is logical discourse. Like Mark Johnson, we can "view moral deliberation as expansive, imaginative inquiry into possibilities for enhancing the quality of our communally shared experience."[7]

Even in the absence of grand projects of grounding our moral values, we are not reduced simply to compiling a catalog of descriptive ethics. There is still room for articulating, contextualizing, comparing, organizing, and clarifying moral systems, as well as showing their internal relationships (of constitutive concepts, principles, metaphors) and external implications (for practice or inquiry). Let us call such programs of moral philosophizing explanative or interpretive ethics—something less presumptuous than objectively normative ethics, yet more discursively systematic than an ethnographic recording of various moral beliefs and practices.

How might this sort of approach redound upon the issue of interspecies ethics? It would be helpful to consider the context out of which reflections on the ethical consideration of animals (human and nonhuman) occur. The major terms of debate are generally organized around whether nonhuman animals should be included in the realm(s) of moral consideration already staked out for human animals. The burden of proof lies at the feet of those arguing for inclusion.

Over many years of discussion and reflection concerning the nature of transhuman morality, I have noticed a pronounced and repeated rhetorical feature in exchanges with interlocutors (an aspect, in fact, even of the interior dialogue philosophers notoriously conduct within themselves). The set-up starts out like this: what justifies inclusion of other animals in the ethical sphere—what, in other words, gives them moral standing or considerability? Then the inquiry or debate proceeds to look for and contest certain morally relevant properties as candidates to fit the bill, for example: having a higher intelligence such that they are at least minimally rationally competent (and thus approach a kind of autonomy); having something like a will and thus deserving of credit and blame, etc.; or being sentient and thus capable of feeling pleasure and pain. Because of a prevalent psychocentric bias in favor of mentality's moral significance, this move typically mobilizes investigations into and applications of philosophy of mind or comparative psychology.[8] Despite the best efforts of many animal ethologists and ethicists, however, there persists—at least amongst philosophers and scientists (less so in the public at large)—widespread resistance to or reservations about attributions of morally robust mentality to members of most, if not all, other species. In a conversation that impacted me, one philosopher objected that we just don't get enough "traction" for such attributions to legitimate them.[9] Here, "traction" refers to that which could serve as a basis of comparison for claiming that animals are sufficiently like us in a way that is morally relevant. Animals are obviously like us in many ways, but the issue at hand is usually framed as one that asserts or challenges similarity in the specific characteristics upon which human moral worth is measured. Those seeking to support a case for inclusion, then, have at least two challenges: they must identify the characteristic(s) that make human animals worthy of moral consideration (about which there is certainly not unanimous agreement), and they must then show that nonhuman animals, or some particular members of that set, have the requisite characteristic(s). Thus, assuming a certain (and special) kind of separation already exists, the interspecies ethical theorist must bridge the gulf to and from other creatures.

My approach suggests that this way of framing the issue has the experienced phenomena and the ethical problem entirely backwards. We do not, either as a matter of firsthand experience or of now fairly well-established fact, initially find ourselves as discrete objects whose original problem is to figure out how to connect with the world. We are not in some abstract, retro-Cartesian position of species solipsism where our minds seem to just float in a rarified space of pure spectatorship apart from all ecological enmeshment and social connection with other organisms and persons, wondering, as it were, if "there's anybody out there." That is a portrait borne not of philosophic rigor but of psychological malady or hyperintellectual pretense (or both). Where we begin, quite on the contrary, is always already caught up in the experience of being a live body thoroughly involved in a plethora of ecological and social interrelationships with other living bodies and people. That, I hold, is our native position, and it deserves—existentially, phenomenologically, and indeed (as I shall later argue) scientifically—to be recognized as such and consequently to be taken as our philosophic starting point.[10] The ethical upshot of such a gestalt-shift in the ontological background is profound, because it effectively transfers the burden of proof from what has been denigrated as ethical "extensionism" or expansion[11] to, instead, what we should rightly refer to as ethical isolationism or contraction (i.e., homo-exclusive anthropocentrism). From this perspective, the problem of traction for moral consideration of nonhuman animals dissolves, because the moral motion at stake is no longer felt to be a pull (into the ethical sphere) but is reconceived as a push (out of or away from it). It is the movement toward dissociation and nonaffiliation that needs to be justified against a background of relatedness and interconnectivity.[12] Put another way, it is relinquishment or disavowal of our aboriginally constituted bodily being with others, or our "somatic sociability," if you will, that would require defense. The goal of this book, then, is to describe, explain, and interpret the constitution and interspecific implications of such somatic sociability —and leave it to the anthropocentrists to justify, if they can, why we ought to renounce, give up, or let go of that primordial experience.

It is the fact that we have or, rather, are animate bodies—bodies that are experienced and come to be known through interaction with other animate bodies—that I will take as primary. I emphasize one route into the investigation of the ontology of animate modes of body as applicable to humans and at least some other nonhuman animals alike. Certain historical and methodological orientations lend themselves quite readily to this inquiry. I take what I consider to be a late-modern rather than a postmodern approach insofar as I rely upon a number of nineteenth- and twentieth-century figures of classical Continental philosophy rather than more recent or contemporary figures usually identified as postmodernist or poststructuralist. My approach is chiefly phenomenological, drawing heavily on existential philosophy and hermeneutics.

A brief comment on Nietzsche's relevance is appropriate from the start, since Nietzsche sent up the battle cry for philosophical investigation and appreciation of the body, and so greatly influenced significant strands of twentieth-

(and now twenty-first) century philosophy of the body and reflection on human animality. David Michael Levin goes so far as to claim that "Nietzsche is really the first philosopher since the beginning of the Judeo-Christian influence to espouse the human body in its truth, its beauty, and its goodness," and, indeed, Nietzsche prefigures a veritable corporeal turn taken of late by much intellectual inquiry.[13] Seen in nineteenth-century context, Nietzsche was an avant-garde sniper, waging lonesome guerrilla warfare against those traditionalists he dubbed "the despisers of the body."[14] Toward and during the middle of the twentieth century, admirers of the body began to join forces and mount a positive program for philosophy of *bodiment*—a term that deliberately resists the inner/outer distinction that abides in the more familiar term of 'embodiment.' Reflective research projects for studying the lived ontology of the body-phenomenon had early practitioners in vitalist Henri Bergson and religious existentialist Gabriel Marcel and a vigorous exponent in psychological phenomenologist Maurice Merleau-Ponty. But it was Jean-Paul Sartre who truly brought the body to the center of philosophical inquiry with his meditations on sadomasochistic sexuality.[15]

The theoretical point of Sartre's treatment of sexual attraction and manipulation was to dramatically highlight a generic thesis about (human) bodiment —namely, that there is a radical, ontological rupture between the *body-for-me* (qua conscious subject) and the *body-as-other* (qua perceptual/practical object).[16] To further explore my main query, I have found it necessary to depart from this central claim of Sartrean somatology. Values are not items or ideas (furniture of the world or mind), but rather field-phenomena: they arise within and are made up out of relationships between certain entities. Since I favor an axiological context of (constitutive or internal) relations, any ethic of bodiment that would do justice to such an axiology would have to bridge the very gap between bodies that Sartre believes to be an impassable gulf.[17] More precisely, an ethic of bodiment would have to deny Sartre's dualistic divide in the first place. I think that, with the assistance of Merleau-Ponty, this move is possible—and, saving philosophic priority, I think it is also preferable as a matter of ontology.

Before moving on to Merleau-Ponty, however, it is helpful to consider Martin Heidegger's influence on the enquiry at hand. The homo-exclusivist anti-vitalism of *Being and Time*'s project of fundamental ontology is stimulating but ultimately limiting insofar as it exerts an arresting gravitational pull on those phenomenologists who would move beyond Sartre's false dilemma of bodily being into a zone of "transpecific intersomaticity" in the spirit of Merleau-Ponty. Despite Heidegger's admirable effort to give priority to being-in-the-world, the ontology of *Being and Time* is too coarse and its *Daseins-analyse* is still too disembodied. We shall also consider relevant elaborations furnished by Heidegger in his 1929–1930 lecture course on the foundations of metaphysics. Still, as Jacques Derrida points out, the early Heidegger's onto-logical framework remains fairly ill-equipped to deal with animality.[18]

Three modes of being are significantly discussed in Heidegger's earlier writings: being-there (*Dasein*), readiness-to-hand (*Zuhandensein*), and presence-at-hand (*Vorhandensein*). How shall we regard the animal, given this division? Strictly speaking, unless an organism is ontologically oriented—that is, unless the organism *cares*, in the special sense that Heidegger gives to that term, about the question of the meaning of being—it cannot be (or be called) properly *Dasein*. In other words, a being that lacks such care about being does not exist in the special way that Heidegger appears to think that human beings do. A fundamental characteristic of the kind of being attributed to human beings, that is to *Dasein*, is that their primordial experience as being-in-the-world is the condition for the possibility of all other experience. But if that is so, then all (or certainly most) nonhuman animals must be deemed either ready-to-hand or present-at-hand. Yet surely these designations do not exhaustively ac-count for the existential being of many (if not most or all) other animals.[19] Natural familiarity with animals who share the same perceptual sphere or scale with humans, what Paul Shepard calls "phenomenological fauna,"[20] is sufficiently convincing that other forms of life are not merely tools-to-use or objects-of-study (or contemplation). It would, indeed, be quite strange if we decided that in terms of their ontological status, animals could be properly heaped alongside hammers and minerals. As Czech philosopher Erazim Kohak remarks, apropos of existentialist ontology (glossing Sartre, but with relevance to Heidegger as well): "Only from a very great conceptual distance could one mistake a porcupine for a boulder and lump them both together under the common label of *l'être-en-soi* [being-in-itself]."[21]

Nonhuman animality suffers this ontological reduction if we follow Heidegger in disembodying the living worldhood of *Dasein*. In fact, the disap-pearance of *human* being's animal nature is likewise the result of this tendency in the *Daseinsanalyse*, the phenomenological investigation of how being there

(*Dasein*) occurs. In this analysis Heidegger places great emphasis on time—particularly insofar as the prospective death of *Dasein*, which it can anticipate and ultimately dwell upon as its ultimate possibility, serves as that in which all other possibilities can appear in relief and thereby acquire their significance. The kind of end that death appears to represent for Heidegger is a decidedly temporal one—our "finitude" indicates the limit of our duration. The possibility of "death as mine" does not bring forward, in Heidegger's analysis, the fleshy vulnerability that live bodies experience in each moment. This move forces him to diminish interpretation of the dimension in which embodiment has purchase (i.e., space).

Heidegger certainly considers the significance of spatial relations in the worldhood of *Dasein*—the very name of the entity under discussion emphasizes its having what we might call *em-placement*, that is, it is always already located somewhere. This is a significant advance over philosophical stances that characterized the modern period in which disembodied thinking subjects bedeviled the philosopher trying to figure out how such an entity could "inhabit" a body and then "connect" with the world. In my own effort to shift the burden of proof off the inclusion of nonhuman animals in the moral sphere, I am to some extent reenacting, in a crude form, a philosophical turn that Heidegger takes with regard to the mind-body problem. For Heidegger, there is no problem of explaining how a discrete mental (or spiritual) substance interacts with a discrete and separate physical substance, because the supposed separation is overcome in the analysis of the pre-reflective condition of being-in-the-world —which we might also say, albeit problematically, is being-(in)-a-body. However, the immersion in a world that provides the condition for the possibility of ethical relations (in Heidegger's terms, being-with, or *Mitsein*) appears predicated on the anticipation of *Dasein*'s end or temporal finitude. While other animals clearly take actions to avoid mortal danger, it is not clear how many (if any) can sufficiently anticipate something akin to taking death "as their own," as a possibility that ends all possibilities (which is what Heidegger considers to be the case for *Dasein*). Yet it is precisely this interpretive or hermeneutic possibility of "death as mine" that supplies the basis for *Dasein* to forge relations (including ethical ones). Thus Heidegger's ontological framework provides fewer opportunities for the vitality of organic animate being to emerge for serious consideration.

The possibilities that are available to *Dasein* emerge and acquire their significance precisely because of the fundamental way in which *Dasein* can "stand out," or achieve a kind of ecstasis, in its realization and contemplation of its ultimate possibility of death—and it is this feature of Heidegger's analysis that ultimately pushes his work toward even greater dissociation from the body than his predecessors. As Didier Franck puts it rather starkly, "The ecstatic determination of man's essence implies the total exclusion of his live animality, and never in the history of metaphysics has the Being of man been so profoundly disincarnated [as it is in Heidegger's thought]."[22] Even when Heidegger seems to become aware of this problem, he only reinforces the fact that his interest is exclusively human when he insists that "the human body is something essentially other than an animal organism."[23] Thus we are left largely alien to other animals, and little understanding of our incarnate interrelationships with them is allowed.[24]

I suspect that this sundering of the human-animal nexus may actually be intended by Heidegger himself. Only a couple of years after publishing *Being and Time,* he taught a course at the University of Freiburg in which he lectured precisely on the phenomenology of animality.[25] Here Heidegger treats the question of animal constitution in much greater detail than the mere hints he supplies elsewhere in his corpus. Yet, despite the care with which he addresses the question, the ultimate result further betrays, rather than transcends, the life-philosophical limitations of *Being and Time*'s *Daseinsanalyse.* The very approach Heidegger undertakes is dubious, inasmuch as his stated concern is with "finding out what constitutes the *essence of the animality* of the animal."[26] Such essentialism is likely to conceal much more than it could reveal, for it tends to enshroud the existential manifold of animal be(com)ings in a conceptual abstraction—assigning and consigning them, that is, to a generic philosopheme of "animality." (Jacques Derrida characterizes the term "animality" as "an immense group, a single and fundamentally homogeneous set that one has [presumed] the right, the theoretical or philosophical right, to distinguish and mark as opposite" to humanity.[27]) But an essence of this sort does not appear to exist in reality. In cannot be the basis of phenomenological investigation; there are no generic animals roaming the earth, and pure/perfect "animalness" as such can be conjured in Plato's heaven only by speculation. Consequently, I concur with Derrida's excoriation of the concept when he declares that "this agreement concerning philosophical sense and common sense that allows one to speak blithely of the Animal in the general singular is perhaps one of the greatest and most symptomatic idiocies of those who call themselves human" (or *Dasein,* I would add).[28]

While it is heartening to see Heidegger seriously engage the issue of animal worldhood, the categories he chooses to frame the discussion are worrisome. The clearest example of terminological liability is his description of animal world as "poor," and it will strike all but the most charitable audience as disingenuous of him to insist that such "poverty" does not imply or at least suggest "hierarchical assessment" or "evaluative ranking."[29] In claiming that "every animal and every species of animal as such is just as perfect and complete as any other," Heidegger appears to be echoing Nietzsche's revaluation of animal difference in *The Anti-Christ(ian):* "man is absolutely not the crown of creation: every creature stands beside him at the same stage of perfection."[30] However, it becomes hard to take Heidegger at his word on this score when he goes on to characterize animal being as essentially a condition of "deprivation."[31] Hard, but perhaps not impossible: in subsequent chapters I will have recourse to and critical elaboration of some useful insights as well as some inadequate notions that Heidegger unfolds in the course of these lectures. At this point, it suffices to note that *The Fundamental Concepts of Metaphysics* does not constitute in its basic outlines a readily serviceable framework for articulating and interpreting primordial experiences of sharing lifeworld with other species. My appraisal in this respect is not unique. Commenting on the discourse at issue, for instance, Michel Haar has observed that "the aim seems to be an exorcism, a demystification of the 'link' with nature"—indeed it appears that "Heidegger wants . . . to destroy the idea of an *animal lineage*" altogether.[32] These moves away from evolutionary theory, however, invite an older mystification of humanity under the imagery of divine descent. It may be that, in spite of his desire to deconstruct the Occident's ontotheological tradition, Heidegger rebinds his thought within the confines of that tradition's anthropocentrism. In this light, Heidegger partakes in a counter-Darwinian tendency that seems to run through much of the hermeneutic movement—an inclination toward what Hans Albert calls "excision of the human realm from the natural world," and which he criticizes for being "rooted in [the] socio-cosmic thought of the unique status of man in nature—an idea of predominantly theological significance."[33]

Returning more specifically to the issue of Heidegger's metaphysical antipathy for animalic genealogy, even a sympathetic reader such as David Farrell Krell is forced to acknowledge in Heidegger a kind of retro-religious backsliding—namely, that "when Heidegger tries to separate Dasein from the animal, or to dig an abyss of essence between them, he causes the whole of his [phenomeno-hermeneutic] project to collapse back into the congealed categories and oblivious decisions of ontotheology."[34]

Beyond exegetical questions regarding the internal consistency of Heideggerian discourse (in its critique of ontotheology), the more relevant issue is whether philosophy rightly ignores or excludes humanity's animal aspects and associations in its traditional preference for the supposedly divine dimensions of human existence. Nietzsche's Zarathustra endeavors to recast such associations when he famously claims, "Man is a rope, tied between beast and overman —a rope over an abyss."[35] Such an image suggests connection, perhaps even interpenetration, between humankind's animalistic and superhuman capacities.[36] Krell tries to resurrect the notion of bestial divinity as he attempts to walk a neo-Nietzschean tightrope over the abyss that Heidegger digs between *Dasein* and the living (as such).[37] What Krell calls "daimon life" (the physical pulsion of vital energy) is supposed to imbue Heidegger's phenomenological hermeneutics with organic drive. Thus we see one of the foremost contemporary Continental scholars advocating a more subtle reappropriation of "the quest for the essence of animality and of life in emphatic disclosure." Doing Heideggerian violence to the etymology of the ancient Greek *zoon,* Krell denominates this search *za-ology* in order to show that the enquiry he engages "is neither altogether independent of the science of zoology, nor simply a part of it."

Although Krell does not reach the goal of this quest, his work provides clues that could serve as a catalyst for the continuance of (animal) life-philosophical inquiry. For example, one could take up the concept of daimon life precisely in order to graft life into the notion of *Da-sein* so as to furnish "za-ological" interpretation with the working concept of "*living*-in-the-world" instead of Heidegger's reorientation of inquiry on the focus of "*being*-in-the-world." Certainly, the liveliness of such a conception would be an improvement (over regular Heideggerian discourse). Still, the proposed replacement of 'da' with 'za' is objectionable in that it nevertheless would maintain, if the Heideggerian focus of analysis otherwise remains intact, a monological version of worldhood (whereby world is always only thought as a universal). And this would too readily lend itself to a variety of hegemonic interpretive approaches that draw upon further exclusionary ideologies—as when speciesism, ethnocentrism, and the like insist that "the" human or "the" white world(view) constitutes or describes "the" totality of "the" universe as such or at large. Agnes

Heller reminds us that our (human) being is not existentially life-in-*the*-world but rather—more modestly and tolerantly—life-in-*a*-world.[38] To be human might very well be, at least in part, to have a world—or even, as per Heidegger, to emerge phenomenologically "in-*the*-world"—but it might very well be that other varieties of world organization are available to different kinds of sapient or sentient being *and* that some beings just might have the possibilities of "world-traveling" to some extent.

We who would undertake ontologically transpecific inquiries would do better to begin our study from some form of "being-in-*a*-world."[39] A caveat is in order for those reading with Ockham's razor ready-to-hand: loosening the circumscription and uniformity of worldhood risks proliferation of worlds beyond necessity. For example, Heller eventually slides into egological worlding as she concludes: "there are as many wor[l]ds as persons: a world is subjective."[40] Despite being dubious—even, that is, if it fails to supply compelling evidence for personalistic subjectivism—her evidence remains intriguing. Heller appeals to Wittgenstein's observation (in the *Tractatus*) that a happy man's world is "entirely different" from that of an unhappy man. Perhaps this remark is too extreme. Yet, although affective differentiation may not radically *fragment* worldliness, it may nonetheless place worldhood on a *continuum* and broaden that spectrum's constituency.[41] Such an approach, at any rate, affords at least the possibility for considering the different ways different species reveal their worlds.

To gain ontological access to the varied life-modes of different animals, one must enter environments not wholly of human making. This means beginning without making the assumption that there is just one world, permitting the possibility of other *Umwelten*—foreign, yet potentially familiar, forms of worldhood. Indeed, starting out this way may itself contribute to the revelation (or even constitution) of other animal worlds. Approaching others as if they are capable of relating or being related to us, in other words, can help enable the cultivation of that very relationship.[42] It may be instructive to reconsider why it is that this sort of move does not come to full fruition within a strictly Heideggerian horizon. One factor is the emphatically temporal nature of the *Daseinsanalyse*. But what is it about temporality that is so world-retentive that its overemphasis would obscure otherwise evident worldliness from the manifold environment(s) of other organisms?

The history of philosophy provides us with a good illustration in the system of Kant, for whom time-without-space would spell implosion of interiority away from the outer world as such. For Kant, although time is a form of both internal and external intuition, its "expansion" into the outer world requires the formal intuition of space to lend exteriority to phenomenal experience. Without spatiality, a Kantian time-keeper would be left dwelling upon its own temporality, suspecting that being *is* time, becoming full of angst as it fretfully counted and contemplated the disembodied moments of its denatured existence. To readers of *Being and Time,* this scenario should sound familiar. If Heidegger is operating against the background of Kantian temporality, then his emphasis on time and diminishment of (or at least comparative inattention to) space leaves *Dasein* dreadfully disincarnated and deanimalized, unable to understand any *Umwelt* qua world. Although an "ek-statically" worlding entity, *Dasein* "stands out" into a world largely bereft of breathing beings; it stands *apart* from most environmental conditioning. *Dasein* knows little of any living *oikos.*[43] Kantian time-without-space is a recipe for the transcendental unity of apperception's self-enclosure;[44] Heidegger's *Dasein* tends toward a twilight zone of time alone, which establishes its "ownmost possibility" as a wholly individualized being-unto-death.[45]

Linking Kantian and Heideggerian philosophy in this way can be justified as a heuristic device—for it leads one to reflect on how the false person/thing dichotomy of Kantian ontology, though mutated by Heidegger, is essentially replicated in Heidegger's own ontological researches. Certainly the notion of *Dasein* is meant to get beyond or behind such metapsychological concepts as personhood and consciousness; likewise, Kantian "thinghood" is dismantled into Heideggerian "handiness" of the present and ready varieties. Several commentators have noted that *Dasein* is a primordially "handed" being. Accordingly, and expanding from this observation, some have seen in Heidegger's work a salvageable philosophy of body. While there is (barely) enough textual testimony to permit such a rereading, hermeneutically the overall enterprise strikes me more as reconstruction than as rescue.[46] All the phenomenal variety of nonhuman and immature life, neither fully *Dasein*-people nor (merely) "handy" things, must either be mangled ontologically to fit into misshapen categories, or else be retired from ontological discourse (and thus have its philosophic treatment aborted). In recognizing this impasse, I am indebted to the work of Mary Midgley, both for the person/thing characterization of Kantian ontology and for highlighting the artificial alienation inherent to the anthropic, adults-only lifescape conjured by much existentialism.[47] The former ontology coupled with the latter "community" pretty well precludes the development of an inclusive moral conscience. Kids, not to mention kittens, must fall by the ethical wayside of *Dasein*—an ontological loner whom we cannot easily imagine will be much worried about ontically humane or ecological matters.[48]

What is the upshot of these critical observations regarding the Heideggerian difficulties in dealing with the phenomena of bodiment and animality? Simply this—that we ought to accept Didier Franck's seemingly severe conclusion: "*Dasein* institutes the abyss that separates it from the animal . . . . It is therefore necessary to cease to determine the essence of [the hu]man as *Dasein* if due consideration is to be given to its incarnation and to its life."[49] Despite his attempt to break with the ontotheological metaphysics of Western philosophy, Heidegger retains a core tenet of that tradition, namely, belief in the absolute uniqueness of humanity.[50] Maintenance of this belief in our post-Darwinian context is possible only through an antiscientific predilection toward a priori methods that involves dismissal of the most reliable knowledge currently available from empirically based enquiries such as evolutionary biology and ecology. Conversely, as Franck phrases it, "only the relegation of ontological difference can render our bodily animality thinkable."[51]

Having sacrificed Sartre's dichotomy between the subjectively conscious body-for-me and the practically or perceptually objectified body-as-other, and having also surrendered Heidegger's homo-exclusive *Daseinsanalyse,* where are we now? In return for abandoning these two strongholds of traditional phenomenology, we gain entry into a possible *Lebenswelt,* configured as the zone of shared and interactively sensed "live bodiment." In what follows, I shall suggest that we look more toward Merleau-Ponty as a guide to such a zone. In the spirit of Nietzsche's call to remain faithful to the earth, Merleau-Ponty advises: "There is a kinship between the being of the earth and that of my body (*Leib*). . . . This kinship extends to others, who appear to me as other bodies, to animals whom I understand as variants of my embodiment."[52] A central part of my project aims to show that this kinship is a more promising setting within which to work out philosophically satisfying and empirically responsible bioethical views.

How, more precisely, are we to understand this sort of kinship? Merleau-Ponty makes somewhat sketchy references to Portmann's ideas of *Tiergestalt* and "interanimality."[53] Is there anything in the corpus of Merleau-Ponty's own work that might provide a philosophic context for thematically elucidating such notions? In his early work, there is a kind of "vital order" acknowledged in *The*

Structure of Behavior. Gary Madison has claimed that, "it must be said that [for Merleau-Ponty] animal behavior has a meaning (*sens*)."[54] But, as Madison himself recognizes, one may wonder whether Merleau-Ponty believes animal behavior is meaningful *to* us (humans only) or also *for* the animal itself. Merleau-Ponty apparently opts for the former, certainly against the latter— without implying thereby a dichotomous collapse of animality into the Sartrean alternative of inert stuff. Denying that the nonhuman organism is an entity cognizant of self-realizing complexity does not entail reducing it to mere thinghood: "it is a whole which is significant for a[n external?] consciousness which knows it, not a thing which rests in-itself (*en soi*)."[55] Still, not much importance is accorded animality, and, at least at that stage of his career, it can be said with good reason that Merleau-Ponty's philosophy centered on a decidedly human perspective.[56]

But once Merleau-Ponty introduces the notion of *flesh* in his later work, he begins to talk of carnal chiasm and sensate intertwining (e.g., the felt nexus of touching and being-touched simultaneously, noticeable within oneself). Indeed, he seems to hint at cross-species carnality when he rhetorically asks, "Why would not the synergy [of perceptive reversibility] exist among different organisms, if it is possible within each?"[57] Satisfied that such synergy is not solipsistic in scope, Merleau-Ponty concludes that "there is finally a propagation of these [intersomatic] exchanges to all the bodies of the same type and of the same style which I see and touch." Upon closer inspection, however, these statements do not carry any necessarily transpecific implications. The token/type distinction of linguistic analysis may be of use here. Clearly Merleau-Ponty's reference to intersomatic exchanges among *all* bodies deals with intersubjectivity as it is experienced across a *type* of organism; his question about possible perceptive reversibility among different organisms is most plausibly interpreted as treating synergistic similarity between different *token* organisms (within a given type). In other words, one can become aware of the nexus of active/receptive sensation (only) within oneself and as regards members of the same species. Using this interpretation, it would seem that the subtextual domain of discourse—what is implicitly written *about*—is here entirely *intra*typical to the species *Homo sapiens*. That is to say, in writings published during his lifetime, Merleau-Ponty's thought remains leashed to anthropocentrism.

Although he was tantalizingly ecological in his last years of lecturing, Merleau-Ponty met an untimely death before he could flesh out the transpecific somatology toward which he gestures.[58] Following Merleau-Ponty's penchant for probing ever more deeply into the density of Husserl's philosophy, it might be supposed that we should mine phenomenology's historical source for further guidance. Husserl does grant somatology ("the science of animate organicity") a significant liminal niche between properly material and spiritual studies.[59] Methodologically, somatology's "foundation is finally the direct *somatic perception* that every empirical investigator can effect only on his own body and the somatic interpretation that he performs in the interpretive apprehension of perceived alien animate organisms as such." Following this special study, we are afforded three salient insights (building successively): (1) acknowledgment that "in experience, in the sphere of original constitution . . . also [besides material objects] originally given are *zoa*";[60] (2) interpretation of these "animalia as primally present [living] bodies with appresented interiority"; and (3) recognition that "human animate organism . . . is with regard to essence a particularization of animate organism generally."[61] Here, however, the transpecific ontology comes to a halt. Husserl's inquiry instead proceeds along its customary egological horizon and returns to its preoccupation insofar as it remains fixed on human psychic phenomena.[62] Such egology's fatal philosophic flaw (and the ground of Husserl's residual anthropocentrism) is the mistake of positing solipsistic experience as phenomenologically *originary* when in actuality it appears always only *abstracted* from the more basic *Mitwelt* of "mixed community."[63]

Elsewhere in Husserl's published reflections on the theme of intersubjectivity, he reveals a welcome yet ambiguous and abortive awareness of animality. Although his text is comprehensive enough to take notice of other organisms, it runs the risk of degrading them conceptually and, in any case, fails to develop the philosophic significance of their being: "Among the problems of abnormality the problems of non-human animality and that of the levels of the "higher and lower" brutes are included. Relative to the brute, man is, constitutionally speaking, the normal case. . . . Brutes are essentially constituted for me as abnormal "variants" of my humanness, even though among them in turns normality and abnormality may be differentiated. . . All of that, to be sure, needs a more thorough phenomenological explication."[64]

Approaching the animal kingdom thus, "man" does not roam across an existentially enriching realm of related otherness but rather wanders down a hallway of mirrors, bombarded by isolating images of deviant similitude.[65] At least this is the conclusion one might draw when exercising hermeneutic suspicion (in the vein of Foucault), for in such a case one sees that Husserl appears to take normalizing thought (which sets up a standard in light of which "the other" is known) as bound to categoric demotion of difference (abnormal variance implicitly occupying an position of inferiority).

Parenthetically, it should be noted that more charitable perspectives are possible, and those intent on doing exegesis of Husserl's work have made admirable strides toward such an end. For example, the concepts of normality and abnormality in Husserl, one might argue, do not set up a violent devaluatory dualism but rather engage a mildly tolerant pluralism.[66] Still, however we construe this distinction, it seems to me that Husserl's thought remains resistant to thematizing interspecificity, and since I am less interested in strictly or solely providing an analysis of Husserl's work than I am in borrowing genuinely helpful insights and approaches, I am reluctant to strain the texts under consideration to make them suit my objectives. Where I encounter resistance of the sort I find in Husserl and in Heidegger (and later in Levinas), I am content to move on and to look elsewhere.[67]

To Husserl's credit, he is struggling against an ideological heritage of anthropocentrism—witness the subtlety of his designation ("*non-human* animality"), the trepidation of his punctuation ("higher and lower"), and finally his admission of deficiency in articulation (de facto, albeit, thematic abortion).[68] Yet Husserl has not quite managed to overcome that repressive heritage; his philosophy remains solipsistic within a sphere of human concern, developing an ontology that is decidedly and specifically human.

Since the father of phenomenology, then, is unlikely to furnish us with an interspecific somatology of animal being and value, it would appear best to take whatever cues we can from Merleau-Ponty. In his early work, *The Structure of Behavior,* the vital order of being is patterned by styles of worldly orientation or address.[69] This concept of existential theme or style stays with him into the late lectures on nature, where he describes its somatic mediation: "The body belongs to a dynamic of behavior. Behavior is sunk into corporeity. The organism does not exist as a thing endowed with absolute properties, as fragments of Cartesian space. An organism is a fluctuation around norms, which are events enframed by a structure that would not be realized in another order, but has relations with these events."[70]

Now Merleau-Ponty allows that there can be an existentially intercorporeal zone between live bodies "of the same type and of the same style." The notion of existential equivalence implicitly invoked here is best interpreted as

Merleau-Ponty

a spectral concept of phenomenal resemblance. 'Sameness' is not precisely syn-onymous with 'identity'. (If it were, we would not employ such phrases as 'ex-actly the same' or 'selfsame.') The concept of sameness designates a relational fit not necessarily as absolutely "tight" as identity. So, as a matter of somewhat charitable interpretation, Merleau-Ponty cannot coherently mean "same type" and "same style" in the strictest sense of identity—for, textually, the philo-sophical mileage required of the intercorporeal zone is (at least) the overcom-ing or undermining of solipsism. If the text's most plausible meaning calls for "same" to be rendered as "strongly similar" (more loosely, i.e., than "literally identical"), then it is permissible for *degrees* of similarity associated with the relevant sameness to become an issue.

By the end of his life, Merleau-Ponty was set to abandon residual anthro-pocentrism inherited from Husserl: "precisely what has to be done is to show that philosophy can no longer think according to this cleavage: God, man, creatures"; the new focus of interest for him was "description of the [hu]man-animal *intertwining*."[71] Hence, the issue of cross-species exchange of somatic sensibilities related to material bodies can be explored with these cues from Merleau-Ponty as starters. How is it that some species' bodily modes of ad-dress to their world are similar enough to others' to allow and account for an overlay of what we might call *intersomaticity*, a characteristic of animate expe-rience in which felt senses of bodiment are shared and potentially in dynamic relation? Answering such a question would elucidate an animal ethos that is close to lived experience. It is the chief task of the rest of this book to pursue this question and trace its implications.

A helpful answer to the sort of question I am asking comes into focus against the background of an ontology of organisms as such.[72] What exists most inclusively is "Being," though this manner of speaking is too abstract and requires a more determinate formulation. Depending on whether one takes a universal or planetary point of view, the whole of existence can be conceived either cosmocentrically or ecocentrically. Among all beings that exist, some have the special mode of existence that we call *life*. A necessary and sufficient con-dition of life is the possession of worldhood—that is, having a self-generated perspective (in scientific parlance, "autopoietic orientation") on being-at-large. This condition points to a biocentric definition of the phenomenological concept of world—a definition that significantly broadens the interpretation of "world" beyond its original meaning in the work of phenomenologists and hermeneuts such as Husserl, Heidegger, and Gadamer (for whom world or *Welt* is, for the most part, coextensive with humanity only).[73]

One kind of minimal worldhood occurs within the horizon of plant life. For example, consider the sunflower's display of diurnal vectorality. The sunflower can be said to dwell in its surroundings, since it has an environment (or *Umwelt*) in a living, orientational sense unavailable to inorganic things such as stones.[74] There is an intensification of worldhood in an animal's mode of living. Kenneth Shapiro identifies this worldhood as habitat, in the sense of incorporating one's environmental niche through an active awareness.[75] One especially illustrative example of this zoöcentric conception of ontologically constitutive habitat is *territoriality,* whereby an animal ranges within its territory so intimately that it is no longer just spatially *in* or *on* the land but rather becomes a conscious part *of* it.[76] With the self-consciousness of human beings, a robustly cultural world emerges. Humans, in ways that are more complex than those of any other animal, can change and symbolize their environments and habitats by relocating and redefining them and themselves. Cultural processes take two directions: one whereby we inhabit someplace with ever-intensifying degrees of domestication, and another whereby we "dehabit" our usual domicile via various ecstatic techniques.[77] Certain aesthetic or ritual practices could serve as examples of these techniques, such as Native American vision quests, Buddhist meditation trances, psychoactive drug trips, and perhaps even Mardi Gras carnivals. The positive functions of this cultural modality are: (1) to encourage exploration of other non/human lifeworlds, and (2) to continually revitalize our own cultural home by transgressing and reshaping its boundaries.

It is important to realize that this hermeneutic phenomenology of biotic worldhood demonstrates an important multispecies linkage. The types of worldliness considered—environmental dwelling, conscious habitation, cultural domesticity—all revolve around some sort of residential relation to being-at-large. Different species have an appropriate scale or spectrum of worldly address style that can be used to intelligibly discuss (at least the hypothesis of) what I shall call *transpecific* intersomaticity. To strictly satisfy Merleau-Ponty's criterion of somatological evidence, one would have to show a similarity of worldliness sufficiently strong to qualify the comparable modes as being of "the *same* style."[78] What needs to be concretely investigated, then, is whether this theoretical possibility of transpecific worldhood actually receives phenomenological grounding in some existentially significant experience of intersomaticity. In more precise terms, the question can be framed: Would well-attuned familiarity with flesh put us in touch with a living fellowship of ontological residency? Or, to ask this more poetically: Can our bodies nourish biosophic neighborliness with other organisms?[79] In attempting answers to such questions, it would be wise to heed Carleton Dallery's advice. "Ironically," he remarks, "the[ir] rightful ontological place is the one they [all animals] already have in perception—though in an alienated, abstract society one has to look to children, painters, poets, 'primitives', and other exceptional people to find thought and practice based on concrete perception."[80] Following Dallery, one may become attracted to ethnophilosophy (of historically submerged or "uncivilized" oral traditions) and away from the ever-sedimenting exegesis of European texts. Consider, for example, the words of Austral-Aboriginal ("primitive") storyteller Bill Neidjie:

> Eagle there!/ e make you "oh" . . . and how you feel yourself/ how your
> body. . . .
> I feel it . . . my body same as you. . . . no-matter what sort of a animal,
> bird or snake . . . all that animal same like us. Our friend that.[81]

Neidjie gives perceptive witness to a bodily co-presencing (or *Mitsein*) between human, and among all, animals.[82]

Western philosophy's readiness to "go native," however, is limited. It remains important to tap multiple springs of thought, particularly those historically sidelined by the mainstream heritage.[83] In that spirit I refer to two figures from natural philosophy in the twentieth century. The first is the little-known and underappreciated philosophical biologist Jakob von Uexküll. Courageously speculative, Uexküll resisted the contemporary surge of mechanico-behavioral reductionism; he created, instead, an imaginative yet empirical somatology of animal worldhood:

> We who still hold that our sense organs serve our perceptions, and our
> motor organs our actions, see in animals as well not only the mechanical
> structure, but also the operator, who is built into their organs, as we are
> into our bodies. *We no longer regard animals as mere machines, but as sub-*
> *jects whose essential activity consists of perceiving and acting. We thus unlock*
> *the gates that lead to other realms,* for all that a subject perceives becomes

his perceptual world and all that he does, his effector world. Perceptual and effector worlds together form a closed unit, the *Umwelt. These different worlds*, which *are as manifold as the animals themselves*, present to all nature lovers new lands of such wealth and beauty that a walk through them is well worthwhile.[84]

Here Uexküll issues a veritable declaration of phenomenological independence from the entire Cartesian tradition of automated animality (and its by-product, ghost-in-the-machine humanity).[85]

Consider also the work of Frederik Buytendijk, a phenomenologist who worked on philosophical anthropology in the context of comparative psychology. He held: "if one views without prejudice the structure . . . of the relation between an animal and its surroundings as it manifests itself to us, then this relation can only be described by . . . defin[ing] the animal organism as a subject *whose* life we understand insofar as it demonstrates a relationship with our own life."[86] Certainly, such a position sounds favorable to inquiry concerning transpecific interanimality. Curiously, however, Buytendijk goes on to commit himself to the doctrine of (corporeal) human uniqueness: "*The human body*, because of its cultural and social ties with personal-mental existence . . . *is absolutely different from the animal body*."[87]

Showing how profoundly this textual paradox plays itself out is instructive. If human and (nonhuman) animal bodies are "absolutely different," then there can hardly emerge any significant cross-species relationship at all. But then we would be utterly unable to understand other animal life (except perhaps by weak analogies)—since, as Buytendijk conceives it, nonhuman animality is intelligible only to the extent that it displays exactly the sort of relationship that has just been excluded. Yet Buytendijk makes positive claims about how to sensibly (even cognitively) interpret animal being. He states: "the animal organism shows in [its] behavior . . . that it *exists*—even if only in its species-typical way—and that the behavior is perceived by us as belonging to a *subject*." Moreover, he further maintains: "the animal organism as meaning-giving existence manifests itself as a subject that occupies a position with respect to [its] surroundings which is evoked by the meaning of things." Finally, he allows: "we can understand the animal as a 'body-subject', and consequently as a 'knowing-body', as a way of being, ensouled by *its* world and ensouling it."[88] All these unqualified claims are idle (or tenuous at best)—if our own mode of bodiment

Buytendijk

is radically distinct from other animals', and if understanding alien animality is limited to (presumably corporeal or somatic) relations therewith. Thus does Buytendijk's text become self-inconsistent as it endeavors to pay due attention to the lifeworlds of other animals while also maintaining homo-exclusivity of outlook.[89]

Maintenance of anthropocentrism here appears suspiciously dogmatic. Ultimately, the conviction behind the scenes of belief in absolute human uniqueness is the dogma of a radical conceptual split between nature and culture. Many recent critics, however, believe that the nature/culture dichotomy is an article of humanistic faith no longer tenable in the context of contemporary liberal arts and sciences.[90] Avoiding what I take to be the (inconsistent) anthropocentrism of Buytendijk's otherwise admirable and subtle stance, and thereby clearing the way for explanation of my basic thesis, I am inclined to agree with Carol Bigwood when she argues: "the way life articulates itself has as much to do with the response of other nonhuman beings, with the currents of the earthly and skyly environment, and with temporal contingencies, as it does with our subjectivist cultural wills. The crux of the matter, then, as I see it, is to 'renaturalize' the body, truly releasing it from a dichotomized nature and culture. We need to work out a new "natural-cultural" model of the body that goes beyond both the fixed, biological body and the poststructuralist culturally inscribed body."[91] Bigwood nicely maps the task before us—avoiding the false methodological dilemma of an old-fashioned, naively scientific, or romantic return to pristine nature versus a new-fangled, overly abstracted cultural decoding of hypertextualized embodiment.[92]

Interpreting the phenomenon of transpecific intersomaticity in the company of Bigwood's Merleau-Pontyan sense of place, I will construct an ontology of body via the phenomeno-hermeneutic route of making manifest and rendering thematic the fleshly vitality of animate beings. I will use phenomenology of body to supplant the standard recourse to philosophy of mind that animal ethicists have usually thought it necessary to rely upon when arguing for interspecies morality. Of course, this makes it sound as if we can maintain the old Cartesian dualism and retreat from affairs of mentality to turn our attention onto matters of bodiment. But a simple inversion (or reversion) of principles that preserves the original dichotomy would neither do justice to the phenomena at hand nor be very helpful to the transhuman ethics I eventually want to explain. Since somatic phenomena present a field of experience always already intertwined as conscious materiality, I will refer to the work of body-oriented psychologists and cognitive theorists when it comes time to analyze such modes of awareness.[93] Because our consideration of somatology is motivated by an overarching concern with animal relation(ship)s, I will also return to an engagement with and more extended criticism of Heidegger's reflections on animality in *Fundamental Concepts of Metaphysics*. All these ontological preparations will provide some mooring for subsequent axiological researches.

I will articulate values pertaining to the flesh of animate life, some of which are instrumental or extrinsic, and others of which are subjectively or socially intrinsic or inherent (i.e., a person or culture values *x* for its own sake, not as a means to anything else). Consistent with the amoralist metaethic outlined at the start of this chapter, I do not think any of these values are wholly objective (i.e., none are entirely intrinsic to or inherent in the object of value itself). Instead, I challenge the dichotomy of subjectivism and objectivism in axiology and outline a relational account of valuation that is pragmatically process-oriented rather than property-based. As a historical illustration of bodily/zootic values, and because it sets the stage for so much of more recent and contemporary somatology in general, Nietzsche's revaluation of the body and animality is examined at some length, as well.

At that juncture, I will be in a better position to set forth and explain the somaesthetic nature of the phenomena that generate animal ethics. In the spirit of Luce Irigaray's testimonial on her experiences with other animals, I want "to bear witness through relating" and through the explication of cross-species relationships.[94] I will join the company of those thinkers who see compassion rather than rationality at the root of interspecies morality,[95] but suggest a novel explanation for this idea. Behind or beneath the imaginative means of empathy usually appealed to, I will show that cross-species compassion is mediated by somatic experiences that I will denominate *symphysis* (to emphasize its corporal component and to distinguish it from sympathy[96]). In relating morality primarily to compassion, I stand in a philosophic tradition of some repute (e.g., Hume, Schopenhauer, and Schweitzer to name a few) with the support of much contemporary child psychology and primate ethology.[97] In relating moral compassion to corporal provenance and propagation, I move out of mainstream intellectual traditions (at least of the West).[98] Finally, in relating corporal compassion to interspecies ethics, I may be pioneering (and consequently, more susceptible to encounter stumbling blocks).

Flesh-and-Blood Being-in-a-World

Toward a Transpecific Ontology of Somatic Society

All ethical theories or statements regarding the moral significance of
animals are explicitly or implicitly grounded in an ontological assessment of the animal's way of being.

HUB ZWART (1997)

WHAT IS IT LIKE to be a bat? Thomas Nagel's famous question is the critical fulcrum of his now classic article against physicalistic reductionism in
philosophical psychology.[1] In the course of his argument—aimed at demonstrating that it is impossible for reductively materialistic theory to provide a
phenomenology of conscious subjectivity—Nagel claims that the phenomenon of "mind" (quite close to, though not exactly coextensive with, what I
have been calling "world") is widespread throughout the animal realm. About
animate individuals, including many nonhuman ones, he is prepared to say
that "there is something that it is like to *be* that organism—something it is
like *for* the organism." One may believe that the singular experiential viewpoint of another, especially nonhuman, individual is unyielding to description
and hence unintelligible. But Nagel counters, "The fact that we cannot expect
ever to accommodate in our language a detailed description of [e.g.] bat phenomenology should not lead us to dismiss as meaningless the claim that bats
. . . have experiences fully comparable in richness of detail to our own." Still,

understanding transpecific phenomenology—what it is like to be a bat, for example—"may be permanently denied to us by the limits of our [human] nature."

Nagel's agnostic warning on this point is not absolute—he allows two possible avenues of inquiry: (1) a "degree of partial understanding [of alien subjectivity] may still be available" by "transcend[ing] inter-species barriers with the aid of the imagination"; (2) an "objective phenomenology not dependent on empathy or the imagination" may forge new concepts applicable across species boundaries. Paul Taylor has furnished an example of the first route. He argues that if we shed the stereotypes imposed by human purposes, and adopt the unique existential standpoint of another (nonhuman) organism, then:

> [O]ur consciousness of the life of an individual organism is characterized by both objectivity and wholeness of vision; we have reached the most complete realization, cognitively and imaginatively, of *what it is like to be that particular individual.* We have let the reality of another's life enter the world of our own consciousness. We know it as fully and intensely as it can be known.[2]

Of course, the question raised by this position is: just how fully can another organism's lifeworld be known thus? For instance, Yi-Fu Tuan replies radically in the negative:

> The uniqueness of the human perspective should be evident when we pause to ask how the human reality must differ from that of other animals. Contrary to appearances, a person cannot enter imaginatively into the life of his dog: canine sense organs diverge too far from our own for us to leap into the dog's world of smells, sounds, and sights.[3]

Because he shares such pessimism about the imaginative mode of cognition, Nagel lays open the second option: the development of an "objective phenomenology." What that would amount to is left unclear by Nagel; therefore, I shall creatively take up Nagel's phenomenological challenge and see where it might lead.

It is important to realize the exact nature of the task. We want to understand more about another animal's worldhood (waiving its *a priori* preclusion, for the sake of inquiry). In order to accomplish this, there is no need to conduct fanciful thought-experiments or to attempt supernatural exercises in identity-shifting. One does not have to actually become somebody else to be familiar with that other.[4] Further, it is not necessary even to know precisely what it is like (hypothetically, in thought) to be that other subject-of-a-life *in its own right*.[5] For our present purposes, it will suffice "merely" to arrive at some comprehension of what it means to *be-with* other individuals of different yet related species, because that experience of "being-with" gives us all the mileage we need for tracking cross-species community.[6] Hence our mission is to articulate a transpecific form of a fundamental characteristic of experience, namely what Heidegger calls *Mitsein*. More specifically, what we seek is familiarity with cross-species "conviviality,"[7] a shared experience of interactivity. Indeed, as Michael Steinberg notes, "we can understand what animals do— including animals like ourselves—only as a continuing transformative interaction with each other and the world."[8] While "what it is like" to have such experiences might differ among the participants, consideration of such experiences at least provides a shared point of reference, one that potentially provides for there being at least some points of overlap in the varying phenomenal experiences of those involved.

It is instructive to return to Heidegger's lecture course of 1929–1930 for clues both about what to do and what not to do in pursuing this investigation. Helpfully, he reminds us: "In our existence as a whole we comport ourselves toward animals . . . in such a way that we are already aware of being transposed in a certain sense—in such a way that a certain ability to go along with the beings concerned is already an unquestioned possibility for us from the start."[9] If we want philosophy to be faithful to experience, then, it is important not to alienate ourselves from the actual lifeworld we share with others. It is not necessary, from the start, to figure out how we could possibly share experiences with other animals. They are part of the community of others populating the world in which we find ourselves already immersed. Being in the world with others is one of the major ways in which our experience is structured. It partially organizes what it means to have an experience at all. Only under highly contrived methods of contemplation, following Descartes' *Meditations* for example, does one entertain the possibility that she lives in a social and ecological space of humanoid zombies and organic automata. Alasdair MacIntyre echoes this point: "Interpretative knowledge of others derives from and is inseparable from involvement with others, and the possibility of Cartesian doubt about the thoughts and feelings of others can arise only for those deprived of such involvement either by some grave psychological defect, or, as in the case of Descartes, by the power of some philosophical theory."[10] Our regular behavior and interactions assume, for their very intelligibility and efficacy, what we might call the *worlding* reality of other lives in whose midst we act and are ourselves constituted. Put succinctly, "To be *someone* is necessarily to be *with other someones*."[11] It is important not to deflate this essentially hermeneutic capability by qualifying it, for example, as noncognitive, because, as MacIntyre explains: "It is a form of practical knowledge, a knowing how to interpret, that arises from those complex social interactions with others in which our responses to others and their responses to our responses generate a recognition by them and by us of what thoughts and feelings it is to which each is responding."[12] MacIntyre goes on to acknowledge the animal parameters of such interactivity; and, in a salutary moment of cross-species sensibility, Heidegger anticipates this kind of admission in his comments about being able to "go along with" animal others.

Heidegger frustrates a project such as ours, however, when he claims that the existentially constitutive possibility of transposition he admitted is not genuinely actualized for other animals. This is the case, according to Heidegger, because nonhuman animals are "deprived" of world—and that is so because "we must say that world . . . implies . . . the accessibility of beings *as such*" and other animals lack this kind of accessibility. "When we consider the dog itself," Heidegger asks rhetorically, "does it comport itself toward the table as table, toward the stairs as stairs?"[13] What Heidegger is asking is whether the dog, and, by extension, other-than-human-animals generally, have recourse to the same interpretive possibilities that humans do. He presumes a negative answer, which is problematic on either of two plausible interpretations of the query. Treating *x*-as-*x* can mean behaving toward it in such a way that its cultural signification is understood and honored. While most wild animals do not do this, some do (in their own protocultural social groupings); further, most, if not all, domestic animals are capable of this (in the context of shared forms of life with humans; for example, domestic animals comport themselves toward certain containers of material and liquid as feeding and drinking vessels, certain surfaces as places for sleeping and lounging, etc.). MacIntyre has also criticized Heidegger on this score: "The thesis that nonhuman animals lack the as-structure is compelling in the case of moths, crabs, lizards, and the like. But it is much more open to question, when we consider dogs, chimpanzees, go-rillas, dolphins, and a number of others."[14] On another rendering, treating x-as-x can mean thinking through x's identity and/or reflecting on x's place as a being among other beings (or against the background of Being at large). But this would be too narrow a delimitation and tends in the direction of exclud-ing worldhood from all but those whom we might call ontologicians. It seems to me that Heidegger here is captivated by the philosopher's prejudice of in-sisting that another being must approach the world metaphysically or onto-logically in order to exist in it (at all).

If we drop this unwarranted restriction, then new possibilities open. Con-sider the example mentioned by Heidegger himself, a companion animal on the household staircase. Suppose that certain items have been left on the sides of the first few stairs (a signal to the next one who ascends to take with them some of the stuff-in-waiting, or at least avoid stepping on any of it). I am not the only housekeeper who has had a cat or a dog who successfully maneuvers through this sort of situation. Cats will normally take care not to climb the staircase in spots occupied by things-to-be-brought-up, stepping only in the empty spaces of each stair; some well-trained dogs will even bring one or more things upstairs (if such items can withstand teeth and slobber). Many interpretations might be offered of this scenario, but I think the one that does most justice to the habits and dispositions of those who share the home to-gether is to read what is going on as a certain kind of orientation toward, or attunement to, the contextual function of the items-in-waiting. The cat or dog senses, in Heidegger's terms, that those items are not neutral objects or merely present-at-hand, but are rather ready-to-hand (or to-mouth, as the case may be) and are either not to be messed with or else to be picked up and moved in proper fashion (including time/direction/destination . . .). The nonhuman animal, I am suggesting, is aware of the object(s) *as* something with a certain *status or meaning* in the running of the household—it is not just there before the animal, registering as it were mechanically in some blank field of undiffer-entiated spatial perception. Further, anybody who can thus negotiate a shared setting is *ipso facto* a worlded and worlding entity—regardless of whether they can attain the abstraction of knowing beings as such. In other words, sensi-tivity to metaphoric "*as*-ness" (even without ontologic "*such*-ness") suffices to mark somebody as being-in-a-world—and some/many other animals are thus attuned.

Next, it is necessary to consider what dimension of reality is to be explored in the search for transpecific conviviality. Typically, phenomenologies of intersubjectivity are not what they claim to be; more accurately, they are limited to the humanistic and intellectualistic level of interpersonal mentality.[15] Beyond and against this crypto-anthropocentrism, in keeping with the focal thread of my study, I will instead pursue the matter on the level of bodiment, via the phenomenology of comportment that issues from having a body at all. Since it will not be constricted to a homo-exclusive horizon, my intersomatic domain of description should be broad enough to allow—at least in principle—for some measure of cross-species congress, or glimpse of shared experiences with other animals.

Does this manner of proceeding dictate the abandonment of references to mind or mental attribution? To a certain extent, it may appear so—but my approach need not entail an absolute rejection or bracketing of mentality. It does require a redefinition of consciousness away from dualistic purity (ontically distinct, essentially private, hidden or mysterious) and toward embodied and enactive conceptions of experience. Such conceptions are gaining ground amongst contemporary psychologists. Discussing "other minds" in terms of artificial analogies or theoretical inferences is less than satisfactory lately: "For we do not merely infer, or theorize, about the minds of others;" as one team of researchers puts it, "rather their mental experiences are 'something we are obliged to engage, to tread through, to handle, and to live by.'"[16] Moreover, "far from being exclusively abstract, propositional and linguistic," mentality is coming to be seen as "fundamentally based on sensory-motor experience."[17] The upshot for studies such as mine is encouraging: "Seeing thought as structured by bodily experience puts our task to understand nonhuman subjective experience on a sounder footing since we share much of our basic bodily awareness with other species."[18] Despite differences in some sensory modalities, members of various species retain enough somatic commonality to make sense of one another.

As we try to constructively interpret Nagel's challenge to animal phenomenology, let us consider the promise of detecting transpecific worldliness *in actuality*. Such detection, as I have discussed previously, is a real (not merely logical) possibility, inasmuch as existential residency is a primordial mode of constituting worldhood found throughout the biotic realm. Yet what about the issue of grounding residence not only in a determinate essence of life, but also within a flexible patterning of bodily worldhood—what I have been calling "somaticity"—susceptible to recognition of family resemblances between individuals and across species differentiation? Does this constitute a conceptually oppressive "return of the Same"? Only if we insist on a hard and fast definition of sameness—and I have already argued against interpreting 'same' as 'identical': the concept of sameness could (in general), and should (in the specific context of assessing Merleau-Pontyan intersomaticity), incorporate degrees of similarity. Such an interpretation permits a "play of difference" to emerge within the category *same*. It is important that strength of similarity remain significant in order to avoid the dangers of post-structuralist fragmentation (particularly cynicism vis-à-vis community).[19] Yet, recognizing difference arising in the context of sameness-that-is-not-identity, what is sometimes described as internal alterity, allows us to steer clear of repressive homogeneity or hegemony.[20]

Fusing, then, Merleau-Pontyan concerns with my current interest in meeting (or beating) Nagel's challenge, we can question whether an objective phenomenology of bodily being can establish existential residence as a similarity of lifeworld sufficient to carry intersomatic experiences across speciated difference. Several post-humanists have supplied accounts of cross-species conviviality that effectively answer in the affirmative, although they have not thematized their own studies in accord with the precise formulation of this question. With respect to biocultural worldhood,[21] Vicki Hearne's treatment of training work-animals, drawing on the views of Wittgenstein and Cavell, and Kenneth Shapiro's psychosomatic kinesiology of relations with companion animals both furnish compelling testimony of intercorporal cohabitation between members of different species.[22] Likewise, from the perspective of wilderness experience, David Abram and Danne Polk convincingly bear deeply ecological witness to "flesh of the world" as an earth-home replete with the commingling of various organisms' material and live bodiment.[23]

Yet the planet's phenomenal range of vital reality is not composed according to a dichotomy of lifeworld: bioculture versus wilderness (as mutually exclusive monoliths).[24] Much biotic community occurs along a continuum of place between these two extremities. Even to say this much, however, is to beg the question previously posed—(how) do we know there is "biotic community" here? We might intuit that there is, as F. G. Asenjo eloquently describes: "because lives open to one another in a continuum of existence, others live in our depths, participating in our sentient and motivating processes. . . . [Maybe] this communion of existence, in which barriers disintegrate, reveals . . . the overlapping processes of life as a whole. In-between is a realm of movements, with no fixed hierarchy."[25] Still, to more discursively discharge this kind of intuitive assumption or suspicion, we need to consider our original query with reference to the "interzones" between (or even the interstices within) comparatively civilized and wild regions of life: do such ecotonal biotopes support a somatic society of species?[26]

Our new question is somewhat ambiguous—is the sort of society in question to be conceived as a distributively general phenomenon or as a collectively singular entity? The issue at stake may be profitably pursued on both levels. Considering such a society as a collectively singular entity, the somatologist would inquire into the global character of world-flesh as an existentially universal element for the totality of earthbound life. Edward Casey has articulated an interzone as follows: "in that middle region where the natural and the cultural are co-implicatory and com-present, we recognize the situation of sympathy where *all of nature* is akin: . . . naturo-cultural density is not human alone."[27] In order to avoid committing a phenomenological fallacy of misplaced concreteness, it is important not to overemphasize this totalizing conception. Reducing the risk of hyper-theoretical abstraction, the perceptive somatologist returns to bodily things themselves and so finds it proper to "reassert the experience of the earth as a heterogeneous mosaic of places and of subjects as place-limited participants in the planet."[28] This returns us to the distributive understanding of the enquiry.

If we follow the latter author's salutary move to reconnect somatology with the lived reality of bioregion, it would appear that an important—perhaps primary—part of what it means to share a convivial context with another animal is to belong (at least temporarily) to some common, relatively localized environment. However, our surroundings will never become truly thematized so long as we overemphasize (with Heidegger) the temporalizing historicity of human being. Apparently one of the first (and still, by my estimation, most astute) readers of *Being and Time*, Watsuji Tetsuro finely yet forcefully critiques Heideggerian temporality:

It was in the early summer of 1927 when I was reading Heidegger's *Sein und Zeit* in Berlin that I first came to reflect on the problem of climate. I found myself intrigued by the attempt to treat the structure of man's existence in terms of time but I found it hard to see why, when time had thus been made to play a part in the structure of subjective existence, at the same juncture space also was not postulated as part of the basic structure of existence. Indeed it would be a mistake to allege that space is never taken into account in Heidegger's thinking, for *Lebendige Natur* was given fresh life by the German Romantics, yet even so it tended to be almost obscured in the face of the strong glare to which time was exposed. I perceived that herein lay the limitations of Heidegger's work, for time not linked with space is not time in the true sense . . .[29]

Watsuji's text highlights the significance of "climaticity" in our search for cross-species somatic society, thus introducing a new term that will allow us to consider a specific way in which space is relevant for the phenomenological investigation I am undertaking.

Climate, as Watsuji defines it, is the primordial dimension of natural environment internal to intentional being-in-a-world that is sensed most strongly when we stress the spatial character of such being. Watsuji states, "the space-and-time structure of human existence is revealed as climate and history: the inseparability of time and space is the basis of the inseparability of history and climate."[30] We can now try to understand climaticity as the existential dimension that opens up our lived experience to the convivial context shared by animate organisms occupying the same ecoregional environs. (This is so if, that is, we can at least entertain a robustly biocentric, rather than a constrictively anthropographic, sense of natural history.)

Watsuji's neo-Nietzschean way of conceiving climate is somatological. He thinks through his topic with a bold bodily sensibility, and thus comes to place climate as an existential category equiprimordial with history.[31] Under this rubric is included sensitivity to weather as well as landscape, where the latter encompasses both soil and scenery.[32] We might well believe that these matters are properly the province of meteorology and topography. Weather and landscape, Heidegger would claim, are areas for "regional ontology," not topics for fundamental ontology, as per "true philosophy"; they are mere ontic phenomena worthy only of "existentielle" status, a possible Heideggerian condemnation might run. Yet we are *always already* under-the-weather and over-a-land. Even when we are ensconced in our architectural hideaways, we do not escape these dimensions of our being—for the built environment is itself forever in contact with the elements of earth and sky. It might be supposed that this is a mundane contingency. It is, but not merely so—for mundane contingency is itself an "essential" or "necessary" component of [vital] existence as we know it. Consider the following as thought-experimental evidence: any serious plan to project humanity into "outer space" on a permanent basis always includes some (albeit artificial) context of biome reconstruction. This is not due in the final analysis to science fiction's fancy, but rather to a strictly scientific recognition that our (or any) form of life is quite unthinkable without climaticity. Nor is this simply an affair of material dependence—as a matter of ontology we would existentially need "geotectural" engineering to preserve the living character of humanity in an extraterrestrial context. Thus, if it is with us wherever we go, we must conclude that climate may not be given short ontological shrift.

The reason why climate cannot properly be eliminated from an ontological account of humanity is because human beings are terrestrial animals embedded in evolutionary reality. Consciousness of evolution has existential consequences in that it leads us to the self-knowledge that we are earthbound organisms—and, as such, conduct our lives in climatic conviviality with other animals. Somatic phenomena become particularly pronounced in the felt presence of climaticity. As Watsuji notes, "it will no doubt be evident that there are certain points of similarity between the problem of climate and that of 'body' . . . the self-active nature of climate must be retrieved in the same sense that the self-active nature of the [live] body has to be retrieved." Qua ontologists, in spite of traditional metaphysics, we transcend neither terrestrial nature nor the carnal-cum-visceral experience of physical living. Quite to the contrary: "Transcendence also 'stands outside' climatically. In other words, man discovers himself in climate. . . . this becomes consciousness of the body . . . [and thus] . . . climatic phenomena show man how to discover himself as 'standing out-side' (i.e., ex-istere)."[33] More recently, this insight has been underscored by Eliot Deutsch: "A body must always be some place;" he observes, "and indeed has its very being only in relation to natural conditions and to other bodily beings."[34]

Once outside, speaking in terms of phenomenological vitality, we must admit certain speciated distinctions across the spectrum of existentially embodied awareness of environment. As one ethologist, Sven Dijkgraaf, has put it: "Every animal perceives the external environment only through what its senses can find out about it. It lives in a world of its own, which is more or less distinct from that of other animals and that of human beings. Such distinctions are partly based on differences in construction of the sense organs; but they are primarily evoked by different modes of life."[35] In contrast to Tuan, Dijkgraaf rightly places emphasis on life-mode rather than on sensory equipment. On the basis of his account, it becomes possible to explicate what Tuan's misreading of interspecific conviviality leaves a mystery: why anyone even entertains the hypothesis of imaginative transpeciation. Interpreting Tuan's own example from Dijkgraaf's perspective, what tempts transpecific imagination is that—despite differences of perceptivity—a dog-keeper and her companion animal share a certain lifestyle based on the common performance of many household activities.

Even so, some skeptics might suppose that the sensory differences involved overwhelm any other bases for comparison—there is just too much perceptual drag, as it were, for a satisfactory impression of the other animal's experience to get off the ground. A good deal of the skepticism here is *a priori* in nature, and there are intrepid phenomenologists who have attempted what may only seem to be impossible. For example, following a Goethean methodology of qualitatively descriptive science, Craig Holdrege has mounted phenomenological studies of several animal species. "Any human being who has not been totally blinded by [Cartesian or behaviorist] dogma knows that cats, squirrels, mice and deer are all creatures that experience the world," he claims. "This knowing is not intellectual; it is a kind of felt-knowing based on the direct interactions we have with animals."[36] Holdrege does not relegate such understanding to the status of mystical experience, however; instead, he mobilizes a powerful method for articulating its content.[37] One illustration of his to which we may refer is the worldhood of moles:

> In imagining the tactile world of the mole, we must strip away what is so familiar to us—our colorful and airy world of sight and hearing. We can picture ourselves in a dark, quiet, enclosed space where the surface of our body touches myriad objects. Since our sense of touch is most refined in fingertips and tongue, we can imagine concentrating our perceptions of weight, texture, and temperature through these organs. In this way we can begin to acquaint ourselves with a tactile world, which normally stands in the shadows of our more dominant and focal visual and auditory experiences.[38]

Yes, the imagination figures here—but it is grounded (pun intended) by rigorous acquaintance with the habits, anatomy, and physiology of the species. The star-nosed mole is so called because it is literally headed by an exquisite organ of haptic receptivity: "Under a microscope, the star's surface looks like a honeycomb of about 25,000 little dome-like structures called 'Eimer's organs.' Each Eimer's organ, in turn, consists of three different types of sensory receptors—for detecting vibrations . . . , pressure on the skin, and the texture of objects."

A kind of dialectic between empirical and imaginative study leads not directly into the mole, of course, but nonetheless beyond total agnosticism and away from cartoon caricature. It is an epistemologically legitimate method, responsible both to experience and for creativity: "The point is to build up vivid pictures of the animal from as many sides as possible. By continually immersing ourselves in concrete observation and then connecting our observations to vivid inner images, we enter into a conversation with the animal. The animal begins to show itself."

Some readers may remain wary of this method, unsure whether or not important cognitive boundaries have been overstepped. For them, especially though not solely, it might be useful to consider the application of a similar technique in situations "closer to home" (figuratively and literally). In *Diary of a Baby*, Swiss psychiatrist Daniel Stern admirably attempts a hermeneutic phenomenology of a developing infant's experiences.[39] A real virtue of this method is its capacity to sketch alien experience in vibrant scenarios that bring the most reliable science to bear.

We are brought, at least partially, along the quasi-transpositional path of phenomenology that Heidegger identified as "going along with" the animal. We thereby neither achieve nor pretend, of course, to a colonization of another's consciousness. Still, it is important not to lose sight of the basic biocommonality that serves as the necessary context of similarity for intelligibly making what distinctions are warranted world-wise. Different species' varying sensory modalities are embodied in lifeworlds: they all subserve some form of living incarnation. It is live bodiment, then, that can function as a conduit for interspecific conviviality. As we move more deeply into this kind of being-with, let us recall the lessons we have learned from Watsuji and Bigwood to better fix our phenomenological parameters. In actuality, the two thinkers strike— one side each—the same conceptual coinage. Watsuji reminds us that climate and history interpenetrate; Bigwood eschews the notorious nature/culture dichotomy and urges us to seek an integrative model of body. To state the general point in Greco-Germanic terms familiar to traditional Western philosophy, the embodiment-environment complex of (human) being-in-a-world must be treated as comprising at once both *physis* and *Geist*. Hence, we should pay attention to the natural history and climatic culture of (transhuman) bodily vitality.

One experiential and conceptual context for such chiasmic attentiveness has already been mentioned—the late Merleau-Ponty's notion of flesh-of-the-world.[40] (As I use it here, the term *chiasmic* refers to the crossover between nature and culture, history and climate; this usage, I am suggesting, is in the semantic neighborhood of Merleau-Ponty's sense of *chiasm*—which involves "the blending, the reversible exchange between my flesh and the flesh of the world that occurs in the play of perception. This interweaving, this ongoing communion between divergent aspects of a single Flesh, is to be found at every level of experience."[41] To deepen our comprehension of this notion and reality, we need to understand it is a world of holistic carnality that immerses (surrounds and permeates) the individual's lived body.[42] Thus, in the words of David Abram, Merleau-Ponty "dissolves the traditional division between the human animal and all other organisms of the Earth."[43] The flesh-of-the-world is the consanguinity of organisms on the level of ecosystem and even biosphere; as Abram says: "no thinker can really move from his/her bodily self-awareness to the intersubjectivity of human culture, and thence to the global transcendence that is "the flesh of the world," without coming upon myriad experiences of otherness, other subjectivities that are not human, and other intersubjectivities."[44] World-flesh, then, constitutes a thoughtscape and lifeworld broad enough to conceptually and experientially incorporate intercarnal phenomena that traverse species.[45] In this lifeworld, disclosures of "organic history" and "a description of the [hu]man-animality *intertwining*" become possible.[46] Abrams's synopsis sets the stage: "Merleau-Ponty's phenomenology of the flesh provides a way to describe and to disclose the living fields of interaction from our experienced place within them."[47] We have already seen that the problem with this dimension of Merleau-Ponty's project is that it can be interpreted as a totalizing project. Instead, I would now like to explore it in greater depth of localized detail.

We can place this phenomenological lifescape on a hermeneutic plane of description by interpreting it through the thematic lens of residence. In this view, the flesh-of-the-world becomes manifestly earth-as-home. The danger in such an interpretation is that the diversity of world-flesh might be over-domesticated by the earth-home concept into a romantic vision of nature under the aspect of harmonious holism. Jane Bennett has argued persuasively against ecosophistical faith in this sort of worldview; in its stead, she proposes a more multivalent or plurivocal sense of "fractious holism."[48] The idea may sound cryptic at first; a good metaphor to convey its sense is that of *mosaic*—which presents a whole in piecemeal fashion, qua "fragmentary Gestalt." Perhaps the best simile for world-as-body is that of *stew,* comprising a common medium that permeates even the cores of nonetheless identifiably separate chunks of matter. Certainly, such imagery is better (truer to the phenomena) than that available from the conventional imaginary of cultural diversity and integration, which is usually discussed in terms of the assimilationist "melting pot" or the aggregational (still *externally* relational) "salad bowl" image.

However, as Shannon Sullivan has noted, even the metaphor of stew is imperfect—because it seems to presuppose a decided passivity on the part of the individual ingredients, whereas the elements of nature's stew include organisms who/that are active agents contributing to the flavor of various social and ecologic systems.[49] Hence, Sullivan turns to musical metaphors: she considers and rejects orchestral imagery, because it is too beholden to a supervisory conductor and/or overarching score; finally she offers and settles upon the metaphor of jazz improvisation, which has the advantage of playing up individually spontaneous yet holistically loyal co-constitution of parts and whole.[50] This image is indeed suitable for social situations, amongst which there are some that are interspecific. Yet, other natural settings do not necessarily feature agents as *self*-conscious as the improvising performers in a jazz band. So we may have to content ourselves here with metaphoric imperfection.

If this extended talk about metaphor strikes the reader as much ado about nothing or little, recall that I have repeatedly indicated the current vocabulary for discussing these issues is problematic because the terms that exist either imply or explicitly invoke concepts I am arguing have an unwarranted basis. For example, the word "embodiment" literally evokes the idea that what a person is is something different from their bodies, something which is *inside* of the body one calls one's own. Thus, *bodiment* has become the term that I wish to use. So, as part of explaining and interpreting a bodily basis for ethics, this study must supply the language that facilitates such thought, that opens new pathways for the flow of relevant and appropriate ideas to circulate. It is in this sense that my project must engage in a kind of poetics, which involves but is not exhausted by coining neologisms.

In a different context I have already discussed the philosophical significance of metaphor. In my coauthored introduction to a volume of essays that considers the philosophic value of Nietzsche's animal metaphors,[51] I began by citing Michéle Le Dœuff. She kicks off her treatment of "the philosophical imaginary" with a question about the role of imagery in philosophy's self-conception. Le Dœuff wonders, "If someone set out to write a history of philosophical imagery, would such a study ever be as much an accepted part of the historiography of philosophy as histories of philosophical concepts, procedures or systems?"[52] She continues, "If one further argued that existing histories of philosophy are at the very least incomplete, not to say mutilating, in that they never present us with any individual philosopher's image-album, would such a reproach be deemed worthy of serious consideration?" Images are considered by most professional philosophers as *extrinsic* to the real theoretical labor of a philosopher's writings. (Recall Socrates' famous, and perhaps ironic, denigration of poetry in Book X of the *Republic* when he describes images as a debasement of things as they are in themselves and poetic images particularly as images of images of images, "thrice removed from the truth.") Conventional wisdom posits that philosophers are supposed to present truth, and that to focus on images is to dwell in a kind of ornament that only literature should engage. Yet (as the reference to Plato suggests) this rough view imports a kind of metaphysics that I am explicitly calling into question. Le Dœuff's work demonstrates that images are not only rhetorically interesting but that, despite various philosopher's protests to the contrary, imagery plays an *essential* role in the properly philosophic development of ideas (aside, that is, from questionable persuasive functions, such as subtly inserting unjustified claims or smuggling in dogmatic positions). In this light, then, one of my motivations is to enable an appreciation for the philosophic purposes of metaphorical expression by focusing on particular and problematic terms ordinarily used in the language of ethics and by illuminating different paths for others to follow. Here I take my cue from Mark Johnson's work in this area, in which he states, "most of our moral reasoning is reasoning based on metaphors."[53]

Returning to the main thread of our discussion, whatever metaphor one prefers to employ—the stew or the jazz ensemble—endorsing the view of fractious holism suggested by Bennett would mean giving some weight to the phenomenal fact that terrestrial carnality (world-flesh/earth-home) is not experientially lived as an undifferentiated or placid whole. Rather, it is fraught with all the existential tensions arising out of its spatiotemporal divisibility into relatively individualized organisms and biomes. The convivial challenge for humans, then, is to interpret the skin-boundary not as an impermeable *barrier* encapsulating corporeality but as a surface of somatic *contact.*[54] In Paul Shepard's words, "the epidermis of the skin is . . . like a pond surface or a forest soil, not a shell so much as a delicate interpenetration. It reveals the [human] self ennobled and extended . . . because the beauty and complexity of nature are continuous with ourselves"; as John Compton puts it, "what is characteristic of embodied, inter-subjective, world-related human life . . . is structurally analogous to what is found in other [living] regions of the natural world."[55]

In meeting this challenge, it becomes possible to transcend our strictly *körperlich* limitations and thus to more broadly define the *modus vivendi* of flesh-and-blood being-in-a-world as "*Leibesheim(welt)*" (home[-world], or territory, of live bodiment).[56] Continuing in this vein of residentially hermeneutic phenomenology of body, one could articulate interpretive descriptions indefinitely. I shall therefore focus the present discussion within a certain setting. In choosing a site for this ontology, we should be mindful that thematizing embodiment of residence is no arbitrary affair. It flows rather from a fundamental recognition of the primordial constitution of worldhood; for, as phenomenologist Bernd Jager reminds us, "the house, body and city do not so much occupy space and time as generate them. It is only as inhabiting, embodied beings that we find access to a world."[57] Given this insight and the fact that most of the world's (human) population now lives in metropolitan areas, it is apt to ecophilosophize in and about a citified context—to do environmental phenomenology, more specifically, from the perspective of urban parkland.

Phenomenology of the Park

There are at least two reasons to focus on the park: (1) the park is an "interzone," a place in-between urban and wild; and (2) the park is the quintessential place of interspecific interaction. Hermeneut Joseph Grange observes, "the human body in such a place is fleshed thought seeking the identity of the difference between city and nature," and, thus, "to wonder about place through fleshly thought is to seek our home."[58] In the midst of the urban, parkland clears an open space that enables a residential dialectic between nature and culture.[59] It is precisely in between these principles that we need to situate our articulation of what I am calling *Leibesheim* (somatic home). The urban park is the cityscape's prime setting for cross-species conviviality (including interactions with a wide variety of nonhuman animals—from the thoroughly domesticated through ferine forms to the relatively wild). As biocultural environments, parks present a promising and especially ecotonal locale for tran-specific phenomenology.[60]

Grange offers a useful pheonomology relating to parkscape's *Leibesheim*:

> A person sits in a park. He sees and feels the contrast between city and nature. In experiencing this contrast, he does not so much understand the differences as sense in a relaxed, dim way the fundamental unity of all reality. It is not a question of causal explanation or, for that matter, rational effort. His body recognizes the organic rhythms of nature and at the same time the powerful thrust towards order and symmetry which characterizes human building. These dimensions of human experience are different; the natural is not the urban, but the two connect because the body is able to inhere in both regions of value. What unifies these experiences is the active presence of the body. By being there in a fleshly way, the human body is one in the presence of a soaring skyscraper glimpsed through the leafy vista of summer foliage. *This unification of experience is achieved through the somatic act of being in place.* That is why city and nature are not opposed entities warring for our allegiance. The human body in its generosity can experience both contexts as real and laden with value.[61]

This text draws to our attention at least two significant aspects of park experience. First, ecotonally (as an "interzone"), it illuminates the way in which the park is an "urbanatural" site of paradoxically citified wilderness—wherein the city and the wild interpenetrate, qualifying but not annihilating each other. Second, somatically, it suggests that what permits such interpenetration is the carnal character of bodily being-in-a-park. Building on these insights, I will now specify their scope to deal with "humanimal" conviviality.

"By being there in a fleshly way, the human body is one in the presence of a soaring skyscraper glimpsed through the leafy vista of summer foliage." So writes Grange of park-experience's embodied, seasonal sense of built/arboreal environment. Sensitivity to the cycle (or dialectic)[62] of converting seasons tunes us into the phenomena of weather basic to climaticity (in Watsuji's sense of the term). There is a park in New York City's outer borough of Queens in and from which one can experience just the scenario described above: Kissena Park, in the summertime, affords a greenly tree-framed vision of Manhattan's sky-scraping towers on the horizon. Late in the season of heat and humidity, this sight—to further flesh out the scene—is accompanied by the sound of cicadas drumming their abdomens. The insectiphonic concert begins with maybe only one or two individuals rattling their bellies in the rising temperature of mid-morning. Through the sweaty hours of afternoon the day drips hot moisture that throbs acoustically with the pulsing crescendo and decrescendo of a ci-cada chorus grown now to collectively huge proportions. You do not merely notice or register this bio-percussive phenomenon, as by some attenuated audition—you feel it fully and resonate with its intensity.[63] In such a context the "hermeneutic hearing" of David Michael Levin becomes phenomenolog-ically pregnant. "If we listen well to ourselves," he suggests, "we can hear within our embodiment resonances and echoes that confirm the interconnectedness of all beings and already bring us into communication with all other mortals, gathering us together for the making of a more thoughtful history."[64]

As I resume my park phenomenology, I will try to maintain Levin's sense of somatic thoughtfulness. In my thematized scenario, notice, a life's story is given testimony in certain manifest signs of emergence and metamorphosis: at its base there are little, cylindrical holes in the ground around the tree trunk; on its bark there cling small, empty shells skeletally shaped in bug-form, cracked open along the back-line. Digging deeper,[65] scientifically, one discovers that the cicadan cycle of life is here in evidence: the tiny animals begin living below the parkland's surface, larvally burrowed into the earthy depths of some tree's root system; literally radical sapsuckers, they remain submerged for years; when the time is right (as long as thirteen or even seventeen years after birth), the bloated bugs belly up into the air-world above-ground; there they slowly climb their arboreal hosts, wriggle out of their dirty skins, dry their winged bodies in summer heat, and finally fly off to crowd the branches of available street-trees and parks' copses; thence cicadas of the city sing. If one is lucky enough, she will spot an individual splitting and shedding its old crusty flesh or an-other drumming its tummy under a leaf. And if she cares to, she might look and listen long enough to learn of the insects' chthonic chronicle—which is sensorily present before her eyes and becomes reconstituted within earshot's temporal range.

Now, as the summer draws to a close, so too do the lives of the sonic in-sects. Not only its trees, but also the park's bushes and shrubs begin becoming empty choirs, "where late cicadas sang" (as one might be tempted to think). Yet the passage of seasons does not strip a parkland of its corporally channeled encounters between the species. In Kissena Park, for instance, autumn is signaled in the sky by the honking flight pattern of Canadian geese. The geese alight upon the park's pond, becoming avian observers of the observing human traffic that rings the water. When winter comes they will have gone, leaving the watery scene before it freezes over; then, when it has hardened, the skaters and squirrels will share ice time. Eventually, a thickly fecund aroma of fall's decomposition will yield atmospherically to a crisp, wintry clarity of sight and smell. Warmer weather at last returns in the springtime, of course; and this warmth, though similar in objective temperature to the "coolth" of fall, is palpably different in terms of lived climaticity. Spring is alive with a felt sense of thaw and reinvigoration absent in autumn. In this season the park's faunal and floral environment alternates in tempo and tone between lively action and pleasant calm, and it is also filled with the promise of another summer. Thus do this parkscape's phenomenal seasons turn.

The phenomena of climate and culture, nature and history, are existentially interpenetrating.[66] and form the backgrounding context of interspecific conviviality. Against this backdrop, experiences of transpecific intersomaticity come into greater relief. Chiasmic illustrations like those of Merleau-Ponty include the sensately intertwined "haptic hearing" of cicadas by "enparked" people (and vice versa?),[67] as well as the reversibly observatory encounter between humans and geese. On the level of what I dub "municipal ontology," such interanimalic instances of metropolitan *Mitsein* phenomenally display the somatic and cross-species nature of flesh-and-blood being-in-a-world.[68]

The example of the reversible gaze between human and goose may seem innocuously quotidian, lacking any special significance. What is at stake here —what is important about two different animals noticing each other? My point, stepping outside pure description, is that between the geese and the humans there passes a perceptual process laden with pragmatic potency, an experience not reducible to the "merely" visual event: man-sees-bird/bird-sees-man.[69] Perhaps a contrasting illustration will help clarify. Commenting on the zoo's milieu, John Berger observes: "The visibility through the glass, the spaces between the bars, or the empty air above the moat, are not what they seem—if they were, then everything would be changed. Thus visibility, space, air, have been reduced to tokens. . . . All this is what makes [zoo animals] marginal. The space which they inhabit is artificial. Hence their tendency to bundle towards the edge of it. (Beyond its edges there may be real space.) In some cages the light is equally artificial. In all cases the environment is illusory."[70] One wonders just what "real space" is or could be. (After all, haven't good philosophers learned the Kantian lesson that space itself is always already ideal, at least transcendentally?[71]) Berger's hint is the suggestion that the circumstances would change if irreality did not mark or taint the observational media. The real space of encounter, as I would elaborate this clue, is live space—that "living room" which permits genuine con-frontation complete with all its motile possibilities of adversity, avoidance, and free association. Of course, the zoo annihilates or interrupts these possibilities (that is why it is a site of illusion, one which marginalizes its inhabitants). Yet all those potencies for activity—of fight and flight, of becoming foe or friend, of leaving off or moving in—remain in place in the wild and even at the park such as I have described it. This, then, is the existential import and philosophic upshot of watching animals watching you "in the field": that perception across differences of species is there charged with pragmatic concern or regard, at-tention becomes con-tention, and thus it is difficult to spectate simply (neutrally, reductively) because survival vision and social sight must be literally re-spectful of another living being—taking care, through fear or love, to deal with the other in a phenomenally physical dimension of vital exchange and intercourse.[72]

Associated Analyses

How does my treatment of transpecific intersomaticity compare with current life-philosophies of body? One such philosophy is adumbrated by Douwe Tiemersma, a Dutch interdisciplinarian who conducts his own enquiry into embodiment from a phenomenological approach he characterizes as "inclusive existential ontology."[73] Tiemersma develops a somatology with two dimensions. The first one proceeds on the level of anthropological modeling. The second, which is more germane to the concerns at hand, is a field theory of what we could call "*Leibswelt.*"[74] (In fact, Tiemersma's life-field theory of body can be conceived as an attempt to make more scientific Merleau-Ponty's poetic metaphor flesh-of-the-world.) The three categories of this theory have multiple points of contact with the current discussion. Regarding spatiality, an existential body schema is charted, which establishes a perceptively and affectively sympathetic awareness: "the [body-]subject has in principle an inner connection with and feeling of everything which appears anywhere in the [life-]field."[75] This is the space of cross-species conviviality. In respect to substance, the reality of lived bodiment is pluralistic—the fleshly *res victa* of *Leibswelt* is ambiguously atmospheric, capable of being experienced as either "fine materiality or gross mentality."[76] The Merleau-Pontyan realm of world-flesh discussed previously fits this description. Lastly, there is a factor of force: intentionality orients *Leibswelt* according to various vectors (e.g., felt muscular tonus).[77] This force factor represents a corporal reinterpretation of existential phenomenology's standard account of intentional orientation.

Neil Evernden provides a more generally accessible, yet scientifically updated, presentation of the traditional field-self theory supplied by earlier existentialists. He develops the account by furnishing a sequence of metaphors that become progressively less reified markers of selfhood: body image, "organic thought," and region of care or concern.[78] This last phrase in the series demarcates a self-field of organism-cum-environment "revealed as a gradient of action." Evernden philosophically grounds his existential metaphors in biological bases. The "force-field" of selfhood is realized (and recognized) through the (awareness of) mutualism in symbiotic co-evolution; thus human egology and natural ecology intertwine, and humanity becomes more attuned to animality (qua identity and/as alterity). "What all this suggests," Evernden continues, "is that our [anthropocentrist] assumptions of separateness are unacceptably simplistic, and that we might more closely approximate the facts of [living] existence by regarding ourselves less as [homo-hypostatized] objects than as sets of [transpecific] relationships." Naming attunement of this sort runs all the risk of neologism, but *biosophy* might be the best descriptive term of art.

Such biosophy—like Tiemersma's inclusive ontology—trades on notions of living force fields, and thus can provoke suspicion regarding vitalistic mysticism. Both Evernden and Tiemersma want to dampen doubts in this regard, and so they each deny that their respective theories conjure any even quasi-mystical *vis vitalis*. Still, whether or not these thinkers are successful in avoiding the charge of mystification, the issue of vitalism might be an abiding source of philosophic problems for the project I have engaged.

In order to see if vitalistic philosophy need be an intellectual worry of ours, I would like to examine Michael Weinstein's contemporary defense of vitalism.[79] Weinstein traces the history of philosophic vitalism and identifies a lineage of vitalistic philosophers that includes Bergson, James, Unamuno, Nietzsche, and Santayana. These thinkers all attempted to ground comprehensive reflection in the life-process itself; in response to biological evolutionism and metaphysical idealism, this endeavor supplied a synthesis of scientific mechanism and historical teleology. Although Weinstein admits that early vitalism harbored an irrationalist impulse (evident in Bergson's absolutistic interpretation of life), he warns us against overgeneralizing dismissal, because "the vitalists' irrationalism, however, was never as comprehensive as their critics made it out to be."[80] This apologia is issued in order to vindicate incarnate and animate more plausible rendering of organismal activity found finitude —according to Weinstein's novel reformulation, "a critical vitalism restricts attention to the [existential] evidence provided by life grasped from within a body, by a particular organism or self." In this vein, then, I think we need not fear—indeed, should rather celebrate—being branded vitalists for a willingness to consider and explore phenomenology of live bodies' transpecific intercourse.[81]

A key part of what has worried philosophers and scientists about vitalism is its perceived (and, at times, actual) tendency to overestimate the versatility of and/or agency in organismal activity. For example, Heidegger tries early on to quarantine this vitalistic tendency from his own account of animality by drawing a sharp distinction between human "comportment" and animal "behavior": "The behaviour of the animal is not a *doing and acting,* as in human comportment, but a *driven performing* [Treiben]."[82] In fact, this essentially instinctual account of animal activity is at the root of animality's "deprivation" in the sense of world "poverty." The animal is deprived of genuine world, according to Heidegger, because it is "captivated" by its instinctive drives: "Captivation is the condition of possibility for the fact that, in accordance with its essence, the animal *behaves within an environment* [Umwelt] *but never within a world* [Welt]." Of course, we may still ask whether this kind of account is itself adequate. I believe it is not, and will appeal shortly to a more plausible rendering of organismal activity found in a contemporary life-philosophy.

The operative term in the citation above is *Benommenheit*—but translating it as "captivation" carries too much connotation of lively entrancement (as in fascination); it is more literally equivalent to "benumbedness." In this sense, closer to the original, I believe it becomes obvious that Heidegger is underestimating the flexibility of at least some/many animals' actions (e.g., relationships that comprise animal communities such as porpoise pods, elephant herds, and primate bands are difficult to read solely in terms of instinctual or rote behavior). In developing his allergic reaction to vitalism, in other words, he has overcompensated in his interpretation of animal activity and erred too much on the side of mechanism. Pointing this out is not really a matter of blaming Heidegger (who, after all, was writing and teaching at a time when almost hydraulic concepts of instinct were still viewed as central explanations in biology[83]); rather, it is significant for the present study because it provides a heuristic foil for an alternative interpretation. Contemporary pragmatist Shannon Sullivan articulates a more promising account of the structure of organisms' behavior. Following Dewey, she rejects the notion of instinct for marking certain actions as too ready-made and instead speaks of more malleable "impulses" that are capable of being ordered into "habits" conceived as styles of body-mind comportment. Body and mind, in turn, are de-reified in terms of processes of organic activity ("bodying") and the manufacture of meaning ("minding").[84]

Using Sullivan's terminology, it becomes possible to pick up on relevant distinctions that (do and must) go unnoticed in Heidegger's account. For example, he misses (and so can lead his readers to ignore) a crucial difference between automatic functions and relatively flexible actions, as in the following passage: "This manner of being [*Benommenheit*] announces itself in the case of the animal in the familiar terms of seeing, hearing, seizing, hunting, fleeing, devouring, digesting, and all the other organic processes. It is not as if the beating of the animal's heart were a process different from the animal's seizing and seeing, the one analogous to the case of human beings, the other to a chemical process. Rather the entirety of its being, the being as a whole in its unity, must be comprehended as [non-worldly] behaviour."[85]

This totalizing interpretation of animal activity fails to articulate important aspects of the phenomena at hand. Is it really the case that there is no difference between circulation and seizing, between digestion and feeding, between respiration and hunting/fleeing? I think not, and Sullivan's hermeneutic is better able to distinguish between these pairs' respective functions and actions —by characterizing the latter in each case more plausibly as Deweyan habits rather than as quasi-robotic instincts or spellbound behaviors (as per Heidegger). Certainly, this would do greater justice to the structure of much vertebrate and most mammalian activity.[86]

THREE

Appreciation of Animal Nature
under the Aspect of Bodiment

A sheer exuberance of vitality and a celebration of [its] value and . . .
of physical existence is about taking delight in what we can do, what
we can experience, and what is about us.

GLEN MAZIS (2002)

It is on the basis of this primordial "feral vision" that our sense of kinship with all life develops, along with the sense of self and the capacity
to empathize.

MICHAEL W. FOX (2001)

Introductory Outlook

MY SPECIFIC AXIOLOGICAL concern is with how values are bound up with
ontologies: I seek to investigate appraisals that emanate from, and in turn circumscribe, our conceptions of what and how the world is. Ordinary speech
and action mobilize word and deed into an economy of necessity, for the purposes of survival. Just staying alive, however, is obviously not the only aim of
life. Organisms appear to be oriented toward more than sheer survival or mere
persistence. Preservation differs not only from flourishing but also from what
might be characterized as vitality—in other words, the static energy of staying
power, remanence, rests beside livelihood's impulse to increase. (Consider
Georges Bataille's suggestion that life is patterned according to its utilization
of surplus energy, which is beyond mere maintenance.[1]) There is a kind of
transcendence that occurs within the existential horizon of immanence: an

overarching economy of excess organizes around the axis of an extra-ordinary process of prizing. Prizes can be described as quanta or qualities of energizing appreciation when they take form as values the pursuit of which one positively esteems worthy of effort.[2] Etymologically, the word 'prize' has connotations of competition that invoke the notion of a contest of ideals. Something can be prized only because it has achieved a priority in relation to other possible objects of esteem. Any axiology's articulation is possible only on the basis of a similar contest of possible goods and desires.[3] The prize I currently seek is philosophic evaluation of cross-species somaticity, or experienced bodiment. In this pursuit, I hope to find an enlivening and animating appreciation for bodily being.

As discussed previously, Husserl's phenomenology identifies two ways of conceiving an animal: as deviantly similar, or as relatedly other, to humanity. These conceptual tropes for difference—deviant similitude and related otherness—are not value-neutral.[4] Since they constitute the dominant modes for thinking of and being with animals aside from ourselves, it is worthwhile to investigate their multidimensional meanings. When we conceive the other in terms of related otherness, their difference is potentially valued positively, as possessing unique or distinctive characteristics that are admirable in their own right. Furthermore, a perspective of related otherness evolves into a more basic sense of broad relation beyond those of one's specific kind; it often focuses on shared characteristics and possibilities rather than on marking out polarities or irreducible opposition. Deviant similitude registers when another being is viewed as somebody or thing who/which should be similar in kind yet manifest differently insofar as they fail to manifest the characteristics that are considered to be normal, healthy, appropriate, or advantageous to other members of the same kind. Such an other is regarded as an irregular entity whose being is characterized by its abnormality in relation to "us" or to "me." Out of these experiences arise certain cognitive attitudes—what Habermas would call "epistemic interests" and Foucault would call "power-knowledge" alignments—that configure opposing ontologies. Conceived in terms of related otherness, the alien is deferentially understood as first-rank Other. When the other takes the cast of deviant similitude, it is conceived as an aberrant freak, mistakenly dominated as second-rate Same.

Such configurations have subtle yet decisive axiological consequences. Deviant similitude and related otherness project aesthetics of the monstrous and the marvelous, respectively. The latter calls forth admiration of strange beauty; the former evokes avoidance of grotesque perversity. Morally, the following ramifications ensue: on the level of ethics, that which appears relatedly other encourages development of familiarity with the foreign, whereas that which seems deviantly similar exhorts debasement or degradation of alterity. On the level of politics, the perspective of related otherness charges us to make and celebrate cultural contact with wild(er)ness, while that of deviant similitude frames a situation in which upright citizens are led to incarcerate their backyard denizens (e.g., exotic pets who cannot make it on their own in a new setting).

These examples can be taken to indicate various modalities of differentiation. "Deviant similitude" is intended as a category that crystallizes Foucault's insight that normalizing rationality thematically converts difference into deviance.[5] In deciding which of these positions is better or more accurate, it might not be possible to conclusively argue against deviant similitude. Still, the standpoint of related otherness can be preferred over against its rival on the basis that the former stance is a better one from which to appreciate the other encountered in its own right (thereby allowing it room to emerge appropriately into a space of respectful relationship), whereas the latter standpoint imperiously colonizes and thus mangles that which is other (forcing it into submergence by assimilating it as deformity).

Adopting the standpoint of related otherness does not have to be a decision dependent upon some free-floating ideology of "tolerating the Other"; instead, it can be transcendentally legitimated by appeal to the necessarily public dimension of (the intelligibility of) intentional experience itself. That is to say, our connections and relations to others are conditions for the possibility of having a meaningful sense of ourselves as subjective entities. As J. N. Findlay puts it, "fellows and objects are necessary to one another, and it is only in relation to both that we ourselves can be subjects and can make significant reference to things, people and our own mental and bodily life."[6] If this is so, then respect for our relativity to others is warranted by the semiotics of subjectivity alone—that is to say, making sense of one's worldhood at all requires careful attention to otherness because what one is emerges and is continually (though not exhaustively) constituted in and through one's relations to others. Thus, accepting relationality as such need not involve any arbitrary presumptions about how discrete entities may possibly relate to others.

Formal Analysis

Once this outlook is adopted, one must come to terms with the nature and source of those values propagated by framing encounters with alien animals through the experiential filter of related otherness. This point may be generalized—any means of indicating difference will raise the need for some form of axiological analysis. To ask a standard question—Are these values subjective or objective? Putting such a query forward begs for some prior statement about axiological subjectivity and objectivity.

Whether or not pure objectivism is metaphysically "true," it is certainly existentially empty. Just how inapt it is can be discerned under the lens of lived experience. Why should we care about the putatively nonrelational character of any value that impinges on our lives? Indeed, who would or could care (or even know) about those virtual (aspects of) values that may exist apart from our lives? As a matter of conceptual fact, no one can care about (or cognize) a wholly external or independent value, because caring (like cognizing) is itself an internalizing relation—indeed more intimately so than cognition, and, hence, especially evidential in this respect. (I maintain that the phenomenological point here holds for any [existentially finite] mode of appreciation, not just caring.) In the spirit of Wittgenstein's late work, we might say that the practical zone of valuation and evaluation renders the language game of objectivism idle (within, at least, the parameters of that zone). Unlike (perhaps) mathematical reality, the being of values is coextensive with *praxis*.

Do ideals have force above and beyond our valuing activities? This is a pseudo-question: sanctity, justice, beauty, respect, and compassion all acquire meaning for us only within the evaluatory practices of religious worship, political/civil society, aesthetic experience, and ethical or moral living. As phenomenologist James Hart states: "Values are not what we experience but how we experience the world . . . valuing in its manifold forms, e.g., of desiring, loving, willing, wishing, delighting in, being enthralled by, admiring, finding pleasure in, etc. is an ineluctable and fundamental way that humans exist."[7] Since this study employs a method of existentially hermeneutic phenomenology, axiological objectivism will be left to the metaphysicians. I will focus instead on the activities of valuing, claiming that even if values (in the nominative) do not have independent existence, our lived experience of them can still be checked by intersubjective analysis of the processes of valuing.

The position of axiological subjectivism—the polar opposite of objectivism —attracts charges of anthropologism on various levels. It seems to conflate illegitimately the desired with the desirable, as Frondizi states: "Any inquiry into what people actually desire belongs to psychology or sociology; only the 'desirable' is strictly axiological."[8] Another way of framing this critique is in terms of the notorious naturalistic fallacy, sometimes glossed as "the is/ought problem." Critically, then, the point is that subjectivism appears to muddle the discourses of description or explanation with justification-talk—yet "the axiological problem does not consist in finding out how or why we valuate, but how we *ought* to valuate." Furthermore, it is held that an ought-proposition cannot be validly derived from is-propositions. In other words, the logical relations (if any) involved in discursive movement from is-statements to ought-statements do not sustain truth-preserving deduction.

However, even if one abandons pure subjectivism, "the 'desirable' retains its umbilical cord which unites it to the 'desired.'" How can this be the case, in the face of is/ought cleavage? The vital link in question, the connection between what should be and what happens to be, is not—nor need be—one of ratiocinative derivation. It might be said that the alleged schism between ought and is itself is vulnerable to the charge of axiological "syllogocentrism" (designating an excessive expectation of, and demand for, deductively rational argument).[9] As Frondizi expresses the doubt, "Why should we deny value to what cannot be proved logically? Can one prove that what is proved has greater value than what cannot be proved?"[10]

Linkage of value to fact is not a nexus of rationalistic proof. Its nature is not probatively argumentative, but rather is poetically interpretive. The poetic *as* stands between the scientific *is* and the axiological *ought*. Radically, fact is filtered by perception, which is patterned hermeneutically by inherently evaluatory metaphors or tropes. In the vocabulary of another philosophic dialect: if the factual is theory-laden, and if theorizing is value-laden, then factuality is value-laden.[11] If facticity is always already valuated, then the fact/value split is compromised, and consequently it becomes less plausible to find fault with the naturalistic "fallacy." The is/ought problem thus tends toward dissolution, or else is resolved on the basis of altered terms (as indicated below).

What then becomes of axiology, if it surrenders as false the exclusive disjunction between what happens and what ought to be? Value is now felt to be a relational *Gestalt,* exhibiting both subjective and objective aspects as well as interlocking facets.[12] This conception gives reasonable play to the duality of values, yet without submitting them to a dubious dualism. That duality can be phrased: (1) "a value has no existence or meaning without a real or possible valuation"; but (2) "valuation requires the presence of an intentional object."[13] Valuating, that is to say, is an axio-poetic process bound (albeit somewhat loosely) to claims of (relative) givenness manifested by the object of appreciation—which is to say, along with phenomenologist Don Marietta, that "values [are] not merely subjective in the sense of being reducible entirely to the act of valuing itself."[14] The process of valuing is neither arbitrary creation *ex nihilo* nor the capricious whim of an agent of appreciation.[15] To elaborate: valuation results neither from some subject's freely artistic shaping of a mutely inert object, nor from the deliberately calculative consideration of both subjective and objective contributions—rather, it occurs as an organic process of growth or emergence that happens when valuer and valuee come into interrelationship. (Another, similar way of conceiving its occurrence would be in terms of what Findlay calls "the essential 'drifts' of consciousness.")[16]

Nevertheless, even accepting the hermeneutic account of provenance outlined above, the question remains as to what value *is*. However it comes into being, what is value such that its appearance as a phenomenon does not produce an axiological chaos of interpretations? What is the ultimate nature of value? Since the standard alternative is an all-too-dubious intuitionism, I bite the empirical bullet and respond by thematizing value as the pervasive or profound probability of appreciation.[17] An entity or event is worthy if it is widely or thoroughly likely to be prized.[18] Nothing rational is gained, no philosophic advantage is served in underwriting this widespread or deep-going likelihood of praise by weaving into its pragmatically strong fabric the gilded threads of metaphysical postulates. With reference to somatic axiology, for instance, David Michael Levin furnishes an idealistic illustration: "we are *capable* of a moral existence only because our bodily nature is *always already informed* by the inscription of the *Logos* as a primordial, universal *Nomos*."[19] Levin's Heideggerian mien would resist calling this stance "metaphysical"; nonetheless, it remains an appeal to some supersensible notion of value and thus reconjures quasi-mystical principles previously well-dispelled.[20] Let us philosophize without taking away the pain of disvalue, assuming whatever discomfort arises in the absence of valuational unanimity or guarantee.[21]

Absolute justification for our value judgments may not be forthcoming.[22] Yet, even if we forego the temptation to eternalize our value intuitions, normative chaos need not result. "Understanding that values are not [purely] objective does not take away our ability to make rational moral choices," according to Marietta, because: "Personal experience helps us check the fittingness of our values with the actualities of life. A rich intersubjectivity allows us to learn from our contemporaries, and a knowledge of other cultures and of people's lives in the past gives us perspective on our values."[23] There is generally enough axiological agreement to support broad consensus on most major issues. Where there is not, we may attempt to resolve value conflicts by comparing the situational comprehensiveness, internal coherence, and external consistency of rival evaluations.[24] These criteria are emblematic of philosophic demeanor, logical hygiene, and scientific mien; they issue from intellectual instincts for finality, order, and stability of inquiry and deliberation.[25] In this way we can negotiate disputes with intersubjective and cross-cultural satisfaction, while yet exorcising our collective conscience of the misleading compulsion to bring our troubles before some mythically transcendent tribunal of Reason or Divinity.

Returning to my definition of value, I would like to trace its disciplinary parameters, clearing the way to further the present discussion. If "x is valuable" refers to the plausibility of appreciation, we may leave it to the social sciences (such as psychology and sociology) to determine how likely "x" is to be prized.[26] It would then be the axiological task of phenomenology to discern what appreciation itself is or could be—in strict terms, that is, to provide its *Wesensschau* (i.e., make manifest its ideal type). Achieving this would constitute no mean accomplishment, and yet pursuing it represents a more modest mode of philosophizing than one whose grandiose ambition is to provide final normative consolation for the justificatory pangs of a conscience that always asks "why?"[27] Against this latter tradition of transcendent(al) thought, I prefer to go forward inspired by the Humean sort of humility that seeks "merely" to methodically reflect upon the ordinary affairs of common life. Thus I proffer a typology of somatic valuation and then analysis of the cultural dynamics of animal appreciation.

Substantive Treatment

One twentieth-century axiologist of some repute, Risiero Frondizi, makes the point that "values do not exist by themselves, but depend, rather, upon some value carrier or support, which is generally of a corporal substance."[28] I wish to concentrate next on the specifically somatic entities that "bear" certain values. At this juncture I want merely to indicate the possibility and presence of "embodied ethics," reserving deeper investigation for the next chapter. Now, in the process of conducting his hermeneutic recollection of bodiment, Levin has broached the subject of bodily axiology—specifically concentrating on ethical evaluation at first.[29] He thinks there is a "somatic *basis* of a[ny] moral 'consciousness'" and grounds its positive normativity in "a basic *trust* in the innate potential for goodness carried by the universal body."[30] His (phenomenologically, not biologically) genetic account absorbs the discourses of several psychologists, and his normative conviction leads him to propose changes for pedagogical practice. This source for display of the somaesthetics of ethical value will be further explored in the following chapter.

Levin has prepared the ground in the area of politics as well. He suggests that certain "corporeal schemata" furnish the fundamental "intercorporeity" for his Merleau-Ponty-inspired vision of an ideal community of somatic subjects.[31] Levin's belief is that since "the flesh may be said to schematize a priori a possible body politic" there arises in carnal axiology a civic ideal of somaticity. More specifically, his argument is that "Merleau-Ponty's conceptualization of the 'flesh' can be understood in such a way that it will function as a radically ontological schematization for a new body politic." Although Levin's thought has a tendency to wax utopian at this point, it is concretely grounded, especially in cross-cultural experiences of children. As evidence for his position, Levin points out that reversibility of active and passive modes of sensation can substantiate a primordial feeling of reciprocity. Furthermore, the phenomenon Merleau-Ponty designates "intertwining" attests to "the fact that human existence in its most elemental dimensionality is a field of bodily awareness pervasively determined by interactions with other beings that conclusively demonstrate our interdependence and interpenetration." On these bases Levin claims that an inherent "organismic grammar" of the felt body incites public achievement of consensus formation.[32] The chief political value or virtue implicitly at work here is that of mutual respect. In this way, then, Levin furnishes an indication of the possibility (if not the actuality) of what might be called "incarnate politics."

In addition to ethical and political values of bodiment, it is conceivable to envision a somatic axiology of aesthetics. This makes "good sense"—at stake in this area, after all, is perception of beauty. In the words of Kate Rigby, the post-humanist task of ecological aesthetics is to help those of us bound by the inveterate ideal of pure thought "to experience with our senses, as well as to understand with our minds, how we are part of nature and how nature is part—and not merely a secondary, 'primitive' part—of us, of our very humanness."[33] In this way eco-aesthetics would resurrect a Baumgarten-style discourse of the body, thus displaying how the beauty of "nature shows itself to human beings precisely insofar as they themselves belong to it through bodily sensuous presence."[34] One example is Gernot Böhme's attempt to demonstrate how organismic "ecstatics" can affect existential "atmosphere" via ocular, tactile, and aromatic cues.[35] In addition, Ben-Ami Scharfstein's endeavor to ground universal aesthetics biologically may profitably be read (at least partially) as a reply to the corporal challenge of ecological sensibility.[36] Scharfstein illustrates, by reference to birdsong and "chimpainting," how a somatic sensitivity to artistic expression in various cases involving other kinds of organisms can suggest multi- and transpecific dimensions of aesthetic (e)valuation.[37] Probably the most rigorous project of direct and clear relevance here is Richard Shusterman's attempt to mount an entire program of "somaesthetics," which he defines as "the critical, meliorative study of the experience and use of one's body as a locus of sensory-aesthetic appreciation (*aisthesis*) and creative self-fashioning."[38]

Conventionally, the three areas treated so far (ethics, politics, and aesthetics) comprise axiology's standard philosophic purview. In the interest of comprehensiveness, I shall now briefly extend the present discussion to include more pedestrian arenas of bodily value. Very obviously, perhaps so much so that it often evades our thematic notice, bodies have survival value qua flesh-as-food (or "meat," as speakers of English gloss it). This value has historically brought forth hunting exercises as well as domestication activities. Carnivorous humans prize other animals' body parts, whether as game parcels or grocery items. It may also be that the diets of meat-eating persons are not organized strictly around the value of survival but rather reflect culinary taste, and/or such diets could be directed by other spiritual, religious, or cultural interests. Consider, for example, the association of "meat" with machismo in our culture.[39] In addition, human herbivores fancy the "flesh" of fruits and vegetables and the "meat" of nuts. Related to these survival values, symbolic practices, and taste preferences for certain corporeal entities (usually cooked or ripe), there are hygienic values that refer to somatic health (of living bodies). In the words of one phenomenologist, "Each human can focus on her own body or, preferably, her soma as a case of personal human organic life and, with respect to the soma, a difference between wellness and illness can be recognized."[40] Normally, being of sound constitution is valued positively while being sick is deemed negative.

Because bodily values can be stored and (re)distributed, units of flesh are also subject to economic evaluation. Most inhabitants of the so-called developed world are acquainted with this reality only through such intermediary institutions as the supermarket and the stock exchange; the subsistence forager/trader, however, has direct familiarity. Lastly, quite apart from piecemeal circulation of "dead meat," live flesh can enter functionally as a whole into valuable sexual transactions. Depending on context, the value of sexual intercourse is founded on other, more basic forms of valuation. For romance, sexuality is largely an aesthetic affair. As a matrimonial matter, it often becomes genetically procreative. In the marketplace, prostitution prizes sex as economic exchange.[41]

Cultural Dialectics in a Nietzschean Mode

There is a growing body of contemporary philosophy that explores and recasts the Western tradition's estimation of humanity's animal nature and its corollary estimation of bodiment. In order to help exhibit the connections between esteeming the bodily and (re)valuing animal nature, I will elaborate an illustration of crucial historical import via an interpretation of Nietzsche's thought. Nietzsche's philosophy is particularly apropos for my study because Nietzsche was, arguably, more concerned than any other philosopher in the Occidental tradition with the nature of values, the value of values themselves, and the relations among values. In what follows, I consider Nietzsche's explorations of what he calls "prejudices of philosophers" in terms of how certain values have sculpted and deformed some concepts that are basic to both philosophy and folk theories, including the transcendent character of human existence, the soul, and the body. Related to this is Nietzsche's naturalism, particularly his interest in evolutionary biology, which I discuss briefly in relation to Nietzsche's consideration of the revaluation of the body and his views on the process of revaluation generally, namely his hypothesis of will to power. Will to power can be considered a name that Nietzsche gives to the process of interpretation, very broadly conceived, in which he thinks all of existence is involved since all change can be characterized in terms of appropriative forces. I claim that this conception of nature, including human existence, is operative in Zarathustra's tantalizing promotion of the *Übermensch,* who is, we are told, "the meaning of the earth." I consider Nietzsche's announcement of the overhuman as an axiological project, one that has broad implications for the treatment of ethics that follows in the next chapter, and reflect on how Nietzsche's biological framework and axiological shift bear on conceptions of the tame and the wild.

I have highlighted the prizing of bodies as meat in the context of considering how bodies take on values, and noted that the prizing of flesh as food occurs not simply in the register of nutritional values. What we eat and how we eat it reflects what we value and how we value. This point was not lost on Nietzsche, who famously discusses food, food preparations, and eating habits, among a variety of other "small things" such as "place, climate, [and] recreation" in his *Ecce Homo*—such "small things" are what I would call corporal dimensions of live bodiment (inclusive of Watsuji's "climaticity").[42] There are two points I wish to make concerning this focus of Nietzsche's attention. It is relevant to Nietzsche's view that body and soul are not separate, separable, or metaphysically distinct. Furthermore, valuation of so-called small things, that which is deemed as inconsequential, mundane, or accidental in human experience, is relevant to the overcoming of what Nietzsche thinks is the misguided interest and investment in the transcendent at the exclusion and neglect of the everyday, ordinary world in which life transpires.

Although Nietzsche appears to subscribe to a kind of naturalism that is largely biological and scientific, he is not an eliminative materialist, at least not in the way that contemporary philosophers understand such a view. Nietzsche's informal study of his own age's science leads him to endorse a view of human beings (and all animate creatures generally) as collections of forces. Thus, the human organism is not a discrete self-identical entity but rather a multiplicity, organized as an oligarchy. There is nothing extra or more added that accounts for our human subjectivity. However, the way in which the constitutive forces organize differentiates us as distinct and unique individuals and accounts for our feelings of volition and spirituality. The orientations of the forces that are dominant in us account for the particular perspectives we associate with what is our own. As Nietzsche anticipates new perspectives that might be possible on the basis of new insights and new modes of valuation, he also envisions different spiritual possibilities, new formulations of what he calls the "soul hypothesis." As indicated previously, a kind of transcendence is possible as an exuberance or excess of vitality is achieved, and for Nietzsche this seems to be the stuff of which a revisioned spirituality would consist. What is called spirit, for Nietzsche, is the human activity of meaning-making (valuing and revaluing) that allows us to redirect our aims and to realize new and different possibilities.

In the first part of *Beyond Good and Evil,* Nietzsche recounts the "prejudices of philosophers" that reflect an ancient legacy of metaphysical assumptions. These assumptions remain unfounded and unchallenged, contrary to the hygienic pursuit of truth that is supposed to characterize modern sciences of all varieties. The concepts of substance, soul, and causality are three of Nietzsche's targets. The concept of substance, Nietzsche suggests, particularly its latest incarnation in the concept of the atom, reflects the desire to hold fast to something that endures and does not change, when all of reality appears to do otherwise (*BGE* 12).[43] The concept of the soul serves a similar psychological function in providing the unchanging ground for the endurance of the unique individual. But throwing out this particular conception of soul does not mean that we must rid ourselves of every conception of it, as some naturalists might believe. Rather, Nietzsche speculates that "the way is open for new versions and refinements of the soul-hypothesis; and such concepts as 'mortal soul,' and 'soul as subjective multiplicity,' and 'soul as social structure of the drives and affects,' want henceforth to have citizens' rights in science."

The concept of causality is problematic, too. Particularly under the aspect of agency, it can be linked to (a bad) "grammatical habit" (i.e., supposing there must be a subject for any and all activity), and is connected to the concept of the atom. It assumes that behind "operating 'power'" there must be an operator, a cause, what Nietzsche in various places calls the "doer behind the deed" (e.g., *GM* I: 13). Descartes' "I" in his *Cogito* is not the cause or producer of his thinking but rather an interpretation of the process of thinking. There is not something separate standing behind the thinking that acts as thought's cause. Likely this is what Nietzsche has in mind when he writes in *Thus Spoke Zarathustra:* "Thus the body goes through history, a becoming and a fighting. And the spirit—what is that to the body? The herald of its fights and victories, companion and echo" (*Z:* I "On Gift-Giving").[44] What we might call "spirit" or "soul" is not something *extra* or *supra* in the sense of being metaphysically distinct from the body. *Spirit* and *soul* are interpretations of bodily activities, of the becoming that the body experiences, the becoming that constitutes and reconstitutes the body; spirit and soul reflect the perspective of the dominant force or subset of forces within the collection of forces that we are.[45] Included among these forces are those that we have in common with other animals (as well as certain forces of interpretation—tendencies toward spiritualization— that Nietzsche appears to think are unique to human; see, e.g., *GM* I: 6).

These points resonate with some recent work of Shannon Sullivan, who has offered a focused discussion of Nietzsche's conception of the body and how certain conceptual resources available in his work support the development of what she describes as a "transactional" sense of bodiment. Drawing on Dewey's pragmatist and evolutionary account of bodily identity as constituted by and revealed through internally relational exchanges between organisms and their environment, Sullivan endeavors to offer a new sense of what she calls "bodying."[46] To regard bodiment as bodying is to consider the body as a set of activities rather than as a substance in its own right. Bodies are therefore always becoming rather than simply being, because they are continually constituted and reconstituted through their interactions with others in the world.[47] Becoming body is a transaction that takes place as I am eating, riding my bicycle, making love, laughing with my child, stroking the silky back of a cat, etc. I do not just *have* a body, and I am not *merely* body (qua corporeal object).

I have already indicated that Nietzsche's revelation of what he calls the "prejudices of the philosophers" (particularly with regard to their conceptions of the human and its possibilities) emerges out of his reading of contemporary scientific texts; his was a particularly exciting and productive period in the history of science. New branches of scientific inquiry were sprouting (such as the field of embryology), and of course evolutionary theory was shaping the scientific thoughtscape. The subject of Nietzsche's naturalism has received considerable treatment in the recent literature. My own view is that Nietzsche is clearly a naturalist in the sense that he rejects (or at least strives to reject) metaphysical explanations for natural phenomena. But he is not a naturalist in the sense of thinking that the only valid account of the world is the view that is given to us by science. There are several reasons why Nietzsche does not stick to that sense of naturalism. Foremost is Nietzsche's view that many of the basic ideas and organizing principles that are part of the practice of science are loaded with metaphysical baggage. One such famous example is the notion of causality, which Nietzsche scholars have discussed at length. Another reason that Nietzsche does not stick with a strictly scientistic view is that he thinks that science itself is an interpretation of human experience, one that is perhaps more hygienic in the sense that it endeavors to rid itself of unjustified assumptions. But the fact that science is an interpretation (rather than a bald presentation of facts in themselves) means that it is always subject to reinterpretation; moreover, all interpretations are interested in the sense of taking particular aims and orientations that are affected by certain values. Science is a specifically human enterprise that cannot help but be organized around (though not limited to) certain specific human interests and limitations. A good part of Nietzsche's critical comments about science reflects his questioning of these interests and a concern for refiguring those borders, and this is the task of the future philosopher that Nietzsche envisions.

Nietzsche's interest in evolutionary theory has received considerable attention in recent books devoted to understanding the cultural/historical context of Nietzsche's thought and its contemporary applications. I will discuss only one small, but significant, facet of this body of work, namely, Nietzsche's general disapproval of Darwinism in favor of the evolutionary theory of William Rolph.[48] This distinction is relevant to my claim that for Nietzsche, there is a sense in which human beings transcend their specific or given biology, but such transcendence is possible only insofar as this-worldly life is embraced rather than fled or denigrated. Gregory Moore has admirably demonstrated that while Nietzsche embraced evolutionary theory generally, he was concerned about Darwinian characterizations of competitive goals.[49] For *what,* exactly, do organisms struggle?

Nietzsche preferred the view of William Rolph who argued in *Biological Problems* that organisms do not merely seek to preserve their existence or persevere—rather they seek the maximal expansion of their abilities, a surplus, excess, a kind of squandering. Rolph's "principle of insatiability" was the key idea in his expansionist evolutionary theory (and provided his main point of contention with Darwinian views, which he took to be conservative and unable to satisfactorily provide an account of improvement and creative change). These ideas find their expression in a variety of Nietzsche's works. Section 349 of *The Gay Science* is representative:

> The wish to preserve oneself is the symptom of a condition of distress, of a limitation of the really fundamental instinct of life, which aims at *the expansion of power* and, wishing for that, frequently risks and even sacrifices self-preservation. . . . In nature it is not conditions of distress that are *dominant* but overflow and squandering, even to the point of absurdity. The struggle for existence is only an *exception,* a temporary restriction of the will to life. The great and small struggle always revolves around superiority, around growth and expansion, around power—in accordance with the will to power, which is the will to life.[50]

This view, combined with ideas drawn from embryologist Wilhelm Roux concerning the agonistic character of individual organisms,[51] had tremendous influence on Nietzsche's views on development, change, growth, and possibilities for perfection, culminating in his (in)famous idea of will to power.

Of course, Nietzsche does not provide us with a full-blown theory of will to power—just a handful of references to the idea appear in his published writings (most notably in *GM,* e.g., II: 12 and *BGE,* e.g., 36) and also in aborted plans and drafts that appear in his unpublished notebooks.[52] For Nietzsche, will to power is a sweeping interpretation of (especially animate) existence ("in all events a *will to power* is operative," *GM* II: 12) and a view about the nature of interpretation generally ("all events in the organic world are a subduing, a *becoming master,* and all subduing and becoming master involves a fresh interpretation, an adaptation through which any previous 'meaning' and 'purpose' are necessarily obscured and even obliterated," *GM* II: 12).[53] All of existence is embroiled in interpretative activity, generally speaking. Everything —particularly what is living—has an orientation in light of which it seeks to appropriate, incorporate, or absorb what it encounters.

Human beings, for Nietzsche, are themselves interpretative enterprises (the interpretations of various dominant drives in a contest with weaker drives) that engage in second-order interpreting. This second-order interpreting, specifically what Nietzsche designates as revaluation (the exemplary case of this being the slave revolt in morality discussed in the first essay of *On the Genealogy of Morals*), generally garners its orientation from first-order interpretations. Out of sensitivity to such proceeds Nietzsche's theory of types as well as his interest in the "small things" mentioned above. In the case of the latter specific bodily habitudes (themselves the result of interpretations in the form of conditioning by dominant drives) supply the valuational orientation for a person's thought more generally. But Nietzsche also appears to think that second-order interpretations might well affect the orientations of the first order. In other words, Nietzsche hypothesizes that it might be possible to reorganize or redirect the constitutional interpretative vectors of an organism through the adoption of different or "higher" (what I have called "second-order") values.[54] Nietzsche's preoccupation with how metaphysics, and Christian values particularly, have sickened human beings is a negative example of this idea. His positive exploration is found in what I wish to describe as Nietzsche's axiological project, which is inaugurated in *Zarathustra's* pronouncement that the *Übermensch* is the "meaning of the earth."[55]

In his effort to elaborate what is meant by Nietzsche's claim that the transhuman is the (new) meaning of the earth, Adrian Del Caro focuses on how Nietzsche's dramatic rhetoric serves to redescribe the nature of the body and thus what it means to be human. Del Caro writes, "When the body functions not merely as the carrier or container of the mind, but as the ground itself of what it means to be human, the body, its senses, instincts, and its unique physicality in relation to the [natural] environment assumes new authority, new empowerment."[56] What is this "new empowerment"? I have suggested that one of the most important facets of the naturalistic emphasis and characterization of the body that Nietzsche provides is the new interpretative or evaluative prospect it opens up. Graham Parkes provides a detailed introduction to how *Thus Spoke Zarathustra* inaugurates a kind of ecological thinking in which the figure of Zarathustra is essentially grounded in the earthly.[57] This work is extended further in Del Caro's book: once the body is conceived as the basis or "ground" of human existence, *its* goods, *its* potentialities, *its* possibilities take priority and orient or direct other values we might come to hold.[58] When the goods of the body become the axiological basis for the evaluation or prizing of other goods, new orders of values are constituted—including the valuation of animality more generally, and our appraisals of the tame and the wild more specifically.

When Nietzsche proclaims that "apart from the ascetic ideal, man, the human *animal,* [has] had no meaning so far" (*GM* III: 28), the announcement effectively exhorts his audience toward a trans-signification of human being's animal nature that avoids the hatred of animality that ascetic ideals seem to take as their originary gesture. In the process of zoologically retranslating humankind into nature, Nietzsche continually stresses the importance of feeling humanity's kinship to notoriously "evil" or predaceous species—beasts and birds of prey, snakes, etc.[59] The infamy of such species is understandable, "for the fear of wild animals, that was bred in man longest of all, including the animals he harbors inside himself and fears: Zarathustra calls it the 'inner beast'" (*Z:* 4 "On Science"). Nietzsche's point, however, is that "this hidden core needs to erupt from time to time, the animal has to get out again and go back to the wilderness" (*GM* I: 11). Thus *homo natura* is felt to have a distinctly wild side that is keenly needful of expression.

In Zarathustran terms, the childlike creator is to be the noble successor to both the camel (qua beast-of-burden) and the lion (qua predator) in being human; in other words, playful creation is to succeed both the docile existence of the human herd and the raw energy of the barbarian wilderness.[60] Yet, lest we cast a too-gentle glow upon Nietzsche's portrayal (something which the child-image risks), it is worth emphasizing that Nietzschean creativity never entirely sheds, but rather spiritually incorporates, its animal roots (including the wild strains). "The animal is a creature that persists and must continue to live in the human," as Del Caro interprets Nietzsche, "it is not simply an early stage of the human with which we are finished as a matter of volition."[61] In *Human, All-Too-Human,* for instance, the cultural weight of such incorporation is made manifest. There Nietzsche praises the embodiment of great, opposing forces of culture in an individual life's architecture—and he dreams of this cultural genius in zoomorphic terms: "he is a centaur, half human, half animal" (241, cf. 276).[62] Later in the unfolding of Nietzsche's thought, the heroic *Übermensch* figure takes on the task of cultivating and transforming animality through a spiritual overture of sublimation. It is important to remember that a necessary condition of noble overcoming is atavistic going-under (*Untergang*). Recall, e.g., Zarathustra's dictum, "I must go under" (*Z:* 1, P: 1). For Nietzsche, *übermenschlich* (transhuman) cultivation sublimates naturally primitive zoological drives in a way that does not annihilate or eviscerate wildness—in other words, it spiritually (intellectually or artistically) transforms the brutality of Zarathustra's "inner beast" while preserving its wild animality.[63]

With this claim I part company from interpreters such as Kaufmann and Schacht who stress transcendence of animality to the point of denying, or leaving dubious, the preservation part of the *Aufhebung* (synthetic transfiguration) at issue; from my perspective, Del Caro is closer to the mark when he states: "the superhuman adds on to the human a capacity to recapture and complete the animal, combining the highest spiritual refinement with the 'lowest' animality in one person."[64] Seeded early in his work, Nietzsche's (super)humanizing transformation of animality blossoms into the full-fledged redemption

—not rejection—of animal *physis*. In the later image of a Zarathustran metaphor, humanity appears as a rope tied between animalism and the superhuman (*Z*: 1, P: 3). That rope is never cut by Nietzsche—rather, the braiding of its strands is only tightened and celebrated: "*esprit* and happy exuberance in favor of the animal in man is in [cultivated] ages the most triumphant form of spirituality" (*WP* 1019).

The redemptive project anticipated in *The Gay Science* (109), and inaugurated in *Thus Spoke Zarathustra*—"When may we begin to 'naturalize' humanity in terms of a pure, newly discovered, newly redeemed nature?"—is quite *anti*-Christian: it buys back animal nature at a higher human value than had been European civilization's theological custom. Using a Kantian formula to phrase Nietzsche's view, one can say that while animality without humanity may be (relatively) blind, still, humanity without animality is decidedly empty.[65] For Nietzsche, therapeutically interested in the "psychophysics" of culture, the European herd-history of common civilization has produced animals spiritually sickened by becoming all-too-humanly tame; their illness can, however, be overcome by *übermenschlich* individuals who have the courage and the relevant dominating force(s) to instinctually and artistically reappropriate—redeem and transvalue—ancestral animality from the prehistoric wild.[66] In calling for and cultivating an experimental education of the human animal from civilized domesticity to atavistic wilderness, Nietzsche can be seen to develop a feral philosophy of cultural zoology. In other words, he advances his philosophical anthropology within a broader, zoologically natural history of culture.[67] The process has at least two main components: a project of diagnosis followed by a therapeutic application. The diagnostic project aims at the "revelation" of animality beneath the overlays of theological and humanistic constructions (this unfolds in a scientifico-logical fashion). The previous discussion of Nietzsche's revelation and critique of the "prejudices of philosophers" indicates some of the turns in Nietzsche's critical diagnosis. The therapeutic project aims at the "restoration" of wildness in the human animal (this proceeds in an aesthetico-literary mode; for example, in the early Nietzsche, the restoration of such wildness transpired in the new symbolization of the body that the Dionysian presence lent to tragedy).

In *Beyond Good and Evil*, Nietzsche issues a command that provides a strong clue for the correction of humankind's erroneous zoological/ecological self-image: "the basic text of *homo natura* must again be recognized" (230). Given Nietzsche's radically hermeneutic epistemology, to call *homo natura* a "text" (rather than an interpretation) is to cognitively valorize this image of humanity with an astonishingly honorific title. Of course, some of the astonishment vanishes when Nietzsche sets it as the preeminent task of anthropological knowledge-seekers "to translate man back into nature" (*BGE* 230).[68] Methodologically, the proposed translation is to be conducted with "Odysseus ears, deaf to the siren songs of old metaphysical bird catchers who have been piping at him [man] all too long, 'you are more, you are higher, you are of a different origin!'" (*BGE* 230). Substantively, humanity's animal genesis is at stake for Nietzsche.

From the Christian perspective that Nietzsche rejects, animality comes in only two states: tame or wild, and this view has been attributed to Nietzsche himself. As one commentator puts it, "Nietzsche's *scalae naturae* consists of two basic groups: the weaker *Sklaventiere,* or domesticated animals in the service of man, and the *Raubtiere,* the less slavish animals of prey."[69] It is clear that Nietzsche does not want to tame human animality—that has been the task for the past two millennia of Christianity, and for hundreds of years prior, of Platonism and its offshoots. It also seems clear to me that Nietzsche does not wish to have humans become a kind of *superbrute;* this is evidenced by his valorization of different conceptions of the soul in which certain "brutish" traits become something *more* through their spiritualization. Yet, fortunately, these two options are not exhaustive: zoologically speaking, it is possible for an animal to be neither fully tame nor entirely wild, but rather liminally feral.[70]

Ferity, then, is the hermeneutic middle excluded from standard readings of Nietzschean animality; ironically, it is central to Nietzsche's own retranslation of the text he calls *homo natura.* Nietzsche's conception of the philosopher helps to reveal his affirmative vision of human animality positioned between the extremes of pure domesticity and raw wilderness. The philosopher, as a central figure in Nietzsche's cultural zoology, subliminally fuels intellectual activity with a deep draft of wild animality.[71] Philosophy, that is, draws on a whole complex of animal instincts. Far from the stereotype of cool contemplation, the Nietzschean thinker is *la bête philosophe*—at once bestial and noble.[72] This kind of philosopher is a paradoxical avatar of culture, for his flight from civilization is charged with a prized mission of cultivation and education (see "Schopenhauer as Educator," in *Unmodern Observations,* e.g.). Neither a completely docile "herdsman" or "shepherd," nor a thoroughly savage "exception," he is rather a feral "deserter" or "fugitive" (*TI* "Maxims" 37 and *WP* 1009). Tame-gone-wild, the philosopher as cultural critic/constructor looks back at, while running ahead of, his society and epoch: he cultivates (implants ideals) by educating (literally, "leading out"). Thus, philosophy for Nietzsche has the task of riding and remapping the liminal frontier between domesticity and wilderness, culture and nature, human and animal.[73] With its feet in two worlds, "domestico-wild" philosophy demands that its practitioners have a double persona. Janus-faced, feral philosophy must scale and plumb the extremities of surplus and defect in human animality. Its cultural work is agonistic—to think and live, that is, on the creatively tense threshold between principles of outlandish transcendence and civilized historicity.

Because it is not wholly wild, feral philosophy's "cultivated transcendence" can court confusion with the domesticative disease infecting civilization (as diagnosed by Nietzsche). There is, however, a distinction that may be drawn between the residential and the carceral. Perhaps Nietzsche hopes that the house of culture to be built by his free spirits of the future will not be like the jail cell of European Christendom. Construction of a cultural home, in other words, does not have to be *oppressively* domestic—rather than repressing wild animality, it might be flexible enough to let the animal in us emerge and return occasionally to the wilderness (*GM* I: 11). Beyond this point, furthermore, there is an aspect of Nietzsche that positively affirms what could be called "training without taming."[74] Indeed, the (new) philosopher's cultural advent and pedagogical practice is described in terms of discipline and cultivation (*BGE* 203, *WP* 980). More broadly, Nietzsche is clear that an important part of any spiritual growth is a "going-under" that requires taking on burdens of pain and involves deep distress. In *Beyond Good and Evil* he asks rhetorically: "That tension in the soul in unhappiness which cultivates its strength, its shudders face to face with great ruin, its inventiveness and courage in enduring, persevering, interpreting, and exploiting suffering, and whatever has been granted to it of profundity, secret, mask, spirit, cunning, greatness—was it not granted to it through suffering, through the discipline of great suffering?" (225).

This kind of phenomenon echoes the disciplinary virtues described in *Zarathustra*'s "Three Metamorphoses." It is also tied to what Nietzsche calls breeding (*Züchtung*), something that he explicitly discriminates from taming and extols for its vivifying potency: "There is no worse confusion than the confusion of breeding with taming: . . . Breeding as I understand it, is a means of storing up the tremendous forces of mankind so that the generations can build upon the work of their forefathers—not only outwardly, but inwardly, organically growing out of them and becoming something stronger." (*WP* 398)

How, then, can this sort of training be distinguished from the domestication process Nietzsche so often excoriates? One way would be to lean on the distinction drawn between a dispositional mode of being and a directional application of that mode (*WP* 281). For Nietzsche, the Christian/democratic form of domestication uproots our biological makeup and infects us with a life-denigrating orientation (disposition or being-mode), whereas the cultivation he promotes would train (harbor and apply) certain organic drives in a life-enhancing direction or vector.[75] In terms of a Nietzschean bestiary, the beast of burden outranks the herd animal—because working as the former can serve a genuinely culture-building function (as in the camel-like self-discipline of learning, en route to overcoming, a tradition), and thus breeds a vital nobility or dignity that the latter lacks and even counteracts through its debilitating regime of civilization (as in the acceptance of conformity and complacency seen in the devolved figure of the flea-like "last man" [*Z*, P: 5]).

NIETZSCHE holds that in the past, "the meaning of all culture" has been "the reduction of the beast of prey 'man' to a tame and civilized animal, a domestic animal" (*GM* I: 11). Because he evaluates herd-society negatively as the moribund decay of primordially wild animal energies, Nietzsche envisions a need for atavistically reinfusing humanity with its more bestial nature. Positing a Euro-historic duality between life-denying civilization and life-affirming culture (where life is biologically reducible to "will-to-power"), Nietzsche's thought challenges free-spirited philosophers of the future to undertake the naturalistically redemptive task of cultivating human animality in its full richness. Thus the broad project of philosophical education spins out of the creatively fertile agonism between (healthy) culture and (sick) civilization (*BGE* 61 and *WP* 121, cf. *WP* 966). This program requires an understanding of domesticity, a retranslation of *homo natura* as animal, and an experimental willingness to psychosomatically transfigure oneself into a sublim(at)e(d) embodiment of wilderness—it calls, in other words, for *Übermenschen* of cultural zoology to act as feral philosophers. Ferity, then, is a liminal mode of human animality tapped by Nietzsche's project of biological naturalization in order to redeem humanity's animal *physis* while avoiding the tame and wild extremes of civilized captivity and uncultivated barbarity. Hence, transvaluatory maintenance of carnate animality throughout the spiritual overtures of cultural sublimation serves as a corrective for, and a continuing check on, the false evolutionary consciousness manifested in what Nietzsche identifies as the error of homo-hubristic hierarchy over other organisms.[76]

Questions of Conditioning

My extended Nietzschean excursus maps the cultural logic of valuing animality across at least one layer of its historical sedimentation. Nietzsche endeavors to revalue and prize wilder sides of animal nature, and that emphasis leads him to extol fierce virtues: competition, dominance, exploitation (as forms of will-to-power). Obviously, this kind of praise leaves him open to the possibility of critique and condemnation, especially from those who seek to emphasize nurturance and care in their ethical theories. For contemporary feminist philosophers particularly, Nietzsche's harsh vision of *homo natura* is easily read as a masculinist (mis)construction of human animality.[77] Corroboratively, neo-Nietzschean authors such as Spanish philosopher José Ortega y Gasset appear to perpetuate their master's romantically patriarchal mythology of the brutal beast.[78] However, as the work of Clarissa Pinkola Estes shows, celebration of wildness need not be androcentric (or reprehensible).[79] Yet, aside from specific texts' gendered genealogies, what matters here more generally is that privileging wilderness risks losing sensitivity to domestic and civic virtues altogether.[80] The household and society as such are not forms of life to be rejected out of hand—especially not if my earlier phenomenology is right to interpret life itself as ontologically residential and existentially convivial.[81] Somatically speaking, we may applaud the "home-body."[82]

My emphasis on the notion of the feral in Nietzsche also brings forward the broad issue of valuation's embedment in a cultural matrix. We cannot simply value organismic (animal/bodily) being *in vacuo*. Nietzsche shows us otherwise from the animal perspective; under the aspect of bodiment, contemporary critical theories and deconstructions of the body demonstrate the same point.[83] Not naively granted, "carnation" is inscribed with(in) an acosmic array of discursive and practical complexes.[84] This conditionality of embodiment has prompted two vectors of intellectual response: (1) relinquish the very notion of "the body," embrace ever-multiplying difference, and set about inventively de- and re-constructing actual and virtual bodies;[85] (2) resurrect the idea of a

[right margin handwritten note:] "bodies" are within cultures + are shaped by them, of course

[left margin handwritten note:] Haraway

shared body, insist on some form of stability, and hermeneutically thematize the commonality of real or possible forms of "fleshood."[86]

Bluntly put, I think the second of these two alternatives is inclined toward a better track of thought. The first one has a hyper-textualistic tendency to issue from, or else become, a theoretical position that can be characterized as breaking bodiment down into units of linguistic meaning, setting these bits of pseudo-body afloat on a turbulent sea of textual signification, and casting suspicion upon any suggestion that there is some structure of corpor(e)al being below the surface of discursive and cultural symbols.[87] This theoretical posture often romanticizes rootlessness. Helen Chadwick, for example, effusively opines: "released from the bonds of form and gender, flesh is volatile and free to wander in an aetiology of complete abandon."[88] Scratch the surface of such reckless romanticism and the begged questions multiply upon exposure: Do somatic patterns *per se* restrict growth, or do they rather enable it? What sort of "freedom" does volatile, Dionysiac abandonment produce? Are not Apollonian moments of "body-discipline" also necessary and enjoyable? The extreme implications of this stance are questionable, as are its premising maneuvers. That is to ask, is the reduction of somatology to semiotics warranted in the first place? And is the system of signs itself ontologically closed? Answers to such questions are hard to extract from the recent plethora of critical theories of body, upon which conceptual dispersion of carnality is largely based. I suspect that this critical literature arises from a swell of abstract *skepsis* against epistemically totalizing absolutism, which then overreaches its originally admirable cognitive impulse and is misdirected against ontological reality.

Hypothetically speaking, a similar theory is derivable from mixing Berkeley's immaterialism and Hamann's "linguism" with Nietzsche's atheism. This derivation may have not only heuristic value but also historical validity. A strong tide of European philosophy has, since British empiricism and Kant's "Copernican revolution," subscribed to cognitive perspectivism, which became discursive in contour upon taking the twentieth century's "linguistic turn" (presaged by Hamann, well ahead of his time). The mirror-image comparison to Berkeley then becomes edifying: whereas the bishop purchased ontological objectivity at the expense of invoking an epistemic Absolute (God the Knower, cognitive *deus ex machina*), today many theorists abandon epistemic absolutism (Nietzsche's dictum "God is dead" announcing the cognitive collapse of "grand narrative") at the price of surrendering ontic reality (mind, thing, self, body, etc. all erased or elided). "But the search for grounds must not be thrown out with the godwater," responds Martin Dillon—and I am inclined to agree (though not in any naively objectivistic sense).[89]

The reason why I resonate with Dillon's plea is that I do not think somatology is reducible to semiotics, nor do I believe that all systems of signs are subject to ontological closure.[90] First, there are some elementary aspects of different bodies that transcend cultural symbolism. As examples, it is not culture that decides whether some bodies can fly and others cannot, some can get pregnant and others not, etc. Of course, cultural and social systems (as well as individual intentions!) contribute to the causal and semiotic contexts by and in which particular bodies do/not go airborne (on their own) or do/not bear offspring (in themselves) and come to carry a wide variety of (human and/or animal) meanings associated with such experiences. Nonetheless certain corporeal potentialities are rightly classified as natural capacities to begin with. Second, it is possible to adduce all sorts of bodily phenomena that originate outside artificial systems of significance. Illustrations include blushing, suckling, sweating, and so on: though all of these corporal phenomena are usually (at least for most mammals) experienced in the semantic context of some cultural discourse or matrix of social interactivity, *that* they happen in the first place is not a matter *only* of culture or society.

I am neither claiming nor implying that bodies can biologically "determine" identity or practices. Rather, I am concurring with Sullivan "that room be made for the discussion of concrete, had experiences of lived bodies," and going beyond her to suggest that such discussions presuppose (even if they cannot articulate) corporeal contributions of pre- or non-discursive bodiment.[91] In other words, without surrendering ourselves to any egregious biological determinism (Big Body, as it were), we may yet sustain an appreciative sense of the "real terrestrial weight" we bear as corporal animals.[92] Such a restorative sensibility of axiotic synthesis fuses the two value-concerns treated in this chapter (prizing bodiment and animal appreciation). Moreover, this insight is not merely an abstraction, for there is a measure of axiological specificity to be had: as phenomenologist Daniel Guerriere observes, "What is valuable is not life or the body in general but rather its concrete modalities. These modalities constitute [operational] organic or vital values . . . [of] nutrition, growth, reproduction, and irritability."[93] Of these, the most salient for animal appreciation is the last, which is perhaps better denominated *responsiveness* to (especially the living) environment.

FOUR

Ethos and *Leib*

"*Symphysics*" *of Transpecific Morality*

Our concern with the significance of living form not only involves
a deepening and enrichment of our own experience, it also . . .
strengthen[s] our sense of responsibility with respect to the foreign
forms we find in nature.

ADOLF PORTMANN (1990)

Maybe, being ethical is more about being attuned to the earthbodies
which open up to one another in a flow of feeling.

GLEN MAZIS (2002)

DAVID MICHAEL LEVIN has written compellingly on the subject of somatology's morally educative function. He believes there are profoundly ethical
consequences that flow from the "bodily felt sense of our primordial intercorporeality." Broadly stated, his claim is that there is "an elemental, pre-existent
matrix of flesh which is *inherently* social, and which already sets down each
[body-]subject's incontestable and inalienable *kinship* with all other sentient
and mortal beings."[1] So long as we resist any temptation to characterize it in
terms of eternal necessity or metaphysical ultimacy, this claim is consonant with
the somatically hermeneutic phenomenology of life developed in the course of
my ongoing discussion, and it is logically committed to cross-species parameters (despite Levin's humanistic method). That the kinship in question includes other animals can be inferred from Levin's phrasing ("*all* other sentient
and mortal beings") and is confirmed by my own phenomenology's explication of the flesh-matrix's inherently ecological aspect. That such a position is

also implicitly ethical follows upon recognition of the (pre-)moral texture of conviviality. As Carleton Dallery reasons, the perceptual "inter-world" of living experience is existentially proto-ethical: "we are in and of nature through our multisensory coexistence or perception. . . . To see the animal moving in its environment is already to 'care' about the animal."[2]

Another relevant ethical implication of Levin's work is its relationship to traditional moral sense theory: "The naturalism which begins (with Hume, for example) by grounding moral principles in forms of sensibility which 'custom' has tactfully informed needs to be *supplemented* by a naturalism which recognizes the antecedents of our moral intuitions, and our moral sensibility in general, in our bodily felt *sense* of existence."[3] I would like to cast my own moral scheme in the same sensual mold. Indeed, I think a transpecific somatology of ethics is an indispensable complement to conventional moral sense theory.[4] Obversely and additionally, I believe a new kind of thinking about moral sense can be activated by the sort of ethic implicit in the somatology I have engaged. (Such moral mileage is facilitated by lifting phenomenology's provisional suspension of explanation and/or interpretation.) Beneath the lofty abstraction and pallid platitude of sentimentality as articulated in the Scottish Enlightenment,[5] I intend to affirm the earthy physicality of moral life—it is time, as it were, to put the body back into moral sense.

This move is somewhat heterodox in the field of animal ethics, at least from the perspective of its seminal theorists (Singer, Regan, et al.). There has been a fairly pervasive rationalism that runs through much of the mainstream analytic treatment of the subject, not epistemologically (say in contrast to empiricism) but rather in the sense of moral intellectualism. First- and second-generation thinkers in the area usually took or adopted this stance on ethical or more broadly philosophic principle, but behind their foreground theorizing there was a sociohistorical context that placed structural demands of a rhetorical nature on their discourse(s). Before animal ethics became (in the 1970s and 1980s) a subspecialty within the academic discipline of philosophy, there was an already venerable tradition of animal advocacy and activism (in many countries, including the United States and United Kingdom). Many ideological platforms and strategies of action coexisted under various rubrics, most especially those of "welfare" and "humane." The principal message that broke through into popular consciousness, from the nineteenth up until (at least) the mid-twentieth century, can be characterized justly as a be-kind-to-animals sentiment. To the chagrin of its self-consciously serious proponents, this essentially anti-cruelty movement became branded by dominant humanist culture (especially establishment media) as sentimental in the derogatory sense —with the stereotyped advocate portrayed as an overly romantic, bleeding-heart (pejoratively effeminate) "animal lover." Against this background it is understandable, if not entirely excusable, that early on, (mostly male) animal ethicists as well as their immediate interlocutors/commentators would disown embodied emotion and promote a purely rational basis for "animal liberation" or "animal rights." Such a strategy, which was likely only half-conscious in motivation and implications, effectively served as a rhetorical bid for renewed stature and so greater influence.

Over the past few decades both the philosophical and animal advocate communities have learned a good deal, theoretically as well as practically, from the recent rehabilitation of embodied existence and emotional life conducted by feminist thinkers and activists as well as other ethicists. Acknowledging as much, I join company with those who would correct for a certain affective/somatic deficit in animal ethics. Arne Vetlesen points out: "the act of [ethical] judgment we exercise presupposes and rests on an act of [moral] perception that logically precedes it . . . feelings are required in the sense that there can be no successful act of moral perception, or [*a fortiori*] of moral judgment, without the participation of the faculty of empathy and hence of our emotional capacity, our elementary ability to feel."[6] And as Josephine Donovan observes, "It is a particular qualitative experience that is missing in contemporary rationalist theory, the emotional sympathetic understanding of another creature."[7] I would add that this experience is originally mediated by physical sensibility.

Several "senses" or meanings of *sense* are operating in my account of life-worldly bodiment: in order to make somatic sense of moral sensibility (i.e., to render intelligible the significance of its somaticity), the corporal sensitivity of the body's senses or sensory experiences needs to be thematized by ethical thought. Concretely and critically speaking, one may ask if such a move lends legitimacy to colloquial maxims of carnal license—such as, "if it feels good, do it." Certainly this result is a risk, but it is not a necessary consequence. According to Levin, for instance, the child educated into an embodied ethos of living "learns, or realizes, a very basic, very 'natural' procedure for *reflecting* on his experience of the moral claims that various situations will make on him, and for reaching significant conclusions that pass the tests of good bodily feeling, good bodily sense."[8] Levin does not explicate these criteria, and I suspect that he would regard misplaced any move toward discursively expressing them in abstract terms of formulaic prescriptions or propositional principles.[9]

How might a corporally restorative reformation of moral philosophy proceed? For direction, we can take a cue from the ethical implications of the axiology presented in the last chapter. Carnate valuations arise as (internally) relational field-phenomena of the *Leibswelt*. If we are interested in the moral fiber of this field, we need to work out the translation of bodily value into the realm of right conduct and good character. Specifically, the relevant question is whether somatic axiology favors an instrumentalist/exploitive or a participatory/protectionist orientation toward other (than human) animals. It is all too tempting for an interspecies moralist, as animal advocate, to answer immediately on behalf of the latter alternative—obviously, it would be alleged, transpecific protectionism existentially follows from the experience of cross-species intercorporeity. Yet as philosophers, especially if inclined toward amoralist metaethics, we must be more careful and deliberate; thus I shall stay that quick reply, out of cautious reservation and in keeping with the metaethical methodology laid out in chapter one.

In some sense, then, it does seem suitable to endorse (invitingly if not injunctively) a protectionist stance regarding other animals on the basis of an interspecies/incarnate axiology. Yet in just what way is that suitability manifested? Perhaps in the manner identified by Maurice Mandelbaum, who holds: "all cases in which an agent experiences a *moral* demand presuppose an apprehended relation of fittingness."[10] We might posit this kind of fitting-relation between value and deed, appreciation and action, axiology and attitude. Strictly speaking, the relation itself is indefinable (as Mandelbaum notes) and hence not conducive to logical demonstration. Still, its apprehension can be given more or less phenomenologically rigorous descriptions. Typically, when set in a transhuman context, the apprehension is said to occur in or through a mental process of imaginatively empathetic identification: according to this view, we picture in our mind's eye (or "heart") what it would be like to take the place of a given nonhuman, and then we morally "see" that protectionist injunction x or demeanor y is fitting.[11] From the standpoint of the somatic ontology and corporal axiology mobilized in this study, I believe that such an account is inadequate.[12]

In order to supply a more satisfactory elucidation of the apprehension of moral fittingness, I introduce less familiar but more appropriate notions. The moral intuitions of an animal-friendly bioethic of bodiment—the deontic deliverances that comprise it—are mediated by certain soma-based experiences of multispecific, contypical *symphysis*. Existentially speaking, a "deontic deliverance" is the comportmental orientation constituted by a "deontic experience."[13] Second, "symphysis" is meant to convey the sense of sharing with somebody else a somaesthetic nexus experienced through a direct or systemic (inter)relationship.[14] In this way the concept comes to signify a pattern of more densely physical orientation—i.e., by contrast to the more airy, psychic notion of sympathy frequently utilized by moral sense theorists.[15]

Mapped onto the medium of flesh, symphysis can reflect universal as well as personal experiences—from sexual intimacy as carnal concentricity to pan-vitalist, quasi-mystical communion with the planet perceived as creaturely "carnosphere." For my purposes here, I will be concerned with symphysical experiences taking place between these existential extremities of emotional depth and environmental breadth, moral experiences whose intelligibility requires attention neither to erotic love nor to global consciousness.[16] Corresponding morally to symphysis would then be an idea of "ethical sensorium" by or through which symphysical encounters and memories happen and recirculate, existentially and axiologically.[17] I have introduced new terminology here because I believe talking of symphysis is the best way to describe the proto-ethical feeling that assures us of another animal being's morally considerable capacity for conviviality. Inferential reasoning by analogy may rationally justify that assurance and psychology of imagination may scientifically explain it via empathic projection, but only somatologies of "genus-being" (fellow-feeling with other species) can phenomenologically articulate its actual experience.[18]

What, then, are the processes of symphysical morality? One method for articulating the contours of its multi-specific functioning would be to follow Husserl's somatological advice: "The foundation [of somatology] is finally the direct somatic perception that every empirical investigator can effect only on his own body and then the somatic interpretation [lit. clarification] that he performs in the interpretive apprehension of perceived alien animate organisms as such."[19] Two caveats take us beyond Husserl. The amendment I formulated in the first chapter for the application of somatology to transpecific contexts permitted, in effect, the extension of somatic interpretation to all contypical live bodies. Moreover, consider that somatic interpretation is neither exclusively composed of, nor primarily based on, cogitation—in the first instance it is more felt than thought, and it retains (at least residually) affective aspects even upon reflection. Moreover, I do not regard this feature as an automatic liability, despite the general trend in ethical theory to discount, restrain, or rationalize the emotions, at least until rather recently. Oddly, even someone like Donovan—who seeks to recuperate emotive wellsprings for animal ethics—insists on stressing the "complex intellectual" nature of sympathy (inclusive of reasoning and judgment) lest it be consigned to the devalued category of feeling.[20] Such a backslide into moral rationalism still implicitly takes cogitative reason as the effective standard of bona fide ethics. By contrast, I claim not just that embodied emotion is really more rational than we thought—but also, and of equal importance, that it is more valuable (even in its arational aspect) than most moral philosophers have been ready to grant.

What are the bounds of somatology's "contypical" scope? Husserl's student, Edith Stein, claims in reply: "the type 'human physical body' does not define the limits of . . . what can be given to me as a living body."[21] In fact, she takes a step beyond her mentor's mostly homo-exclusive thought by reviewing the following case: "Should I perhaps consider a dog's paw in comparison with my hand, I do not have a mere physical body, either, but a sensitive limb of a living body. And here a degree of projection is possible, too. For example, I may sense-in pain when the animal is injured." Still Stein warns that "other things, such as certain positions and movements, are given to me only as empty presentations without the possibility of [somatic] fulfillment."[22] In this hasty judgment she would seem to be mistaken—at least, that is, if the work of Kenneth Shapiro can be trusted. Shapiro has developed human-canine hermeneutics precisely in the area of "kinesthetic empathy," and his powerfully positive results militate against Stein's residual anthropocentrism.[23] He demonstrates what I have argued at earlier points, namely, that when members of different species share a common living arrangement (for example, a household or workspace), it is possible for them to surmount sensorimotor variance and attain viable practices of nonverbal bodily communication (effectively mutual understanding).

It is important to explain how someone as astute as Stein might not discover the somatological insights at which Shapiro later arrived, because now Shapiro's findings risk being misunderstood by a similar form of oversight.

empathy

Basically, the difficulty lies in conceiving transpecific situations under the rubric of empathy—a mistake that often occurs in phenomenological literature dealing with experience of other animals. Empathetic methodology is prone to be ontologically misleading, for empathy itself normally serves—theoretically at least—as the psychic principle of intersubjectivity (that is, as a solution to the so-called problem of other minds). But to use empathy in this way is to presume an ontology that grants the presence already of subject/object division and subject/subject separation; in other words, it is to assume an egological horizon of original experience. Such an assumption, however, reverses the actual order of existential development; far from being prior, a solipsistic scenario is rather a reflective abstraction away from community context. When that community is multispecific, the primary experiential principle of conviviality is the bodily one that I am calling symphysis.[24]

symphysis

Reversion to empathy-talk will undercut appropriate description; thus, it is important to choose terminology carefully. To her credit, Stein qualifies the experience at stake as sensual empathy, adding that for the purpose of precision we should refer to *Einempfindung* (rather than *Einfühlung*).[25] But sensing-in is still too projective a phrase, for it suggests that convivial experience is had *by* a person *of* something (possibly inert) *into* which that person must, as it were, cast the actuality of animation. Yet conviviality does not come about like this, at least not exactly so. It occurs instead *through* communal experience *with* somebody (already alive), symphysically (where *physis* signifies living matter). Hence, in remaining loyal to Husserlian egology, Stein can grasp only half of transpecific *Mitsein* (its status as sensation but not its property of communion); and Shapiro, by continuing to phenomenologize in terms of empathy, obscures (at least the temporal aspect of) existential priority vis-à-vis human-animal hermeneutics. Empathy is a force that builds bridges of identification across separation, whereas symphysis is a state or condition of merging through commonality (shy of total fusion)—empathy establishes atomic or molecular connections as external relations, but internally relational symphysis has no atoms to begin with.

Beyond critical commentary, my own concern is that we do not misinterpret the biosocial mediation of transhuman morality by letting any aura of alienation appear as if it were foundational. What Mary Midgley has called the mixed community (of adults, children, and animals)[26] is not a figment of nostalgic sentimentality for some fairy-tale kind of coexistence; quite to the contrary, it is our native setting—the symphysical "home-base" for all soma-tology.[27] Along with this realization, we recognize that individuality—never (solely) primordial—is an achievement derived through detachment and self-definition; as philosopher Kuang-Ming Wu puts it, "we ourselves are com-munal first, before being individuated into isolate units."[28] I depart from existentialist ideology at this point. There are those who believe that the per-sonal center of consciousness is *the* "radical reality."[29] Ultimately, however, that being remains rooted in the co-basic reality of pedologic circumstance—the ground of childhood, the soil of earthy nature and of mixed society into which we are born and through which we must develop. Isolation is always impure: hermits and solipsists are refugees from the inescapable. Accordingly, we have to overcome the entire tradition of thought—from Fichte through Husserl and Sartre—that grants ontic primacy to ego or ontologic primacy to egology.[30] The whole modern discourse of I's, their first-person faces wearing soulful eyes of empathy, is (to be) superseded somatologically as a truly trans-human ethos emerges.[31] To the task of charting its emergence, I now turn—first with reference to vulnerability and then to association.[32]

Vulnerability: Finitude of Animate Form

In the abstract, or for "the animal" as such, it is difficult to map an ethos with any phenomenological clarity. In order to gain climatic/cultural context, there-fore, I return to the sort of parkland scenario portrayed in chapter two. Perhaps the quintessential inhabitants therein are the squirrels, to whom I trust most park visitors are accustomed. What kinds of bodily encounters are possible with these rodents? None, the stay-at-home or pet-keeping skeptic might retort—certainly, we do not (ordinarily) cuddle or tussle with them (like we do, for example, with the typical household companion animal). Against such an ob-jection, I hold that at least some of us, sometimes have literal contact with squirrels—there are occasions, however infrequent, on which the rodents nib-ble foodstuffs from human hands. Moreover, tactile intimacy is not necessary to establish the symphysical unity I believe undergirds moral intuitions regard-ing the welfare of squirrels. Symphysis is sufficiently manifested in the somaes-thetic conviviality conducted through the medium of world-flesh. Instances of intersomaticity that (partially) constitute this conviviality include that I: note the passage of seasons in the bushiness of squirrels' tails (effecting a common climaticity), aurally attend to their clucking barks as they play or mate (shaping a shared auditory life-world), watch them forage for food as I also gather edibles (a scene sometimes eventuating in simultaneous eating), etc. How would such experiences lead to an appreciation of "squirreldom"? Much would depend on the tropological filters canvassed in the previous chapter. If I live toward rodents in general as "deviant similars," then they will not be for me truly fellow mammals, but rather perverse pests. However, if I live toward them as "related others," then I come to positively value aspects of their being. For example, taking up the associated aesthetic of marvel, I become appreciative of tail-bearing. I admire the myriad observable operations of "tailing" squirrel-style: screening against wind, shading against sun, balancing on branches, cushioning for falls, guarding offspring, fun-waving, and sex-splashing (and so on). Finally, alongside or through such appreciation I am inclined to feel (in a stewardly manner) obliged to protect squirrels: positively, I experience a moral demand to look after their welfare; negatively, I find it fitting that they go unharmed (subject to the ecosystemic dynamics of the park as biome).[33] This is a concrete, species-expanded object lesson of body-ethical argument recently put forth by Edith Wyschogrod in somewhat more abstract and decidedly more anthropocentric terms, to the effect that "pain and death break into the descriptive and constative character of the body as text to introduce proscriptive and prescriptive meaning."[34] Vulnerability, she observes, constitutes a proscriptive "corporeal plea" against violence, as if the other's body were saying "do not injure me"; likewise, according to Wyschogrod, it is capable of engendering a prescriptive impetus toward "meliorative action," which may even result (with repetition) in a pattern of radically generous altruism.

It may be objected that the illustration given above is too subjective. To this I would reply that the first-person voice is deployed above somewhat abstractly—i.e., not so much (or only) to report my own experience, but rather (also) to invite others to place themselves in that same first-person position. In this twofold maneuver I am following Hans Reiner's phenomenological method for doing ethics, according to which "an indispensable avenue in the beginning is the phenomenologist's *own moral consciousness*."[35] The methodology is filled out—as right now—by publication and audience comparison: "The rest of the procedure consists in *launching,* so to speak, into the world of readers and, more important, of other scientists [or scholars] the descriptions and analyses which are the phenomenological researcher's results, as *propo-*

sitions presented to a number of others to be checked against *their* own (moral) consciousnesses, and then in the propositions' being either *confirmed* and *borne out* or *falsified* by an experienced voice's contradiction and the exhibition of different findings." So the reader is invited to conduct an existential (not merely thought) experiment and compare her own experience.[36] What is called for is not armchair reflection—instead, one would have to get acquainted with squirrels after the fashion described to actually feel what it is like.

What are the pragmatic effects of this sensorial type of ethical experience? The obligation existentially developed above would tend, for example, toward disapproval of wanton tail-chopping and pesticidal poison-laying. The imaginative model of empathic identity deals with ethically troubling scenarios such as these by first assuming an experiential axis of subject/object bifurcation and then allowing a psychic bridge to be built by the subject's cogitative transference of the object's imagined distress. In practice, this would typically mean mentally visualizing self as other (say, as squirrel), then pretending to know the other's suffering (e.g., tail-wound's pain)—whereupon, by explicit or implicit appeal to moral sentiment, there arises the demand to alleviate present displeasure as well as an obligation to prevent identical or similar stress in the future.[37]

The identification model just furnished is off the mark, firstly, because it falsifies the *phenomenological* experience at hand: when I wince at a squirrel with tail freshly cut and bleeding, I do *not* imaginatively "identify" with the animal by a series of mental machinations. What Lawrence Hatab has said about interpersonal empathy applies also here *mutatis mutandis*: "Empathic concern shows moments when we are [directly and spontaneously] affectively in/there/with the person, without a sense of conjuring up feelings or beliefs "inside" and then transferring them to the other person, or processing perceptual data as "misfortune" and then triggering an affect and then casting it out to the Other—all of this in an inferential procedure of external reception, internal processing, and projective transmission. No, the shared affect simply *happens*."[38] Beyond such testimony of phenomenological fact, I suspect that the very notion of psychic identification being questioned is muddled. "If I were that (or a) squirrel . . ."—what can a conditional of this sort mean? Consider: if I were really a squirrel, then "I" would not be the human ego I know as me—I would no longer be my true self; and so it seems that real identity cannot be putatively transferred. A defender of such transference may wish to object that the process does not cancel, but rather "sublimates" anthropic sub-

[margin note:] i.e., this is not a mental operation, but ✴ a psychological one (+ physical too)

jectivity into the zoomorphic persona—but then what imagination yields is either a humanoid squirrel or a squirrelly human, in any case *not* a squirrel *simpliciter.* Though conceptually anthropocentric, my position is not ideologically anthropocentrist; quite generally, I hold that whereas we can and do intelligibly try to understand others' circumstances from their points-of-view, we should give up the pretense that we are capable (under ordinary conditions) of colonizing anyone else's consciousness.[39]

Another reason why the empathic identification model goes awry is because it enforces a misplaced theoretical construct—the subject/object dichotomy—upon the scenario in order to deliver the standard ethical paradigm of moral agent (human observer) and moral patient (squirrel victim). However, lived morality is not always (and seldom exactly) patterned in accord with this paradigm. In the examples under consideration, for instance, my ethical experience is that the symphysical lifeworld shared with squirrels is somaesthetically lacerated when a tail belonging to one of them is cut by gratuitous violence. (Cruel gratuity is distinguishable from vitality of need by attention to the bodily livelihood displayed or lack thereof; to the attentive somatologist, it is symphysically manifest that a bird of prey needs the rodent it strikes down in a way that the human attacker usually does not. So I would say that the falcon's hunger-swoop is a seam in the texture of the lifeworld, in contrast with the tearing of the lifeworld that happens with a superfluous chop.) Likewise, the park *Leibswelt* between, through, and around us has its existential fabric ripped when a normally nimble squirrel twitchingly tailspins into toxic seizure on account of poisoning. In such experiences there emerges at once a moral awareness of ecosystemic fragility beside an ethical sensitivity to organismic vulnerability.[40] These sensibilities have deontic import: they motivate protectionist actions being taken—and principles being formed—on behalf, micrologically, of members of other species (such as individual squirrels) and, macrologically, on behalf of eco-gestaltic forms (such as a park or woodland).[41]

By way of comparison, contemporary hermeneut John Caputo similarly assesses "physical" unfoldings of conscience and he, too, concludes that they do not occur in the space of egology. He asserts that this sort of transaction "is not an operation the I performs—it is not what Husserl calls an ego act—by the magic of empirical empathy or transcendental transfer, which are redundant attempts to cross to a ground on which we already stand."[42] This previously occupied terrain is what I call symphysis. Caputo stresses that this site of "obligation's body" is constructed entirely as an operation of flesh. It is advisable to reflect on this form of paleonymous phrasing (for which I, too, some-times opt), since the old terms of carnality bear histories of usage that risk obscuring the matter. *Flesh* means cutaneous corporeality in ordinary par-lance and marks the matrix of oculocentric perceptibility for (at least Merleau-Ponty's) phenomenology. Yet, what I am most inclined to call symphysis is only incompletely described as a dermal deed or as an affair of in/visibility; expe-rientially, it is as well a whole-body phenomenon—also felt subcutaneously "in the bones," registering viscerally "in the gut," taking place throughout the thickness of live bodiment's material dimension or aspect (*Körper-Leib/ Leibskörper*).[43]

My quasi-poetic formulation is patent and perhaps requires some expla-nation.[44] The field-phenomena I seek to describe are so "panoramic" in scope that their thematic articulation elicits the wide-eyed, even "peripheral" vision especially available through metaphoric discourse. More than this, the life-states treated are "non-positional" forms of awareness—and thus they are particu-larly ill-suited to discursive investigation via (strictly conceptual) propositional analysis. Additionally, my account treats both the holistic dimension and the realm of the individual at once, rather than bifurcating them and then taking sides for one over the other. This feature is helpful for healing schisms in trans-human moral theory between holist and individualist approaches to environ-mental and animal ethics.

In addition, my claims are earthbound and culturally contextualized: I believe they speak to fairly common (potential if not actual) experiences of real people, whose lives are embedded in the contingencies of natural and so-cial history. Dropping transcendent(al) pretenses, I am neither trying to lay an apodictic foundation nor trading in metaphysical truths or eternal essences. Yet, as per Reiner's defense of hermeneutic ethics, I admit that "absolute cer-tainty is of course beyond reach here, but it is safe to say that a high degree of probability . . . is not unattainable in favorable circumstances."[45] In other words, refusal of absolutivity does not necessarily vitiate moral validity. What "normative bite" there may be in my moral phenomenology would derive from its intersubjectival resonance (and not, by counterexample, from its constitu-ents' putative participation with or in heavenly Forms or non-natural properties of The Good or goodness as such).[46]

Finally, the cross-species awareness of vulnerability I have sought to articu-late does not rely on mentation conceived as inherently private consciousness. Indeed, the intersubjectively ethical dimension of transpecific somaticity is precisely attributable to its symphysical nature—and hence, in this way, my phenomenology departs from traditional appeals of moral aetiology to sentiment theory.[47] Cultivating a bodiment ethos of interanimality is not a matter of mentally working one's way into other selves or worlds by quasi-telepathic imagination, but is rather about becoming sensitive to an already constituted "inter-zone" of somaesthetic conviviality.

Togetherness: Forms of Relationship

I would now like to demonstrate how a moral attitude of cross-species caring and respect stems from—or is implicated in—symphysical sensibility about patterns of association such as partnership and neighborhood. Here the relevance of discussing relational dynamics should be apparent: "Togetherness is a mutuality which by nature is something interactive, an active co-partaking in ontological co-resonance."[48] Even as I am wary of traditional ethics of identification, I believe that we should be careful not to embrace uncritically a recently developed climate of opinion in Continental philosophy that favors postmodern ethics of difference. Related to animality, for instance, it has been held that "the animal must remain different, independent and distinct from humans and we are not to make sense of it through human conceptions. All demand for similarity and identification must be forgotten."[49] Driving this and allied trains of thought, I suspect, is an abstract resistance to "the return of the Same," a dubious exoticism according to which anything foreign or strange is *ipso facto* valorized.

Yet, crucial to the intelligibility and value-significance of difference, there must be some comparative ground of commonality. As Elisa Aaltola argues: "We cannot know or respect the animal if it remains [entirely] different and 'other' to us. . . . We have to see it, enter its world with the limited yet genuine methods we have, and come to know it through the interaction that a certain similarity renders possible. We have to understand its viewpoint to have genuine moral consideration for it, and in this way we do have to acknowledge also difference. At the heart of things, however, this understanding rests on similarities, for it is the similarities that make taking the animal's viewpoint possible." It is this sort of common context that my discussion of relationship aims to uncover. Conceptual subtlety and balance are required here: *common-*

ality need not refer exclusively to the equal sharing of an identical property; it may also mean joint intercourse (via complementarity or supplementation, for example) or the crisscrossings and overlappings constituting "families of resemblance" (a la Wittgenstein).

The persistent reticence of Western philosophy to view other animals as (potential if not actual) associates is largely attributable to the belief that interspecific relationships lack reciprocity or mutuality. Since these traits are often taken to be central to morality, Westerners frequently have intellectual difficulty including nonhumans into their circle of ethical considerability or compassion. To challenge the received skepticism in these regards, I would like to consider alternative testimony about animal sociability and its moral significance.

Before continuing, however, I wish to consider the use and abuse of anthropomorphism.[50] A generation ago, the charge of anthropomorphism could be used in a univocally negative sense to criticize a position deserving that appellation. Yet, today, it has become more respectable to make judicious usage of various anthropomorphic figures of speech. It is no longer the case that merely labeling some stance "anthropomorphic" is sufficient to critique it negatively—the word in question has assumed a more neutral (at times even positive) flavor.[51] There are at least two good reasons for this change: we have finally recognized that the (negative) charge of anthropomorphism tacitly presumes that we know (completely) what humanity is and that no other life forms are similar to human beings; but the first presumption is false by ignorance, and the second is false by contrary knowledge. ("Paradoxically," notes Aaltola, "the fear of anthropomorphism turns into anthropocentrism"—because it ontologizes humanity as an essence above and beyond all ties to animal heritage and affinity.[52]) Hence, it is now necessary to show that, and explicitly how, an alleged anthropomorphism is illegitimately used—if the allegation is meant to negatively criticize at all. The upshot of this development, for this study, may be traced as follows: when I adduce evidence of cross-species association that might appear to anthropomorphize nonhumans (or, conversely, zoomorphize humans), it will be with the intention of illuminating the relevant relationship; such evidence has to be judged on its capacity to count toward that purpose, not on its merely seeming or even being "transmorphic" in nature.

To proceed, then: Vicki Hearne, whose work focuses on interrelationships between (members of) different species, regularly handled animals such as dogs and horses as a trainer, and wrote of her experience in (late) Wittgensteinian terms reminiscent of Stanley Cavell's thought. Her main thesis in the book *Adam's Task* is that it makes sense to speak of (some) nonhuman animals as genuine persons who actively participate in a transpecific social space that can be rightly designated a moral cosmos. (This would then suggest, for those who insist on typical theoretical parlance, that these animals are not only objects of ethical concern but are in fact moral subjects.[53]) Various interspecies work narratives told by Hearne, intelligibly use such ethically charged concept-words as 'autonomy,' 'trustworthy,' 'responsibility,' 'commitment,' 'collaboration,' 'character,' 'dignity,' 'virtue,' 'happiness,' 'excellence,' 'nobility,' etc. These stories lead her to a number of fruitful insights, one of the most refreshing and transvaluatory of which is her conclusion that interspecifc relationships can have their own authenticity: the canine-hominid relationship, for example, "is not an incomplete version of something else. It is a complete dog-human relationship."[54]

Hearne can make this statement without committing herself to some Disney-like indulgence in imagining any fancifully humanoid behavior of dogs. Indeed, she dutifully remarks that, because our structure of belief is overwhelmingly ocular while dogs' is predominantly olfactory, "we inhabit worlds with radically different principles of phenomenology."[55] Hearne continues in species-integrating fashion, "But here is the thing: We *do* talk to dogs about scent, and some people do it quite well." She goes on to relate parables of cross-species perception and understanding, the propositional distillation of which can be stated thus: though there are deep phenomenological differences between distinct kinds of animal, these do not constitute an absolute existential divide—for instance, they do not hermeneutically preclude communicative interrelationships. One instance is the symphysical conversation about wind-awareness that develops between a human handler and a tracking dog as they sensorily check and balance, trust and lead each other toward their common goal. Although she herself does not speak of symphysis, just that or something very like it is what forms the positive experiential basis for Hearne's conviction that "in tracking I do not lose myself and become [the dog] Belle . . . my mind has not turned into Belle."[56] What does happen in such working situations is that genuine animal partners of humans (such as dogs and horses) become "kinesthetically legible" and vice versa. In another of Hearne's examples the symphysical/synesthetic mediation is palpable: "In order to inhabit the world knowable to horses . . . they [riders] start 'hearing' the horse's skin, and in doing so become comprehensible in their own skins to the horse."[57] It is the reciprocal understanding implicit in this sort of collaborative conversancy that makes talk of interspecies partnership sensible here—in fact, a somatico-discursive respect is operative between dog or horse and handler or rider.[58]

Another form of togetherness by which associates can be ethically bonded is that of neighborliness.[59] The discourse of neighborhood is better than that of citizenship, another model often invoked or implied in environmental and animal ethics,[60] because it maintains a sense of intimacy lacking from the abstract terminology of *res publica*. However useful for strictly humanistic contexts, that terminology is ultimately misplaced in (most, though not all) cross-species arenas. What we and the great majority of other animals are to each other is not so much citizens-of-the-world as fellow inhabitants-of-the-earth. The ones we encounter in habitual proximity are our neighbors, literally near-dwellers. This relation holds across the spectrum of natural and cultural environments, including even cities.[61]

Of course, tapping the morality of neighborhood in an interspecies context is itself challenging. We cannot, for instance, appeal directly to the mainstream religious traditions of Western monotheism, because the orthodox scriptural usages of 'neighbor' do not readily encompass nonhuman creatures. The Biblical paragon of neighbor in the Western tradition of ethical thought is a fellow human being.[62] Yet, we may have recourse to the revaluations of ontotheological tradition forged by certain contemporary Continental philosophers. Trying to stretch the traditional intuition, for example, John Llewelyn asks: "Is it conceivable that my neighbor might be a non-human animal?" In responding to that query, Llewelyn follows Emmanuel Levinas—for whom "the other . . . can be an other in respect of whom or which I have responsibilities only on condition of its having a face."[63] Interrogating Levinas further, on the issue of *which* other creatures can be one's neighbor, Llewelyn learns "that the answer turns on whether in the eyes of the animal we can discern a recognition, however obscure, of his [the animal's] own mortality"—though such a discovery appears doubtful (to Levinas, that is).[64] Following a Heideggerian course, David Krell is at least prepared to answer somewhat in the affirmative: in a veterinarian's hospital room, alongside a canine companion suffering life-threatening injury, he reports: "I found myself thinking of Heidegger, of his distinction between human *Sterben* and animal *Verenden*. Her [the dog's] head and paw seemed as immanently and imminently capable of one as the other; her eye, now almost focusing in and out of shock, did not accuse; her bruised body unspeakably beautiful still. . . . I felt very close to our own mortality . . ."65 Still, this sort of testimony is as tentative as it is evocative, and so it may be best to look elsewhere for any normativity of neighborliness.

Notwithstanding Llewelyn's and Krell's efforts to open up Levinas's homo-exclusive portrayal of face-to-face encounter, I think insisting even on a broadened notion of face misses the bioethical mark. In Wu's words, "Emmanuel Levinas' 'face' seems to concentrate too much on the interhuman sphere of ethics, however wide the term 'ethical' is interpreted to mean."66 Concentration on the facial tends to reinstate an anthropocentrist gaze that takes the eyes or seeks ocularity as the reflective surface of a morally weighty soul denied to, or diminished in, other animals. As one commentator has put it, "the face of the animal such as a dog has the power to address us ethically in such a way that makes it difficult to ignore. But we are still a long way from the 'epiphany' of the human face described so rhapsodically" by Levinas.67 Indeed, I would argue that the story to which this remark alludes—Levinas's recounting of a stray dog whose friendly behavior bore witness to the dignity of his prison crew in World War II Germany—depends for its rhetorical force precisely upon a crypto-humanist condescension of animality: "even a dog did better than the Nazis" is the underlying sentiment, implying that the latter had sunk lower than an already inferior animal. More generally, since "he persistently pulled on the reins of his discussion as soon as it appeared to him that the animal question was threatening to take priority away from the human," the same critic continues, Levinas "leaves to others the task of providing us with a Levinasian ethics that does not perpetuate . . . hatred of the other animal." Even sympathetic interpreters who have more recently attempted such have foundered on the anthropocentrist ambivalence that appears to be systemic in Levinas's corpus.68 We need to go past Levinas to pursue the neighborly status of nonhuman animals to broaden our corporal attention (beyond the face as such)—so as to become aware of *whole-body* encounters and their ethical significance.

The work of writer Barry Lopez provides a case in point. He relates a story about a pair of feral wolves with whom he and his wife were spending some time. Once, after having their lupine sleep disturbed by the human couple's prying flashlight, "the wolves immediately began to push [Sandy] around, slamming against her with their bodies and soft-biting her arms and legs. . . . Our intuitive feeling was that they were angry. . . . It is almost as if the animals were warning you of the limits of friendship."[69] This scenario takes place in the dark of night, where the visual possibility of face-to-face conversation is accordingly diminished—but where body-to-body communication can still occur. With respect to the interspecific fellowship here intimated, the bodily display of its limitation would seem to prove the moral constitution of its scope (after all, the wolves *could, but don't,* do real violence to repay annoyance).

Of course humans and wolves do not partake in truly friendly fellowship, at least not in the Aristotelian sense according to which ideal friends should live together—as Lopez admits, "Wolves don't belong living with people."[70] Yet recognizing a certain lived space for wilderness's inviolability does not disbar attempting neighborly association with wild or feral animals. Any virtuous endeavor in this direction will, however, honor the neighborhood that is the wild itself: "We are going to have to get out into the woods." Lopez encourages, "We are going to have to pay more attention to free-ranging as opposed to penned animals, which will require an unfamiliar patience."[71] I want then to move on by quoting and commenting upon a pair of extended passages from *Of Wolves and Men.*

> The wolves moved deftly and silently in the woods and in trying to imitate them I came to walk more quietly and to freeze at the sign of slight movement. At first this imitation gave me no advantage, but after several weeks I realized I was becoming far more attuned to the environment we moved through. I heard more, for one thing, and, my senses now constantly alert, I occasionally saw a deer mouse or a grouse before they did. I also learned the several thousand acres we walked in well enough to find my way around in the dark. I never moved as quietly, or with the grace that they did, not with my upright stance and long limbs that caused my body to become entangled, and the ninety-degree angle at my ankle that caused my feet to catch. But I took from them the confidence to believe *I could attune myself better to the woods by behaving as they did*—minutely inspecting certain things, seeking vantage points, always sniffing at the air. I did, and felt vigorous, charged with alertness.

Notice the mimetic (or secondary) symphysis at work here; it helps existentially shape the woodland neighborhood into a form of transpecific togetherness that does not violate the distance of other animals' differentiation. As the other excerpt has it:

The appreciation of the separate realities enjoyed by other organisms is not only no threat to our own reality, but the root of a fundamental joy. I learned from River that I was a human being and that he was a wolf and that we were different. I valued him as a creature, but *he did not have to be what I imagined he was.* It is with this freedom from dogma, I think, that the meaning of the words "the celebration of life" becomes clear.

It is within the common bodily horizon of such celebration that we come to care about and for the other neighboring varieties of organic worldhood that at times somatically overlay our own.[72]

As with any norm, the moral import of being a neighbor is hardly amenable to strictly rational grounding (logicism in ethics notwithstanding). We cannot just read off duties directly from brute nearness. Nonetheless, for social beings such as humans, those who live nearby us regularly awaken compassion and are accorded at least a modicum of respect (often much more) in virtue of their proximity; and if we are prepared to recognize this much, then it will prove difficult to non-arbitrarily delimit neighborly norms at the boundary of the species *Homo sapiens.* We must acknowledge that it is not human sapience but rather proximal residence that qualifies somebody as a neighbor —and that this qualification can be met at least by other animals (if not plants, though this latter case is an extension I will not consider here). After all, we would not ethically discount a less intelligent human. On pain of speciesism, then, we should not negate the neighborly status of any organism capable of residing—and who does in fact dwell—in our midst. Nor should we make light of the communal aspect of such situations as I am considering. As phenomenologist H. Peter Steeves puts it, "the fact that we share a place and have a specific piece of land [or territory] in common is a strong indication of a concrete common good."[73] In this way, then, a multispecific neighborhood, akin to what Mary Midgley has called "the mixed community,"[74] can indeed be constituted.

In addition to the reciprocity of partnership and the mutuality of fellowship, beyond their rise in cross-specific analogues of "society" and "neighborhood" (the latter incorporating shared territory), there are other experiences of relation and metaphors for transpecific togetherness.[75] The *friendship* of personal or household companions is another prominent form of interspecific relationship. (Here the example of pet-keeping is morally ambiguous, for some would claim that the kept does not have its best interests furthered by the keeper—that the keeping, in effect, is like slaveholding.)[76] There is also the sexual intimacy of *mateship,* and by this I do not have in mind the problematic "unnatural perversion" of (human) bestiality; rather, I mean to refer to those instances of cross-species coupling within comparatively close taxonomic proximity (where inter-breeding is possible, for example, wolf-coyote). The metaphor of (extended) "family" is sometimes used to express the real *kinship* we share with our animal cousins, as it were, through evolutionary ancestry, especially other primates. (When kinship is enacted on a parental model, it is susceptible to the charge of encouraging homocentric patronage rather than biocentric respect.)[77] Finally, all organisms are bodily embedded in the material *interdependency* of ecosystemic coexistence; this is a structural relationship that holds regardless of intentionality patterns. One recognizes genetic and ecological ties of interconnection through scientific knowledge of, or folk familiarity with, natural history. These paths of acknowledging our organ(ism)ic interlinkages need not be (radically) reductionistic or relativistic, respectively.[78]

Problem-Solving and Supportive Context

In this last section I would like to anticipate and resolve some worries that might be problematic for the bodiment ethos I am proposing, and to refer to common experiences and scientific studies that support the ethos. Chief among the problems is that of non-interactive instances.[79] Since my transpecific morality is premised upon an internally or constitutively relational axiology, an issue arises concerning the ethical considerability or moral status of those world-aspects with which one does *not* as a matter of fact have direct (inter)relations. Why should we respect, how can we care about, what would lead us to protect, those individuals, species, or systems with whom or which we do not carry on an association of somaesthetic conviviality? Is the morality of symphysical encounter sufficient for, or necessary to, delivering an "ethic of strangers"?

Generically, in answer to the latter question, I hold that symphysis is a necessarily but insufficiently relevant condition. To develop an ethic of strangers, there must also be recourse to some principle of moral imagination.[80] It is here that the employ of imaginative processes has its legitimate role to play in phenomenological ethics.[81] That role—subsidiary and extensive in nature—

is founded upon the somaesthetic advent of more basic, symphysical phenomena. More specifically, in answer to the question above, imagination of (the possibility of) symphysical encounter with individuals outside the orbit of one's somatic conviviality is a force capable of extending concern to those individuals (not by actual identification, but by enlargement of "virtual community"). With respect to species: on the basis of the previous statement we can and do generalize ethically from small sample experiences to regard for entire populations, within a given species; across different species, our ethico-imaginative resources continue to function—but their force dwindles the further we stray from actual instances of paradigm encounters or relations.[82] Furthermore, it is arguable that species are not (morally) valuable as such and what (ethical) concern there may be for them is usually derived from biodiversity interests.[83] Regarding ecosystems, protective care for them is not so much to be logically constructed out of or upon concern for its organismic constituents as it is already existentially latent in a properly symphysical state's implicit context of biome as world-flesh.[84]

Another potential difficulty for the morality mobilized in this chapter is the problem of inorganic counterexamples.[85] For instance, it may be objected that we might in the presence of a doll's dismemberment have an adverse "gut reaction" (manifested, for example, by wincing) that would qualify—absurdly —on my account as moral expression.[86] Stated this way (plainly), such an objection is causally obscure. If we wince when a doll is decapitated because we have momentarily mistaken it for a living thing, then the scenario at hand is simply a case of cognitive error to be corrected by the addition of more accurate information. If, however, our moral impulses misfire because we have entered into a long-term relationship with a doll as if it were steadily live, then the case becomes one of pathology to be treated by psychotherapy (rather than either epistemology or ethics).

Perhaps the next example is more profoundly problematic. It has been held that certain (or all) naturally occurring inanimate objects, say, stalactites, have moral weight.[87] In reply it could be said that though a stalactite "grows," it is not actually alive—in the worlded sense of being autopoietically oriented to existence—and hence cannot really be an object of (direct) ethical concern. Yet, although this response does supply a working definition of life, it fails to engage the thorny problem of life's precise moral significance. The question remains, across the present study's trajectory, whether (sound) symphysis is possible with nonliving nature; and I leave it an open issue whether an ethos of bodiment must delimit its sphere at the edge of the *Leibswelt*—or if, beyond that properly somatic boundary, it should expand its bodily *Umwelt* outward still, including thereby all corporeal beings within a moral kingdom of *Körper*.[88]

Finally, it should be pointed out that several experiences of common life and findings of social and life sciences form a supportive context for the bodily kind of animal appreciation I have been interpreting.[89] Tapping into a symphysical ethos is not an avant-garde gesture, but is rather a re-creative valuation of somatic sensibilities common to most deontic experiences had during juvenile times and in the lifeworlds of other cultures—that is, beyond the recalcitrantly humanist horizons of "maturity" and "the developed world." With respect to the latter, though we have much to learn from the life-philosophies of nature present in indigenous peoples' tribal traditions, we should take up these lessons upon invitation only (instead of conceptually colonizing those traditions in academic or activist endeavors of what could seem to be, or actually become, ideological imperialism). Perhaps then, with regard to childhood experience, it would be best for us to turn inward and, as it were, backward. What Arne Naess has said about the green worldview of deep ecology can be said equally well about the significance of body phenomenology for animal ethics, namely that it "is largely an articulation of the implicit philosophy of five-year-old children who have access to at least a minimum of animals, plants, and natural places"—who thus, in the context of transpecific conviviality, experience themselves as fundamentally similar to, and caring about, other organisms. Like Naess's ideal ecosophists, persons who retain symphysical solidarity with the community of life "may be said to be people who have never found biological, political or other arguments to undermine those [biophilic] attitudes implicit in childhood."[90]

This suggestion is not merely an idle piece of romantic speculation from the rhetoric of environmentalist advocacy. Rather it is an intimation of a fairly widespread phenomenon—namely, a natural affinity for animate others or "biophilia"—hypothesized in, and gaining confirmation from, a number of scientists' research.[91] In the background is what appears to be a tendency toward compassionate morality widespread throughout the human species and rooted in the pervasively sociable orientation of primates generally (in particular among great apes such as ourselves and chimpanzees).[92] Environmental psychologist Eugene Myers, one of the foremost researchers in this area, has concluded that "a naturally occurring consequence of self in relation is the propensity to take to heart the welfare of others to whom we are close."[93] This propensity is at least zoocentric (if not biocentric) in scope and a key component of its source in "animate relatedness" is cross-species attunement to coherence of bodily integrity and similarity (conveyed, for example, by coordination and congruence of movement or contact).[94]

A salient aspect of such developmental discoveries is that children's concern about and for nonhuman animals reveals itself as a "self-organizing dynamic of morality" and indeed "it does so more vividly than does their moral development toward other humans, because in the case of animals the [dominant] culture encourages a [speciesist] discontinuity" through messages and mechanisms of distancing and desensitization, including "detachment, concealing the harm, misrepresentation, and shifting the blame" (compare, e.g., media representations of barnyard bliss at "Old MacDonald's Farm" to actual animal agribusiness and slaughterhouse processes stocking our supermarkets);[95] Myers thus endorses a precursor's claim that "one can only *lose* a moral sense" such as we have been discussing.[96] If this is right, then we have buttressing evidence for the stance I assumed in the opening chapter, to the effect that our moral starting position is *already* one of corporal compassion with other species and so the burden of proof would not be upon anyone to justify transpecific "traction" of moral symphysis but rather on the anthropocentrist who wishes to deny, dissolve, or otherwise dis-tract us from our proto-ethical predispositions toward somatic/animalic ties of conviviality.

Body Bioethics in Realms of the Carnal and the Carceral

However, even before we reach the level of public policies, there needs to be a change in[to] feeling our flesh as inseparable from the flesh of animals.

GLEN MAZIS (2002)

IT IS SOMETIMES held that applied ethics is not (properly) part of philosophy. The extension of morality into local contexts is seen by a certain purist self-understanding of philosophy to be unsuitable to the truly wise thinker. The latter, apparently, should dismiss any project that does not deal all-at-once with the whole-as-such. Since applied ethics usually treats this or that particular sector of moral reality—and not everything-qua-totality—it gets short shrift from the vantage point of "pure" philosophy. Those who endorse this sort of view want, admirably, to pare away any biased partiality from philosophizing. However, in satisfying their totalizing desire for profound purity, they risk cutting themselves off from the world's extensive reach at finer levels of resolution. Full-fledged wisdom, I would caution, requires more than grand knowledge of first principles pertaining to the One or All—it must inquire into the subsidiary details of reality's various patterns as well.[1] Therefore, even (indeed especially) after backing into the more inclusive purviews of axiology and ontology, I think moral philosophy does right to probe further forward into more focused zones of applicative investigation. Application does not denigrate moral—or any—philosophizing; rather, it helps to fulfill philosophic insight and serves toward actualizing philosophic endeavor. "Whatever may be gained in respect of theoretical understanding," one contemporary thinker has observed, "philosophy will have lost at least half of its subject if it neglects the pursuit of practical wisdom."[2] I turn now to consider practical matters of "applied ethics," maintaining that I do not thereby diminish—to the contrary, can fortify—the philosophic status of our discussion.

Perhaps the terminology of *applied ethics* is inappropriate for what I shall be doing. Normally, applied ethics (as a distinct subfield of academic philosophy) is associated with several methodological determinants. My stance differs from this standard usage in subtle yet significant ways. Applied ethics as regularly conceived is concerned with the extension of moral rules to specific situations, frequently according to the parameters of currently controversial issues. First, applied ethics is usually conducted by (at least its professional) practitioners as a juridico-criterial mode of discourse that treats moral dilemmas and conflicts of interest by testing and settling them in almost algorithmic accordance with a certain moral theory's prefabricated conceptual apparatus (including ethical laws of behavior, moral maxims, practical mottoes, etc.). Second, applied ethics is typically given to dealing with well-defined situations; these situations, moreover, are taken to be external to the genesis and status of the relevant rules to be considered. Third, it is standard for applied ethics to be oriented to issues of controversy that current social and political debates have established in advance of the ethicist's concern and on which he or she must reactively yet authoritatively opine. It may be that these three aspects (in decreasing order of plausibility) stem from the application of Enlightenment objectivism to moral methodology and ontology.[3] Perhaps it is this or a like formula that produces what has been referred to as the exclusively applicative "view of the relationship between the philosopher and any given problem according to which the first 'turns up' to sort out the difficulty without letting the nature of the case inform his or her view of the fundamental philosophical issues."[4]

My approach (call it "ethics-in-action") has a phenomenologically existential, rather than a propositionally regulative, bent. Projected from a cross-species ontology of intersomatic overlap and through a felt sense of bodily value, it does not issue the deliberative judgments of codifying consciousness —instead, it invites us to experience the relation of "fit" between embodied conviviality and certain propensities of a broadly zoocentric moral sensibility.

Furthermore, symphysical philosophizing is given to a hermeneutic of situational context concerned less with cases-of-crisis than with sites-of-praxis: the case as such is externally related to a discursive body of (ethical or positive) law; on the contrary, the ecocarnal site or *Leibswelt* is internally constitutive (at least partially, though not exhaustively) of a moral practice mobilized through somaesthetic activation. My interspecies ethos of bodiment is not so much interested in reacting to ethical controversy per se (by position-taking) as it rather enables those character dispositions that help us to negotiate moral living's problem zones.

The issue-oriented nature of applied ethics can look like the parading of special interests and conflicts upon which the moral thinker must duly enter her or his *pro* or *con*.[5] In part to avoid the unseemly image of such a spectacle, many moralists have recently taken a neo-Aristotelian turn toward virtue theory. Although my move is similar, it is performed with the late-modern twist that the relevant traits are not left classically pure but are seen to be embedded in a contemporary dialectic of the carnal and the carceral (for which the work of Maurice Merleau-Ponty and of Michel Foucault are the respective reference points).[6] The *carnal* here refers to the boundary-breaking force of organic or fleshly excess—of swellings and peelings, of turgidity and atrophy, of pumping circulation and oozing excretion, of the alternately in/visible and visceral flow and ebb of embodied vitality's drives and impulses (in the words of Didier Franck, *chair pulsionnelle vivante*[7]). "The *carceral*," by contrast, designates the boundary-building power of mechanical or technical containment—of limited access, constant rigidity, fixed passage, and panoptical surveillance.[8] I will explore certain morally problematic sites of interspecific encounter with reference to the dialectic enacted between these two principles of praxis. Perhaps it is better to consider the following an existential exercise in "practical philosophy"—to distinguish it from the analytic mode of "applied ethics" regnant in the academy today. Whatever their disciplinary appellation, the ensuing studies constitute object lessons in the approach to bioethics I wish to develop.

Laboratory Experimentation

The laboratory is the site that most vividly converts nonhuman organisms' being into instrumentality or reified objects (what Heidegger called readiness-to-hand and presence-at-hand, respectively). In the context of this chapter, the bio-experimental lab is a place wherein animals are pressed into science's or industry's service; put bluntly, they *become* tools or results/products of science or business. The laboratory research setting dictates parameters of behavioral operation that desensitize the practitioner to the bodily spectacles enacted under his experimental surveillance. Indeed, the "culture" of modern, positivist scientific practice seeks to disbar the emergence of symphysis or somaesthetic caring in its very methodology.[9] Emphatically, *detachment* is the watchword of this context—against, say, compassion. One can palpably detect the existential difference between the architecturally confined, psychosomatically partitioned test space of laboratory technicians and the environmentally expansive, holistically structured study space of a field researcher such as Jane Goodall. It is the difference between laboring in the carcerality Foucault charts and working in the midst of the world-flesh Merleau-Ponty maps.

None of these remarks should be taken to imply the nonexistence, still less the impossibility, of interaction or relationship arising—bubbling up, as it were, even through methodic attempts to avoid or suppress it. Admitting behavioral or affective "attachment" is hard for practicing scientists to do, at least officially and publicly. As two researchers observed not too long ago, "Although animals are widely employed as research subjects, only recently have we acknowledged the bond that frequently, perhaps inevitably, develops between subject and researcher."[10] Recognized or repressed, however, compassion has a tendency to come into operation when certain animals spend time together—and it is mediated by the corporal experiences I have highlighted. In fact, findings from comparative psychology and zoology bear testimony to this claim: "Recent work on social attachment in vertebrates has established that one of the most important factors, if not *the* most important factor, in establishing a social attachment or bond to some other organism or object is prolonged sensory contact with it."[11] Such linkage of "social attachment" and "sensory contact" is remarkably similar to the phenomenon I am calling symphysis.

Carcerality reified is the cage, which is the lab animal's actual abode. What is the significance of that animal's housing? What sort of world does it make—or break? Bernard Lonergan has characterized the biological pattern of experience as *constitutive extroversion*: "The bodily basis of the senses in sense organs, the functional correlation of sensations with the positions and movements of the organs, the imaginative, conative, emotive consequences of sensible presentations, and the resulting local movements of the body, all in-

dicate that elementary [animal] experience is concerned, not with the imma-
nent aspects of living, but with its external conditions and opportunities."[12]
Note here how the physicality of living is stressed, and that it serves to project
the organism out into a world externally constituted. Max Scheler's paradoxical notion of environmental existence brings home a similar point: "the animal . . . lives, as it were, ecstatically immersed in its environment."[13] In this
model animal individuality is not an atomistic subject or mental monad (by
Cartesian or Leibnizian analogy, say, to human subjectivity), but is rather a
body-self incorporating its surrounds.[14]

If an animal develops worldhood by appropriating externalities, then the
result for an incarcerated lab rat is internalized imprisonment.[15] The rat's environment is dominated by the overarching fact of bars, or walls, or fencing—
hence the rodent comes to phenomenally assimilate the carceral into the carnal.
A clockwork-orange transmogrification, the product of this kind of metamorphosis might better be denominated a "jailhouse body."[16] Indeed, this alteration is reinforced by the treatment of such organisms in testing protocol as
"living laboratory equipment" run through a historical "process of greater in-
dustrialization, in which lab animals become standardized and increasingly
became a production process and part of the apparatus of science" itself.[17] In
other words, animals in laboratories (most of which are rodents) are not only
physically restrained in literal cages but are also ontologically reduced to the
status of ready-to-hand tools.[18]

On three levels—the individual, social, and ontological—caging appears
to entail seriously deleterious effects, most visible morally from the existential
viewpoint of somaesthetic transaction or orientation. The jailhoused bodies
of individual animals prevent a full and healthy range of corporal expression.
Sometimes practitioners try to sidestep this obvious point, as when one research
designer opines: "It has often been said that the ideal cage for a rabbit has a
floor made of grass, walls made of hedges, a roof of sky and a floor area of half
an acre. In practical terms the well-being of laboratory animals can be achieved
by restricting their movements to areas smaller than this in cages or pens."[19]
Note that the ideal here does not serve its usual function of referring to some
supernatural utopia, but rather is descriptive of nature's actuality. This rever-
sal of reference occurs even as the negative connotation of idealism (that which
cannot be realized) is maintained; hence, acceptance of the author's conclusion
is rhetorically facilitated by discrediting its alternative in advance and without

argument. It should also be pointed out that stunting of bodily expression in animals used for experimentation happens not only in terms of outward barriers but also through interiorized distortions of behavioral repertoire. The zoological "neuroses" that thus arise are well documented elsewhere.[20]

Furthermore, *ad hoc* statements of ethical reform in technique, though superficially encouraging, are negative testimony of the need for more profound change. Take, for example, the following reformist assertion of a published professional: "All staff, regardless of position or qualifications, should receive training in the sympathetic handling of a wide range of species, supplemented with regular practice."[21] Of course, at least on a cursory reading, such instruction merits applause; yet, upon more careful and critical reflection, one is moved to ask: why do personnel have to undergo that sort of education in the first place? Could it be that their very working conditions constantly militate against native sources of sympathy or symphysis?[22]

Regarding cross-species conviviality, its authentic possibility diminishes to the extent that the carceral overtakes the carnal. Under imprisonment, the body's animacy is congealed by confinement, and in this way *Leib* slides into almost lithic *Körper*. Toward the further reaches of such a transition, being-caged precludes *Mitsein*—one can no longer *be with* the caged animal, instead only *located alongside* it (that pronoun now being the most suitable term of thing-like reference).[23] In fact, perversely, this very situation is deliberately intensified and enforced in some contexts. Speaking of a striking scenario of bad faith, an interviewed technician once "recounted that the scientists in that lab insisted that she put the rats in opaque cages." Why? "They did not like having rats in clear cages because 'the animals could look at you.'"[24]

The somersaults of rationalization and emotional misgiving embedded in this illustration are impressive: presumably, experimentation was initially modeled after some analogy between the animal subject and cases of human application; then, it was likely "justified" ethically by drawing a demarcation of moral difference between human and nonhuman beings (usually having to do with an allegation of lesser subjectivity); finally, conscience is bothered by affective qualms predicated again on likeness (tacit attribution of greater subjectivity than one is prepared to admit). Remarkably manifesting "return of the repressed," this example even displays an aspect of Sartre's notorious phenomenology of sadism (wherein, namely, it is felt imperative that the other's gaze not be returned).[25] One need not subscribe to the neo-Hegelian dialectics of

Sartrean existentialism to observe that those in positions of dominance are often uneasy about the status of, and recognition from, those they oppress. Indeed, to realize that such an insight applies as well to (at least our dealings with) other species, one would have to come out from under the shadow of humanism cast by the likes of Hegel and Sartre. Only then would it become possible to register or limn the shortsightedness afflicting the researchers referenced above, to see that what Jacques Derrida once said about the discourse and mien characteristic of anthropocentrists in general applies to their case in particular: "They neither wanted nor had the capacity to draw any systematic consequence from the fact that an animal could, facing them . . . *look at* them and *address* them from down there" in, as it were, the object position.[26]

Third, somewhat more abstractly, ontological violence is done to the incarcerated animal body. All test subjects (of a given group) must be submitted to the same carceral conditions—this in accordance with the very controls of protocol constancy requisite to scientific experimental procedure itself. Such a situation, through the biologically constitutive extroversion characteristic of the animals' experience, homogenizes individual creatures into merely numerically distinct tokens of species-type. This result consolidates complementary habits of speciesist degradation. Indeed, as biologist Lynda Birke notes, "most laboratory animals (especially rodents) are not named but given only numbers" —and this practice betrays suppressed scruples inasmuch as it "reflects a need to establish distance from rats or mice as [subjectively individual and thus associable] animals in the lab" (which, in turn, can be considered negative evidence of underlying yet unacknowledged symphysis or sympathy).[27]

An extension of such reductive and distancing tendencies can be traced as follows. Stereotypically stamped and set on a downward ontological and moral slide, lab denizens are then reduced to generic animals, eventually becoming only lab-functions (to the experimenters) or just inert commodities (to their suppliers).[28] In the worst-case, unfortunately prevalent, scenario, at the end of this process the organism at stake "has become transformed from what most of us would commonly call an animal into something that stands in for data and scientific analysis."[29] From the somatological perspective I have presented, the pivotal downgrade is from the somatic to the corporeal. In the processes both of breeding for specific traits of use to scientific experiments and in the processes of representation as a 'model,' laboratory rodents are reduced to something else—particular gene effects or physiological responses.

This perhaps makes it easier for us to forget . . . [that] these laboratory rodents remain living animals." The ultimate demotion, however, is that of nearly total disembodiment—whereby animal identity is denaturalized to the point of becoming almost immaterial, as a test subject is virtually identified with its provision of information or simply and finally with data as such.

"So, in the production of results from the laboratory," Birke explains, "the animals who ate, slept, and played with their friends—hidden from human eyes—disappear." This last consequence allows me to foreshadow a similar emptying effect on animals of the next site to be discussed, the zoo. There, naturally elusive animals are paradoxically overexposed into invisibility by the conditions of ubiquitous and omnipresent exhibition imposed through captivity. Here, "the lab rat has been [methodically and mathematically] metamorphosed from a rat, with particular characteristics of species-typical behavior, to a 'laboratory animal' representing numbers." Both nature of kind (rodenticity or "ratness") and individuality (subject status of "rat persona") are elided. In the lab, "for scientists to do their [experimental] work, the [essence and identity of] animals must disappear"; at the zoo, for visitors to have their (spectacular) fun, the *wild* animals must be *kept* on display—and so *their* essence also disappears (i.e., becomes impossible to encounter as what it, or its type, originally was or would be like naturally).

There is another salient similarity between labs and zoos that is worth mentioning: both of these institutions self-promote by partaking in a venerable and rhetorically persuasive discourse of redemption—from infection on the one hand, and extinction on the other. In the case of science's reliance on rodents, this promotional rhetoric had an especially difficult challenge, for the rat (or mouse) would have to be transfigured from an emblem of disgust and horror to a hygienic representative of medical progress: "The wild rat of the sewers, terror of so many myths and legends and bearer of disease, becomes iconically part of the struggle of biomedicine to conquer disease."[30] Indeed, it seems that only the ideational power of Christian salvation stories, steeped in transubstantiation of debased flesh into divine glory, has the gospel-magic to perform such a feat of essentially somatological conversion. The labor and lives of rats and mice are, from this viewpoint, referred to as "sacrifices" for the restoration and uplift of human health; thus, these animals come to acquire moral significance through the backdoor of crypto-theistic humanism, by representing "the ultimate triumph of good over evil—a process in which the rodents themselves are transformed from evil, disease-full vermin into sanitized, germ-free angels of mercy."[31] In the case of zoos supplying at least the semblance of sanctuary for many endangered species, the redemption narrative is reversed and digs deeper into older, Judaic roots of Biblical rhetoric: we humans are now the guardian angels of rescue for animals, Noachic saviors at the helm of conservation's latter-day ark.

Finally, notice that it has proven possible to criticize animal experimentation ethically without even mentioning vivisectional measures of greater notoriety. That observation should not be construed to mean that vivisection itself is immune to criticism from the perspective put forward in this study. To the contrary, it is the very vulnerability laid bare by somaesthetic attention that vivisecting agonizes—cutting apart both the innards and interactivity of organic and phenomenal bodiment. The invasiveness of vivisection is already primed in the moment of caging by the laboratorial invasion of the carceral into the carnal.

Zoological Exhibition

> It seems to him there are a thousand bars; and behind the bars, no world.
>
> RANIER MARIA RILKE, "THE PANTHER"

The zoological park or garden is a common feature of urban areas throughout the world.[32] However, being commonplace has not protected it from controversy centering on its highly ambiguous moral status. Usually the debate is framed in these terms: either the zoo is (primarily) a *sanctuary for* animals or else it is (primarily) an *exhibition of* animals—if the former, then it appeals to laudable conservation ideals; if the latter, then it panders to lowly amusement values. Thus the ambivalent nature of the zoo's identity—between refuge and circus—marks it as a site of ethical contest. In fact, there are question marks surrounding its purpose and function even *within* each of the aforementioned characterizations. With respect to conservation, which goal is paramount: preserving species (as types/kinds, entities of genetic abstraction) or protecting animals (as individuals)? In regard to exhibition, do zoos manage to educate people ecologically beyond mere entertainment?

While these sorts of questions are indeed of ethical interest, they do not directly interrogate the relevant issue for the present discussion, namely, the effect of zoo-presence on human as well as nonhuman animal bodies. Referring back to the thematic of caging, if the lab fixes the being of animals at readiness-to-hand, in Heideggerian terms, then the zoo reduces it precisely to presence-at-hand. Traditionally and still all too often, the standard zoo did and does display its keep in cages. Is there anything morally worrisome about this practice, according to the somaesthetic ethos mapped in the previous chapter? Lonergan's principle of biological extroversion is key here. As Shapiro puts it, "an animal's habitat is his or her dwelling place not only in the sense of providing a particular home but in the sense of being the substance of his or her species identification."[33] In this light, ex-hibiting an animal not only renders it homeless, but also—consequently—disembodies that creature of its world-flesh identity. This deconstruction of incarnate worldhood is given testimony by the encaged animal's chronically bored monotony of bodily behavior; broadly stated, the distinctive way in which a particular animal lives her species-identity is existentially flattened out into conduct becoming of generic animality.[34] Speciated individuality of living bodiment disappears from such a scene. An absence of this kind, for the moral vision of symphysical attunement, is to be deemed an ethical deficit.

The contemporary zoo-goer is likely to wonder about the relevance of the preceding discussion to the trend over the past generation toward increasing naturalism in zoological architecture. Lately, many zoos are reforming their exhibition design into greater conformity with their captive animals' original (wild) habitat. Instead of being housed in mausoleum-style buildings sub-divided into small rooms with cage-bars, many of today's zoo inhabitants are kept instead in microcosms of quasi-wilderness, planned and set up with decidedly more biological parameters in place.[35] This change of circumstance has occurred in tandem with a growing concern for, and implementation of, behavioral enrichment features—apparatus and activity ranging from toy-like mechanisms for relief of boredom to actual predation as a near-facsimile of hunting in the wild.[36]

Yet such reforms remain on the level of the virtual: almost natural, but not quite; only artificial attempts that achieve, at most, asymptotic verisimilitude. The problem is not merely one of technical shortfall in the reproduction of reality.[37] Rather, the difficulty is structural: as one expert admits, even "good" zoos—just in virtue of their being zoos—"must reduce nature to the extent that they make residents visible to visitors."[38] This reduction means that even the best practical examples of zoological naturalization are condemned, on principle, to provide sites/sights of simulacra. Zebras and tigers are not beings whose nature it is to laze under the gaze of human observation; usually, if we got too close, they would avoid or attack us. Thus zoos face a dilemma of dishonesty: as they improve environmental realism to impressive heights, with proportionate poignancy they increase the sense that animal preservation is being simulated (i.e., *not* actually accomplished). Our suspicion is aroused: can tigers or zebras exist in the zoo, or do only "tigers" and "zebras" reside there? Perhaps the ultimate creature of naturalized presentation is an artifact of somatological hyper-reality, a disembodied entity reincarnated as a nicer replica of its former self—what certain postmodern critics would call the "real fake."[39]

Still, a defense of zoo-keeping might dismiss such criticism as beside the main point of genetic conservation of species. As for the living individual organism, one apologist allows that "if an animal lives as a member of a social group that is proper for its species, feeds from natural vegetation, finds its own mates and rears its own offspring, it does not seem to matter overmuch if it is also protected from predators, or is amenable to human observation."[40] After all (so the argument goes) we have rescued the animal from endangerment in its external environment. Or have we? Carefully consider an actual limit-case: "If, to save the California condor, it is necessary to imprison every extant example of that being, what have we saved? A singular bird, certainly, but one which can be regarded as saved only by accepting a limited, biological definition of a bird as the physical manifestation of coded genetic information. Were it regarded as the manifestation of embodied limits and therefore the functionary of a particular 'place,' the fact that we have expertly exterminated that place makes nonsense of any claims that the bird has been saved."[41] At stake, here, is the bodily being of animality—whether it is properly reducible to objective corporeality (matter in the form of genetic development), or must also somatically incorporate its ecological habitat (on a phenomenal plane). According to my account of live bodiment, as the former reduction overlooks the latter condition, an incomplete description of the animal body results; hence we have good phenomenological reason to doubt the adequacy of zoological preservation, whatever its rationale may be from the vantage of "scientific management."

Parenthetically, under the lens of this skepticism, I would add that we can further and fruitfully inspect the whole salvific tone of zoo rhetoric. The dream of the most "progressive" zoological conservators is to return future generations of their presently endangered keep into the circumstance of wilderness, "to take them back to the wild at some future, more relaxed and more enlightened time."[42] Geopolitically, however, the near-term prospects for economic relaxation and ethical enlightenment are not very encouraging. On the contrary, all euphemism aside, dedication to an international ethos of growth and greed has become the strongest force of our times, overwhelming pleas for a steady spirit of sharing: as one commentator notes (following critical theorist Peter Sloterdijk), under modernity's aegis, "science, technology, production and consumption, fashion, [and] mass media . . . are all dominated by the kinetic imperative of accelerating acceleration" with little or no regard for qualitative value.[43]

From and to where, then, do the utopian visions that are held to be the highest justification of zoological parks and gardens come and go? It seems that they are birthed from, and aligned with, a dubious faith in the promise of biotechnology. For instance, if it should take centuries instead of decades for the enlightened epoch of zoological paradise to arrive, we will (so they say) ride out the extended time by freezing the seminal and embryonic material of those species threatened with extinction.[44] Eventually, come Releasement Day, biodiversity will be resurrected in its full beauty and splendor—if not here on Earth, then on the surface of some suitably geo-engineered planet (e.g., Mars with its ice caps melted down for water).[45] It should be obvious that futuristic planning of this sort presumes socioecologic stability over a very long term. Yet the measures necessary to prevent collapse of our society and/or biosphere —human population control and sustainable lifestyle—are also precisely the factors that would most contribute to habitat preservation and species conservation in the wild to begin with! The unavoidable answer to mass extinction, then, behind all biotopian dreams of intervention and reeducation,[46] is (human) self-limitation.

Doubly paradoxical, the zoo conceals much about nonhuman animality and reveals at least as much about humanity,[47] including the effects of zoo-keeping and -spectating upon human styles of bodiment. Glossing Foucault's *Discipline and Punish* in their book on zoo culture, the sociologists Mullan and Marvin write a chapter entitled "Containment and Control" wherein they claim that "zoos are about humans, for zoos tell us stories of human power, the exercise of control and domination." How does this insight refract upon the medium of the human body itself? As we saw in respect of our considera-tion of Merleau-Ponty's work, the lived body is existentially larger than the anatomical unit. In terms of phenomenal vitality, it incorporates a live space of potential motility and sensory engagement. For the prison guards, asylum wardens, and zookeepers of centuries past, living their carcerally institutional bodies meant adopting carnal duties and corporal stances that assumed "the techniques of force and fear are appropriate to the management of 'brutes.'"

Various reforms in the twentieth century had the effect of casting a more humanitarian atmosphere over these places. Yet, even today, the visitors who come to see the (human or animal) inmates are constrained by the layout of architecture and the routine of policy to experience their bodies as having outer horizons shaped by an analytical arrangement of space (a la Foucault). Cir-cumscribed separation and continual surveillance interrupt natural processes of transpecific sociality and etiquette (including, ironically, avoidance), and so the space of interface cannot be negotiated neutrally into the zone of existen-tial equilibrium ordinarily established amongst free-ranging animals. This kind of situation cuts across the grain of what Anthony Weston has called "elemen-tary politeness" toward (members of) other species, which involves "working in their media, as it were, not primarily ours, and going to them in a way that allows them to break off the encounter whenever they wish."[48] Diverging from such advice, the visiting body at a zoo unconsciously becomes a locus of hierarchical observation, oscillating between the poles of voyeuristic removal and prying proximity.[49] In these ways, then, the institution retains its morally problematic status—even when viewed through the alternative and bifocal lens of human and nonhuman phenomenology of body.

In the basic structure of my ethical account, I described the moral phe-nomenon of symphysis and then showed that it mediates dispositions of car-ing (through recognition of common vulnerability) and of respect (by sharing bonds of togetherness). What would happen if we centered our zooscopic at-tention not on the somaesthetic elements of experience, but instead on the empathetic identification of a psychologically modernized moral sense theory? By anthropomorphic projection, I suspect, we would come to care about the animals' "imprisonment" on a simplistic, straightforward analogy between the bars of (old-fashioned) zoo cages and those of jail cells. Concerning the contemporary naturalistic zoo (absent gross manifestations of encagement), I fear we would not arrive at more than a dim, attenuated awareness of its carceral element—and in this way would be inclined to mute or silence any moral criticism that may be due. With regard to vulnerability, then, we might impute identical imposition (between human prisoners and zoo residents) by facile inference from similar conditions of constraint, on the one hand; on the other hand, however, susceptibility to incarceration might remain relatively or altogether invisible to our conscience. Thus, in at least this arena of application, an account rival to mine yields too much or too little.

Regarding togetherness, I think my approach is capable of furnishing a strong yet subtle critique. One could say that the typical zoo precludes most, if not all, forms of symphysical relationship. Certainly, the potential for association between visitors and inhabitants is severely if not entirely curtailed. In the words of John Berger, "nowhere in a zoo can a stranger encounter the look of an animal. At the most, the animal's gaze flickers and passes on. They look sideways. They look blindly beyond. They scan mechanically. They have been immunised to encounter."[50] Putatively, there may be some sort of partnership at work between keepers and the kept—but even that possibility has a patronizing profile. As Alexander Wilson puts it, "In a culture in which hunting has become a sport, jet fighters are named after birds of prey, and an animal-rights movement has interjected previously unspoken questions, all relations with our animal companions on this Earth have been thrown into crisis. That crisis is present at the zoo in the very glances traded between animal captives and their human keepers."[51] It would seem that we are led either toward animal indifference and human disappointment or toward animal mistrust and human pity. Whichever the case may be, genuine respect is not realized because the support of admiration is removed from the somaesthetic scene. What we have found by proceeding on a phenomenological/hermeneutic path of praxiology is that the zoological "garden"—despite or even through its peaceful park-like image —is predominantly an institution of power, the specific functions of which are to display and preserve its keep. Notwithstanding the lack of punitive or penal intent on the part of its organizers, the zoo nonetheless may be considered an artificial space of enforced occupancy and demonstration, an island of constraint within the series of social(izing) establishments that Foucault termed "the carceral archipelago."[52]

To some, this characterization might seem too harsh or unfair. In fact, zoos have been defended against such (or similar) judgment. For example, zoologist and philosopher Stephen Bostock responds: "The urge to dominate, to show one has power over others, is doubtless an important part of human nature, and equally, no doubt, this urge sometimes motivates the capture and keeping of animals. But to regard this as the major motivation behind all wild animal keeping is a wild exaggeration!"[53] This sort of deontological remark can counter criticism only on the level of intention, however. It enables one to argue that sometimes such keeping is not motivated by a dominating impulse, or at least not primarily so. Further, moving onto a consequentialist level, it allows one to make the charge that the original critique is itself a form of genetic fallacy: even if misotherist tyrants founded zoodom from an imperial impulse toward biocolonial oppression, it does not follow that there would necessarily be anything wrong with the eventual fruits of their ill-intentioned work—in fact, in spite of doubts regarding their once being reduced to a collection of living trophies, we can rest assured that today's zoo inhabitants reside unmolested in truly wonderful, homey habitats.

Yet, notice that my largely Foucauldian criticism of carcerality at the zoo remains untouched by this response—because it is not based on a genetic or motivational thesis at all, but on structural observation. Whatever the motives of any zoo director may be, the nature or pattern of zoological exhibition abides. The zoo's lifeworld is structured around holding and showing wild animals— essentially characterized by (albeit negative) freedom—in captivity; somatologically, this structure ensures the production of docile bodies (or dead ones).[54] Such production of docility, in and of itself, constitutes and demonstrates a relation of powerful dominion: captor over and above captive, the carceral shot through the carnal. (It is an important feature of this conclusion that the mastery asserted is not total; in Foucault's analysis, "Power is exercised only over free subjects, and only insofar as they are free."[55]) That relation of dominance, regardless of what any keeper has in *mind,* derives from and stays in *place*— zoo as enclosure and stage: animal archive at the least, conservation circus at its extreme.

The doyen of zoo philosophy, Heini Hediger, once commented that animal specialists and criminologists share in common certain methods of professional practice. Further, what he said about holding animals captive both foreshadows contemporary zoological sentiment and has been eerily echoed by paternalistically progressive calls for prison reform: "One wants the inmates to feel as comfortable, as snug, and as much at home as possible."[56] Whatever our impression of efforts at "humanizing" imprisonment (of our own species), it is hard to deny that improvements in zoo conditions have actually occurred over the past few decades. After animal collector Peter Batten made an investigative tour of United States zoos about thirty years ago, his book-length report constituted a damning expose of the institutions' lack of attention even to biological basics.[57] Following his lead in zoo evaluation, I visited Zoo Atlanta periodically from the late 1980s to the mid-1990s to assess its changing conditions. This particular site saw noticeable change for the better—to the point where 80 percent (and maybe more) of Batten's own condition checklist appeared to have been met.[58] Do results such as this mean that the carceral comparison is now misplaced?

I do not think it is—certainly not if Foucault is right to suggest that carcerality has productive effects going beyond simple suppression. Visibility is a key concern here. Bentham's prison design, the Panopticon, was "to induce in the inmate a state of conscious and permanent visibility that assures the automatic functioning of power."[59] The zoo also represents a nexus of power and vision, but with the roles reversed: the function of controlling the animals' placement and diet is to habituate them to tolerate indefinite exposure to the visive presence of humans. (Ironically, because it beats down instincts of alertness and avoidance, this habituation itself undermines the possibility of really meeting animals—face-to-face, or better, body-to-body. The irony, somaesthetically speaking, is that overexposure is tantamount to disappearance.[60]) Flattening Merleau-Ponty's world-flesh dialectic of the visible and the invisible, the "zoöpticon" is a kind of panopticon turned inside out—similar principles are at work, and, although they are arranged in opposite vectors of force, over the long term they tend to produce the same result: an institutionalized organism largely incapacitated for life on the outside.[61] Or, more insidiously still, whether originally human or nonhuman, the transformed product is often an inhuman animal all too ready for the carceral milieux that have socially and ecologically colonized the (no longer quite so) external world. For examples, so-called reintroduction programs must monitor the movements of the released, frequently by remote electronic equipment—and parole boards have already borrowed similar tracking devices. Animals "paged" while on parole? Convicts reintroduced "into the wild"? Would there be plausible distinctions anymore—ultimately and most poignantly, then, between freedom and imprisonment?[62]

Another axis of Foucauldian critique reveals juxtapositions of epistemic activities and political interests, particularly as they configure bodies and inscribe flesh. In zoological park practices, knowledge and power intersect. Hediger's lifelong enterprise, for instance, was to reestablish the zoo on a biological basis (and he explicitly likened this project to the hospital's erection on a foundation of medical knowledge).[63] His program was to be pursued in the style of systematic science, and it was held to empower its practitioners somatologically (i.e., with hermeneutic control over bodily behavior).[64] "They were [to be] technicians of behavior," said Foucault of prison organizers. "Their task was to produce bodies that were both docile and capable."[65] The same comment can be made in respect to zoo personnel's duty. Docile bodies are capable of conservation and demonstration, and so their production is at a premium. As Hediger states, "There are three reasons for stressing the need for tameness in as many animals as possible in zoological gardens: tameness is attractive; tameness is healthy; tameness is expedient."[66]

Notice that, in this last regard, the dictates of exhibition are continuous with those of experimentation. Hediger, like others, promoted perspectives that would incline one toward a contradictory position—that zoos and labs are "diametrically opposite," at least "as far as the sympathetic attitude between man and animals is concerned." My treatment, geared to a somatological perspective, shows to the contrary that symphysis is subject to stifling in both domains and that this is so because the carceral petrifies the carnal in those contexts. Accordingly, an applied ethicist guided by traditional moral sympathy theory might see in zoos a more benign aspect (as in greater opportunity for empathic communion), whereas the practical philosopher following moral phenomenology of body takes a more skeptical view: the attraction of affective attachment (such as pity) in zoo management belies the strength of carcerality there, where transpecific symphysis (whether companionable or predatory) is interrupted structurally.[67]

Inexcusable menageries once upon a time, zoos have developed into cultural institutions capable of defending themselves on scientific grounds—that is, by appeal to aims of conservation and education. Yet such defenses are not strong: the former appeal is weak because heroic rescues to save species by removing specimens from the wild (and holding them or their descendants or genes "on reserve" indefinitely) are inefficient and incoherently utopian; the latter appeal is superficial in that it rests on bad faith (i.e., inauthentic presentation of captive animals as truly wild ones). Incarcerating animals in the name of science does not then appear justifiable, evolution beyond discredited practices of entertainment notwithstanding. A "moral physics" of confinement is operative in the zoological park: corporeally, the zoo is to serve as a repository of genetic material; somatically, it is to function as a conservatory of whole-body conduct.[68] Despite the best intentions, efforts, and achievements toward making these forms of confinement more comfortable for the inhabitants and more palatable to the visitors, zoos still share deeply in an order of prison-like institutions partially constitutive of urban modernity.[69] Violent seizure, forced captivity, thorough exhibition, programmed feeding and breeding, commodi-fied exchange—all these activities testify: to display animals is already to dis-cipline them; to preserve species it is necessary to punish individual specimens (as representative inmates). When we go to the zoo, we *visit* animals not only in the sense of "meeting" them (inspection by ocular survey), but also in the archaic sense of affliction, through imposition and interposition of power (mastery/control). Visiting here, with inquisitive eyes and all the vim of sal-vation, one grasps doubly.

Such "grasping" occurs mostly without reflection, involuntarily or habit-ually, on the level of a cultural unconscious. Though I have submitted zoo-going to structural critique, I do not wish to condemn zoo-goers personally —because we (I count myself) go to the zoo primarily from prerational need. How better to satisfy the evolved yearning for authentic animal encounter in contemporary civilization is precisely the problem toward which practical zoologists and philosophers of culture should now turn their combined atten-tion and energy. Indeed, beyond diagnosis, critics of the zoo have a responsibil-ity to frame institutional or social therapies. In general, deconstruction should not be the terminus of critique, but rather a propaedeutic for reconstruction. In the area of present concern, more specifically, it will not do to condemn zoos and leave it at that. After all, it looks as if we have a biophilic need (a nat-ural or innate affinity) for interspecies animal encounters. The sheer popular-ity of zoos suggests that they fulfill or at least extend the promise of fulfilling a powerful and significant need. Zoos command audiences that exceed those of major league professional sports; in the United States alone, they attract 135 million people per year, a figure greater than the attendance at all major professional sporting events combined.[70] As I have implied, the promotional factors of preservation, research, and education are neither necessary nor suffi-cient conditions for the existence of zoos. Still, what we too lightly (and as yet naively) call "amusement" might very well be both necessary and sufficient. To appreciate this matter more profoundly, we should focus on what E. O. Wilson describes as biophilia and understand how it could lie behind our spectatorship of other organisms.[71] In this light, then, our task would be to develop modes of cultivating that biophilic drive and the associated affiliation with animals in ways beyond and better than zoos do or can.

Hence, working with a comparison I alluded to earlier, transformation of animal encounter might correspond analogically to salutary forms of erotica as contrasted to objectionable pornography. It thus becomes apposite to investigate the possibilities for actually and figuratively re-vising zooscopic practices by examining and weighing relevant phenomenologies and hermeneutics of vision as set forth by provocative and productive thinkers such as Marilyn Frye and Alphonso Lingis. Frye, a theorist of feminist critique, speaks of "arrogant eyes which organize everything seen with reference to themselves and their own interests"; she has in mind the controlling gaze of patriarchy and its effects on women, but her analysis is in several respects quite capable of extrapolation to the gaze of anthropocentrism and its effects on nonhuman animals.[72] For instance, Frye astutely notices that the agent of arrogant vision "coerces the objects of his perception into satisfying the conditions his perception imposes." This pattern, translated to the interspecific situation, is what I have identified as the pornography of preservation embodied in the zoöpticon. It is constituted by capture, feeding schedules, architecture of display, and breeding regimens.

Another example of the linkage between Frye's account of androcentric optics and homocentric zooscopy can be traced from this observation: "How one sees another and one expects the other to behave are in tight interdependence, and how one expects another to behave is a large factor in determining how the other does behave." As we have seen, one can hardly go to the zoo and truly expect an authentic encounter to occur; it should not surprise us, if Frye is right, that none takes place. Overall, what we are presented with in the vision of arrogance is a leitmotif of disintegration: the perceptual consumption of a coherent organism and its breakdown through and into the interests of the spectator. This same dynamic operates under the aspect of patriarchy and under that of zoological exhibition or imperium.

If this is a sort of spectatorship to be avoided, what might a kind to be fostered literally look like? Frye herself calls a salient alternative the "loving eye." Negative descriptions give us some idea of what she means when she writes, "the loving perceiver can see without the presupposition that the other poses a constant threat or that the other exists for the seer's service. . . . The loving eye does not make the object of perception into something edible, does not try to assimilate it, does not reduce it to the size of the seer's desire, fear and imagination." Of course, there are indeed times when we face hostility or hunger and defensive or venatic eyes may be appropriate—but when self-preservation is not at issue, how do loving eyes see?[73] Frye's positive characterization is open-ended; for her, the loving eye lavishes a creative type of attention: "It knows the complexity of the other as something which will forever present new things to be known."[74]

Indeed, there is a certain sort of showiness in nature. For Lingis, the kaleidoscopic manifestations of organic phenomena—especially the blooming, buzzing confusion of colors and shapes displayed by animal forms—exceed the necessities of camouflage and communication. They point beyond those functions, to organisms' participation in a "logic of ostentation" that is driven by a "compulsion for exhibition, spectacle, parade."[75] In the thick of such morphology (described from the perspective of marine diving expeditions) Lingis becomes a voluptuary of visual delight, and discovers a (com)passionate kind of loving sight, the hallmark of which is its maneuvers of caressing: "The voluptuous eye does not seek to comprehend the unity in the surface dispersion of shapes, to penetrate to the substance beneath the chromatic appearances . . . it caresses, is caressed by the surface effects of an alien domain." Forgoing the ego and its projects of appropriation, this species of optics melts into a general sensuousness immersed in the "exorbitant materiality" of the natural lifeworld (the matrix of perception and perceptibility that Merleau-Ponty called flesh-of-the-world) and thereby paradoxically "expose[s] exposure itself."[76] At this point, Lingis suggests, the so-called rapture of the deep spreads itself across a profundity of surface aesthetics.

Although such experiences of sensual immersion are revelatory and valuable, life is not always lived through them—and so it is important to stay in touch with and further refine other practices of perception. Distinct from erotogenic or romantic models of fusion, the loving eye as Frye portrays it maintains the distance of vision itself—one who employs it does not dissolve into the other: "There are boundaries between them [seer and seen]; she and the other are two; their interests are not identical; they are not blended in vital parasitic or symbiotic relations."[77] I have underscored the ethical significance of a jointly held form of bodily consciousness that I have been calling symphysis; here we see a complementary apprehension of separation, which is necessary to engage periodically in order to keep in play an ontological and moral dialectic of difference and similarity.[78] In Frye's words, "it is a matter of being able to tell one's own interests from those of others and of knowing where one's self leaves off and another begins." This power of discrimination is a necessary condition for relationships to be conducted along an axis of optimal freedom, whereby the spell of captivity cast by the arrogant eye is broken and encounter becomes volitional rather than compulsory. The advantage of such a transformation is palpable: "It is one mark of a voluntary association that the one person can survive displeasing the other, defying the other, dissociating from the other." All too often, of course, just the opposite holds in the lives (and deaths) of zoo and circus animals, pets and working animals, and even wildlife who get too much "in the face of" human civilization. Thus, changing over from the vision of arrogance to that of love could produce remarkably beneficial results for not only interpersonal but for interspecies relations as well. Finally, of course, in the twilight of the zoo, it will be up to biologists, animal advocates, and concerned citizens alike to look ahead with new eyes, devise novel and better modes of cross-species encounter, and see them through to implementation and inevitable revision.[79]

SIX

Contexts and Promise of
Corporal Compassion

Humanism is the attempt to recreate equality amongst the mass of humankind while still insisting upon immovable divisions between the different [animal] servants of empire.

STEPHEN R. L. CLARKE (1995)

To PROCEED BY clear argument is the standard way of philosophy. In case the explanative or interpretive aspects of the foregoing reflections appear wanting in discursive clarity or cogency, I will recapitulate the proceedings so far by condensing them into a more perspicuous structure. This move runs the risk of making it seem as if the study's broadly phenomenological method were being violated, but what I intend to construct is an argumentative contextualization or utilization of phenomenological findings. Moreover, the sort of phenomenology at work in this study has already been subject to qualification —namely, through the modifications of existential and hermeneutic thought. Thus my appropriation of phenomenology is neither exclusive nor pure, but rather eclectic.

And what of my appropriation of argument itself? Simply put, argumentation is discursively rational suasion. The standard philosophic recipe for argument is to marshal propositional truths into inferential arrays abiding by certified patterns of logical derivation in order to compel acceptance of new insights.[1] As prefigured in my methodological dismissal of ultimate justification for the bodily ethos of animal appreciation articulated, I must confess that the argumentation operative in this study deviates from the ideal model just characterized.

The crux of that deviation is located in the exclusivity of the current canon of accepted inference patterns, which rules out many discursive maneuvers as fallacies—including one of pivotal importance to my meditation. Typically, an "appeal to common sense" is deemed a pseudorational demerit against the philosophic statement of a position. Yet something very much like it forms the heart of the "explanative ethic" I have presented. Of course, the appeal I make is to shared *sensibility* (an "ethical sensorium" correlative to the moral experience of symphysis)—not popular practice or opinion. Still, if one insists on hard-nosed adherence to canonical purity, then a crucial step in my proceedings will be found fallacious.

According to rigorous application of standards for logical cogency, then, my case for an interspecies ethos of bodiment cannot be judged compelling in the sense of purely rational persuasion. Thus I am disbarred from the role of philosopher-as-legislative commandant; I am unable to force or require by dint of reason alone the points I wish to make. Yet perhaps that heroic role arrogantly romanticizes rationalism; maybe my shortcoming is a blessing in disguise. "Philosophers should be generous enough to refrain from legislating imperatives and confine themselves to offering invitations," says Michael Weinstein in a moment of metaphilosophical humility.[2] Following that advice, it may be best to construe this study not as a persuasive tract attempting to frame or instantiate categorical imperatives, but as an invitational discourse endeavoring to make a transhuman ethos more sensible and existentially attractive.[3] Alternatively, one might view the book as contributory to "moral psychology." Caveats would then be in order to distinguish this contribution from the usual work of that field's proponents and critics: first, the relevant psychology here is more existential than cognitive, and more phenomenological than experimental. Moreover, the "psyche" at stake does not engage with the transcendent(al), a la Plato or Kant—rather, it is so radically embodied/incarnate that reflections regarding its ethical weight would more appropriately occur under the heading of "moral somatology."[4]

This study began with the initial, overarching question: (how) can we sensibly describe, explain, and interpret transhuman morality? A posthumanist hermeneutic of somaesthetic sensibility and the lived force of existential attraction (registering as bodily sensitivity and thus encompassing dimensions of our being behind or beneath that of rational rectitude) were key factors in the sorts of descriptions we have entertained. The time has come to reflectively re-phrase the insights elicited by our query into a positive statement of the study's overall thesis. I believe I have shown, affirmatively, that it is indeed possible to axiologically articulate the ontology of animate modes of bodily being such that it is sensible to incorporate other animals into a transhuman form of morality.

That claim, however, is only the skeletal outline of my position. I shall now review the discursive musculature that holds it together and fleshes it out—a task I will accomplish by recapitulating each chapter's "argument" (such as it may be, with all the caveats listed above). In the first one, then, I posit an amoralist framework of explanative/interpretive ethics. Much of the chapter's initial argumentation is geared toward negative historical critique.

Sartre

Sartrean somatology's flaw is its claim that there is a radical ontological difference between the body-for-me and the body-to-others. I counter that there is no such split of bodily reality (none, that is, ontologically absolute).

Heidegger

With respect to Heidegger my critique proceeds on three fronts, with the combined effect of claiming that he fails to give animality its due. First, his *Daseinsanalyse* does not have enough ontological resolution to bring into focus the being of nonhuman life as a form (or forms) of existence irreducible to instrumentality or objectivity. Second, that analysis is executed in an over-temporalizing, somewhat disembodied fashion. Third, even Heidegger's later attempt at handling animality more directly is riven with aporias. The overall force of these three problems is to make animality opaque (or at best obscure) to existential phenomenology, and thus to debilitate an important field of re-gional ontology. In order to establish the existence and specificity of this "bio-region," appeal can be made to our natural acquaintance with other life-forms (especially those relatively wild ones sharing a similar scale-of-presence with us humans). To do philosophic justice to the animate realm of organic life a broader, more ecological notion of "being-in-*a*-world" is a phenomenological necessity (as a corrective replacement for Heidegger's extensionally homo-exclusive "being-in-*the*-world").

Merleau Ponty

Next, Merleau-Ponty became the center of attention. He posits a common-ality between (human and nonhuman) bodies, speaking of a carnally chiasmic "interanimality." As against Sartre's radical bifurcation of body-consciousness, this seemed a better starting point for our enquiry—at least methodologically

Merleau-Ponty does not provide a full-fledged account of being-in-a-world as bodily animality, yet he does furnish important cues, chief of which are the notions of "intercorporeality" and body-world "styles of address." (Husserl was *Husserl* also found deficient in his dealings with animal nature—for his treatment, though it recognizes the phenomenal foundation of transpecific somatology, dissipates into homocentric egology.)

Using Merleau-Ponty's concepts beyond his own horizons, I took up the issue of whether different modes of worldly address can be intersomatic in a cross-species sense. I laid out an organismic ontology (of vegetal and animalic worldhood) and observed that a residential relation to being-at-large is a life-worldly common denominator between species. This observation served as evidence for the possibility of transpecific worldhood (as various species' worlds share at least one similar existential structure—namely, that of residence). We still needed to know whether there is a *somatic* dimension to the existential overlap of phenomenal world/s.

Since bodiment is submerged in status and topicality by the dominant in-tellectualist mainstream of Western philosophy, I turned initially to "marginal" resources of thought and feeling to deal with the question of cross-species so-maticity. First, ethno-philosophically, I made appeal to the Austral-Aboriginal account of poet Bill Neidjie. I moved on to consider two "alternative" figures on the borders of modern Euro-philosophy: Uexküll, who holds that various animal worlds are based in sensorimotor processes (hence are fundamentally corporal), and Buytendijk, who talks of nonhuman subjectivity, but thinks the human body is entirely different from those of other species.

Unfortunately, appeals to marginal resources either fall on deaf ears or else lead down blind alleys. Ready-made solutions to the problems before us were not likely to be forthcoming and we had, therefore, to become creative. This task would not be met totally *ex nihilo*—it was, rather, both "thrown" and "projective" (in the Heideggerian senses of those words): thrown, negatively, in that it had surrendered the nature/culture dichotomy; projective, positively, in that it sought a "third way" for somatology beyond the false dilemma of sci-entistic biologism and linguistic textualism.[5]

An alternate route between these horns was traveled in the second chapter. There I took up Thomas Nagel's now-classic challenge to animal phenome-nology that it must search for a realism based neither in imagination nor in empathy. My argument for circumventing Nagel's alleged opacity of nonhuman being was that the task before us is not one of transubstantively becoming-other (indeed impossible) but of articulating our already familiar experiences of *being-with* others. This reinterpretation dissolved the original problem, and then I resolved it into a more comprehensible project sufficient for our purposes by returning to Heidegger's (mis)treatment of transhuman *Mitsein* and demonstrating how to work through and think past shortcomings therein, by untangling his tortured reading of accessibility to beings "as such" and its relevance to the transposibility of animal worldhood.

With the focus then on phenomenology of transpecific conviviality, I argued for a phenomenology of body because somaticity is what opens us out into our environment—and that environmental opening is what provides the shared space of convivial worldhood across speciated horizons. I referred to Watsuji, who argues the case for the existential importance of the climactic/spatial dimension of human worldhood. Climaticity as an existential structure includes our appropriation of weather and landscape.[6] Human being-in-a-world is a bodiment-environment complex that has to be treated as comprising, chiasmically, not only *Geist* but *physis,* too.

Such treatment was facilitated by employing the Merleau-Pontyan notion of world-flesh, which describes a holistic *Leibswelt.* I placed the phenomenology of this live body-world under a *residential* hermeneutic, which permitted speaking of world-flesh as a carnal earth-home. I conducted a foray into "municipal ontology" and focused on urban parkland. It may seem to cut across the grain of an ecological phenomenology that it concentrates on an aspect of the city. Yet this appearance holds true only if the nature/culture dichotomy is maintained and we insist on identifying ecosophy with natural communion and civilization with cultural artifice. However, this way of configuring environmental thought is precisely what I—in concert with Bigwood, Böhme, Watsuji, and others—want to think past. In some quarters at least, ecophilosophers have already begun to appreciate the consequences of radically renaturalizing our conception of humanity.[7] If the human being is an animal whose nature it is to be(come) political, then it is proper to view even citification as a zoo-natural process.[8]

Using my parkscape phenomenology, three main points came to the fore: climate and history (or nature and culture) interpenetrate; our environmental experience is transhuman, involving our lifeworld with other species; and these "chiasms" of climatic culture/natural history and cross-species conviviality are made possible and actual by "the somatic act of being in place" (a la Grange). This common worldly residency is itself constituted through somaesthesia —that is to say, it is a bodily phenomenon felt by flesh-and-blood being-in-a-world. Thus existential ontology can speak intelligibly of "transpecific intersomaticity."

In chapter 3, I discussed the Foucauldian observation that normalization *Foucault* tends toward deviant similitude, in effect reducing the other to the status of abnormality; and I invited the reader to adopt, instead, the trope of related otherness, which affords another species its own, respectable positivity. To treat valuation, I first engaged a structural axiological analysis. Objectivism is too metaphysical for its own good—the significance of values, I argued, lies precisely in their pragmatic meaning, and so belief in (or worry about) their putatively pure inherence in that which is appreciated had no import for our study. Subjectivism, on the other hand, falls prey to troublesome relativity (capable, for example, of producing normative chaos). Thus, a relational axiology was found preferable: value arises neither by revelation nor as creation, but rather through a process of growth—organically emerging when valuer and valuee are related (and subject to cultivation or neglect thereafter).

Beyond giving this account of value's source, I also supplied a statement of its nature, namely that it is the "pervasive or profound probability of appreciation." Hence, we arrived at a hallmark of valuability: x is worthy if it is widely or thoroughly likely to be prized. (Such a definition built into the concept of value a requirement of consensus or conscience, but it left room for conflict or doubt—which, I claimed, can be decided by appeal to formal criteria of comprehensivity, coherence, and consistency, or to principles of phenomenological lucidity and loyalty.

What are the connections, one may ask, between my literary, genetic, and structural accounts of valuation? The latter two provide the general characteristics of the "origin" and "essence" of value. The literary one supplies categories helpfully applicable to our domain of enquiry (most especially, the trope of related otherness links well the broad genetic notion of relational axiology to the specific question of appreciating other animals).[9] The structural one is empty on its own and, in order to suit my study's purposes, needs to be applied to animality and bodiment.

I proceeded to furnish a more substantive treatment of appreciation itself when applied to bodiment and animality. This task was pursued on two levels:

typology of somatic valuation and "topology" of animal appreciation's (cultural) dynamics. Typologically, somatic valuation is discussed in six domains: first ethics, politics, and aesthetics; then survival/health, economics, and sexuality. The most significant insight resulting from such discussion is Levin's notion that the experience of intersomaticity (rooted in corporal phenomena of reversibility and intertwining) brings with it a primordial feeling of mutuality.[10]

With respect to mapping the cultural dialectics of animal appreciation, I presented an extended Nietzschean treatment of the history of prizing tame versus wild animality. "Zoovalently," Nietzsche himself privileges and thus transvaluates the feral. Nietzsche's philosophy demonstrated the general fact of valuation being contextual—that, in other words, it is embedded in historical sediment and cultural conditioning. Organismic being—as subsumptive fusion of the animal and the bodily—appears inscribed with(in) an acosmic array of discursive and practical complexes.

Confronting this situation, either we reduce somatology to post-structural semiology and/or postmodern politics of praxis, or else we reinvigorate the phenomenological/hermeneutic project of thematizing fleshood's presence and significance. My study has tended to follow the latter route, which enables us to articulate and appreciate family resemblances of bodily animacy across species lines as well as the real heft or terrestrial weight of organismic being for various earthlings' lifeworlds.

Chapter four pursued the task of making sense of other animals' incorporation into transhuman morality, arguing at the outset that animal ethics had matured enough to redeem its existential basis in affective/somatic experience. Theoretically, the chapter mobilized Mandelbaum's claim that experience of moral demand rests upon apprehension of a fittingness relation between a situation or context and an action or attitude. Phenomenologically, it was seen that that apprehension is in transpecific fields undergirded by a somaesthetic nexus experienced by one or more members of a(n inter)relationship—and I referred to this experience as symphysis for short. Historically, I held that investigation of symphysis is a necessary complement to the sentimentality of moral sense tradition.[11]

After introducing the idea of symphysis, I attempted to illustrate its existential mediation of vulnerability and togetherness in order to show that awareness of the former can explain a felt obligation toward protective conduct, and that awareness of the latter evokes attitudes of care or respect. To illustrate vulnerability, I used the example of squirrel protection (registered as a moral phenomenon). I gave various descriptions of the cross-species intersomaticity possible with squirrels through the *Leibswelt* of parkland. These phenomena are symphysical in nature (rather than ones of neutrality, repellence, or hostility).[12] They lead one generally to appreciate the related otherness of squirrels and specifically to attend concernfully to their vulnerabilities. One thus experiences a moral demand or claim expressible ethically as a protectionist judgment of obligation—in which, that is, a fit is apprehended between the convivial context charted and deeds (committed or omitted) that tend toward squirrels' faring well or avoiding ill. It was noted that this way of conceiving transhuman moral phenomena affords an ethical equipoise between interests of ecological holism and biotic individuality.

In the second kind of situation (illustrative of togetherness), after realigning the issue of anthropomorphism, I appealed to Hearne's and Lopez's accounts of symphysical relationships and encounters with working and wild animals (respectively). Hearne's canine and equestrian examples of interspecific togetherness demonstrate an intimate reciprocity, and the Lopez's association with wolves displays a relational mutuality, both of which render fitting the adoption of respectful or caring attitudes toward other animals. I responded to objections against my somatological ethos of animal appreciation, and furnished supportive scientific findings (particularly as regards the role of biophilia in children's development and other primates' sociability).

The fourth chapter was the argumentive climax of my study's enquiry. I concluded that it is (or at least really can be) sensible to incorporate other animals into transhuman morality—sensible in the double sense of being conceptually intelligible, from the twin perspectives of relational axiology and transpecific/intersomatic ontology, and existentially attractive, on the lived basis of (sensory awareness of) cross-species symphysical phenomena. With this major moral claim in place, it became important to treat (at least some of) its ramifications in the practical realm of "applied ethics." Therefore, in chapter five, I approached some salient sites of moral praxis from the vantage point of my bodiment ethos. I did not proceed according to the juridico-criterial method of standard casuistry (in which cases are regulatively external to law); rather, I looked at the experimental laboratory and the zoological park as sites of praxis existentially internal to conscience constitution. I also explored these morally problematic scenes of interspecies contact under the aspect of a dialectic between principles or forces of the carnal and the carceral (as per Merleau and Foucault). With respect to laboratory animals, I highlighted the morally degrading processes of ontological reduction to which the tested are subject—here the experimental (de)construction of rodent being was especially revelatory. I then focused at greater length on the zoo and concluded that, even in its modern manifestation, it retains elements of ethical equivocation (e.g., structural inauthenticity and a pornographic undercurrent)—enough on the negative side, indeed, to suggest the desirability of eventual eradication or else radical transformation.

Comparisons and Implications

When "interspecies ethics" is mentioned, at least in North American discourse, the position with which it is most readily associated is that of "animal rights." Arguments on behalf of this position can be grounded culturally or metaphysically.[13] The classic contemporary statement for animal rights follows the middle path of reflective equilibrium (balancing pure ethical theory and our moral intuition),[14] and bases rights-bearing on the inherent (nonanthropogenic) value or worth of living subjectivity. While my symphysical ethos likewise centers on a vital value (that of live bodiment), its relational axiology judges the notion of (objectively) intrinsic worth to be at best idle and at worst incoherent. There is another salient point of comparison: from the perspective of the most recent work in animal rights theory, corporal compassion can be criticized for not (being capable of) grounding a normative theory of ethics on its own. Julian Franklin, for instance, claims that "compassion cannot serve as an independent and sufficient ground of rights for animals, or indeed for humans either" because "rules of reason are indispensable for deciding conflicts and avoiding bizarre applications of compassionate feelings" (e.g., to those rightly held blameworthy otherwise, such as the thief wounded in the act of stealing).[15] In response, I would concede that compassion is not the whole story of morality (inter- or intraspecies). However, it is crucial to remember that neither is rationality alone enough for ethics to have purchase in the realm of lived experience. Corporal compassion is a necessary condition for the comprehensibility and appeal of (at least animal) ethics—no more, yet no less.[16]

Another transhuman ethic is that of animal liberation. As theorized by its founder, Peter Singer, it is based upon a biologically egalitarian (species-blind) application of preference utilitarianism. By contrast, in respect of appropriating traditional thought, I have preferred to align my work with the moral sense heritage. Moreover, the emancipatory vision of animal liberation differs somewhat in perspective from my own convivial conception of symphysical solidarity (the difference of letting-go versus being-with). These historical and perspectival distinctions do not, however, make the two ethics incompatible. In fact, as regards their driving principles, I would say that they are best conceived as complementary: compassion (between bodies) is what underlies the very attention to suffering that is the hallmark of animal liberation; calculation (of interests) could help decide conflicting allegiances generated or informed by symphysis.

Both the animal rights and animal liberation ethics are essentially zoocentric extensions of existing moral paradigms. Deep ecology and ecofeminism, by contrast, are attempts to build an environmental ethos on new, posthumanist or post-patriarchal, foundations. Norwegian philosopher Arne Naess distinguished the former fundament from the conservation movement's anthropocentrically instrumentalist reformism by propounding an alternative, revolutionary platform of ecosophic axiology and transpersonal ontology.[17] In comparison, the cross-species symphysics of morals I have mapped also displays a more deeply ecological holism (rooted in a Merleau-Pontyan *Leibsweltanschauung*); on the other hand, it does not ratify the globally absorbing identity of environmental Selfhood—its own existential principle of connection relies rather on relatively bounded bodies' *Mitsein* (via interpenetration, contact, or sharing vital media of being-in-a-world). Ultimately, however, I would see compatibility here too, at least insofar as deep ecology can be supplemented or enriched by "wide somatology" (flesh-of-the-world, for example, is both profound in nature and broad in scope).

Ecofeminist philosophy seeks to juxtapose anthropocentrism and androcentrism, the better to show patriarchal linkages between the domination of nature and the oppression of women. As broached in the present study, my ethic of bodiment does not thematize gender/sex issues. Future thinking might address this lacuna by engaging questions such as: How is the *Leibswelt* gendered? Does fe/male dividuality mediate or interrupt transhuman symphysics?[18] For now, I would like to acknowledge that feminist philosophy's retrieval of bodily consciousness has inspired the present work and that its theorists deserve credit for calling animal ethics to account on the issue of caring's centrality to moral thought and practice.

In the past decade or so, pragmatist philosophy has made significant contributions to transhuman morality—in both environmental and animal ethics. Its pluralism, fallibilism, and flexibility is a welcome intervention into this field (which can sometimes slide into righteously rigid monism), and its tradition of public conscience only helps fortify an already laudable attention to actual problems of present currency beyond mere armchair philosophizing.[19] One pragmatist contribution of relevance, Phillip McReynolds's Deweyan approach to animal ethics, reveals similarities and contrasts to the account I have given in this book. McReynolds observes that "we can share overlapping horizons [of meaning] if the horizons that surround and encompass each of us happen to include the same territory," and he argues that "where there is a basic level of sociality, which is determined by inhabiting the same horizon of meaning, there is, at least implicitly, an acknowledgment of moral standing."[20] This line of reasoning nicely tracks the development of my symphysical ethos, the only difference being that I have stressed the bodily mediation of the process ("shared territory," e.g., translating into *Leibswelt* on my position) whereas McReynolds emphasizes the role of habits in constituting a common field of action. Ultimately, however, these two approaches may be melded: Shannon Sullivan's transactional analysis of bodying, to which I have referred several times before, can be used to show that bodies are lived through their habits —or, from the other vantage, that behavioral dispositions are registered somatically.[21]

Beyond more general alignments and divergences of outlook, it will be illuminating to compare my practical philosophy of the zoo with another recent critique in particular. This comparison differs from those already conducted in that its point of reference is a position substantially similar in its conclusions, here the plane of contrast being rather one of approach. Dale Jamieson, operating along the lines of applied ethics as conceived by most Anglo-American writers in the field, has analyzed the putative justifications for the zoo as an institution.[22] Dutifully and judiciously, he considers the major arguments in defense of zoos and finds them far from compelling. Amusement seems a rather frivolous compensation for captivity; education in the zoo does not appear to happen very often or very well; research activities are, for the most part, farfetched, circular, redundant, or trivial; and preservationist breeding programs "save" animals only "in the thinnest biological sense," sacrificing real individuals' quality of life for the benefit of abstract species.

What is interesting to me about Jamieson's critique is not his intermediate results (which, for the record, I believe are largely sound), but his rationale for reaching an ultimate recommendation of abolition. One of the critical pivots employed by Jamieson is (appeal to) a moral presumption against keeping wild animals in captivity. My own criticism in chapter five implicitly rested on just such a presumption, and it is a virtue of Jamieson's criterial mode of doing ethics that it makes that presumption theoretically explicit. Yet, we may ask, upon what experiential element does such a presumption float? "It is surely true," Jamieson claims, "that in being taken from the wild and confined in zoos, animals are deprived of a great many goods." I would respond that this is surely true for an audience already disposed by symphysical encounter to care about the bodily or behavioral ramifications of other animals' losing their liberty! This is one way in which my phenomenological approach complements an otherwise incomplete account.

The other fulcrum of critique Jamieson uses is the judgment that "zoos teach us a false sense of our place in the natural order." He identifies this as the most important consideration, but confesses that it is "more difficult to articulate." Since zoos capture and organize other animals for our (human) purposes, Jamieson explains, they hinder the zoological humility suggested by ecology and recommended for biospheric survival. In view of the latter factors, we should "learn to live as one species *among* many rather than as one species *over* many." Once again, the approach I have followed is able to enhance the articulation offered by another mode of moral discourse—for the unarticulated difference between "living among" and "living over" is exactly what I have spelled out in chapters two and five under the rubrics of conviviality and carcerality. With those discussions in place, we have a greater capacity to understand and appreciate the falsity and danger of the structural message communicated through zoo visitation.

"Because what zoos teach us is false and dangerous," Jamieson finally concludes, "both humans and animals will be better off when they are abolished." There ends the accounting of a standard analysis that can be associated with the typical format of applied ethics. Yet John Berger, operating more in the mode of what I have called practical philosophy, continues on: the disappearance of animals from modernity's lifescape, which according to him makes zoos possible and necessary biosocially, represents a "historic loss . . . now irredeemable for the culture of capitalism."[23] Regardless of one's mien in respect of Marxian axioms or methods, it is fair to say that this insight—in tracing the socio-transcendental presuppositions of the zoo, beneath its ideological self-promotions—touches not only economic but existential nerves not noticed in the prior analysis, nor even noticeable in that rationalistic type of view.

Finally, I would like to compare the transhuman ethos of my moral phenomenology with certain contemporary currents in continental European thought. Projecting its direction, Edith Wyschogrod once remarked that Continental ethics would reflect further upon the notion that "ethical subjectivity as a primordial responsiveness to the other takes for granted the corporeal being of others."[24] Consonantly, I have strived to examine precisely what is normally taken for granted by moral philosophy, namely, bodily presence and exchange. In retrospect, my aim can be said to have been an interspecific alteration and extension of Wyschogrod's Levinasian argument for the sensate nature of morality, which is based on two main premises: "the body is a sensorium," and "sensibility is bound up with meaning . . . replete with ethical significations" of susceptibility and vulnerability.[25] More specifically, according to Wyschogrod, Levinas "stresses the other's corporeal vulnerability as soliciting one's generosity";[26] my own interpretation of this point takes it beyond Levinas's humanism to include other animals.

Building on Wyschogrod's last claim, in other words, I believe that by thematizing vulnerability, the transpecific scope of morality can be appreciated appropriately. A recent work by Werner Marx may prove helpful here—if it is stretched to accommodate our theme. Marx suggests that a nonmetaphysical, phenomenological ethics could come forth from the capacity for compassion elicited by awareness of human mortality.[27] Grafting my own idiom and insight to Marx's, I would add that such an ethos of compassion becomes cross-specific when mediated by symphysical awareness of *animal vulnerability* (comparing, for example, the specifically human concept of death with a generically animal perception of pain).[28]

Marx attempts to delineate a path for developing nonmetaphysical morality by demonstrating that it is possible—without resorting to transcendent theology or rationalistic systems—to find "a measure on earth for ethical conduct." He believes that this earthly standard is discoverable in the capacity for compassion, which manifests itself preeminently through one's encounter with mortality. Basically, the pattern suggested is that confrontation with death and dying produces a sense of life's transience, contingency, and dependence; this feeling, in turn, breeds an affection of solidarity with those beings who share the condition of mortality. In relation to my present concern, however, Marx believes that the concomitant transformation of attunement—from solitary horror under the shadow of fatality to altruistic joy in the company of others —is "an unfolding of what characterizes man as a human being above all."[29]

This anthropocentrist interpretation rests on two premises: the conviction that the catalyst of compassion, genuine mortality, stems from awareness of self and elicits rational insight; and the assumption that both these forms of consciousness (i.e., self-reflection and intellectual intuition) are exclusively human phenomena. As Marx's mentor, Martin Heidegger, would have it, only humans truly die—other animals, by counterexample, merely perish. One way of challenging such an interpretation would be to marshal ethological evidence for nonhuman modes of "being-unto-death."[30] For instance, so-called covering behavior observed amongst elephants is quite suggestive of burial ceremony.[31] Consider the following ethological report:

> There is something eerie and deeply moving about the reaction of a group of elephants to the death of one of their own. It is their silence that is most unsettling. The only sound is the slow blowing of air out of their trunks as they investigate their dead companion. . . . Just as unsettling is the way that elephants back into their dead. Although elephants use their front legs for killing, by kneeling on their victims, they have a way of walking backward and using their sensitive hind feet surprisingly delicately for waking up their babies and touching the dead. Using their toenails and the soles of the feet, they touch the body ever so gently, circling, hovering above, touching again. . . . Their movements are in slow motion, and then, in silence, they may cover the dead with leaves and branches. Elephants' last rites? A wake, a death watch, the calling up of the elephant spirits? Elephants perform the same rituals around elephant bones. They approach slowly and silently, and then the touching begins, slowly, as they deliberately, carefully turn a skull over and over with their trunks, touching, hovering over the long bones with their hind feet.[32]

Of course, such scenarios illustrate only retrospective awareness of death. What we need for our present purpose is evidence of prospective consciousness, which is lacking here (though there is a hint of it in the mention of presumably anticipatory rousing of the young). It would be interesting to see if similar behaviors are associated with the tending of terminally ill or lethally wounded elephants.

Another tack (one I prefer instead) is to shift the platform of comparison by suggesting that we float moral compassion for other animals upon the somaesthetic apprehension of vulnerability, rather than mortality under the aspect of mental phenomena. (Compare a similar stance of Robert Goodin's: "What gives rise to our special duties to protect animals from pain and suffering is their peculiar vulnerability to us."[33]) From this perspective, an ethos sculpted somatically by symphysical encounters would constitute a character or culture morally sensitive to the existential element of live bodiment as such—including its susceptibilities to damage, disease, and decay.

On a somatic level, then, we have seen that we are aware of our own physical vulnerability—susceptibility to injury and illness—just by virtue of being sentient entities of animate flesh. We might share this sort of somatic sensitivity with another (kind of) organism in the minimal sense of becoming aware that our susceptibility to suffer harm is like that of the other organism. My claim on this construal is that such minimal mutuality of common carnal nature suffices phenomenologically to establish compassionate concern for the other—in the mode of its being the proper object or "patient" of ethical consideration. In another, stronger sense of sharing, the second party might also become aware of our vulnerability being similar to its own; this richer form of reciprocity seems requisite for interspecific compassion to take on the aspect of respect—whereby both parties appropriately regard each other as moral subjects, agents, or actors.[34] Some of our relationships with other primates (particularly apes), with cetaceans (such as dolphins), and most especially with domesticated companion and work animals (such as dogs and horses) feature reciprocally cognizant compassion grown into moral respect.

Finally, I want to cast the concept of symphysical ethos into the form of a transhumanizing task. I borrow the notion of "task" as a guiding principle for (moral) philosophy from Carleton Dallery, according to whom the term is vocational and so means "work owed." From the vantage of existential phenomenology, Dallery suggests, "we discover our debt and our task by being open to the world, and not by deducing obligations or inferring prescriptions or having emotions."[35] I would add that the discovery of work owed to other animals is mediated by a somatic mode of being sensitive to the organismic vulnerabilities within the animate world-home. This sensitivity is made appreciative (and appreciable) by our bodily participation as animals ourselves operating on a zoomorphic register. Thus I maintain that my symphysical stance on bio-morality axiologically avoids deconstructive doubts regarding the ethical enterprise as such, precisely because I resist the temptation of traditional theory to metaphysically vouchsafe obligation.[36]

To trace the wider implications of corporal compassion for culture at large, it is helpful to consider its place within the context of post-humanism. The past few decades have included much change and controversy, especially regarding ecological concerns. As Strachan Donnelley has observed, "we are seemingly in a period of profound flux in our philosophical understanding of ourselves and our ethical relation to the natural, animate world."[37] Most observers would agree that the dominant ideology of humanism has brought modern civilization down a path fraught with ecological danger and bioethical risk. This cultural devolution has intellectual and emotional aspects as well as physical or material ones.

Following the Frankfurt School's (especially Adorno's) diagnosis of the disease coiled within the Enlightenment's reliance on (instrumental) rationality, Marcus Bullock provides an evocative analysis of the cognitive/affective dimension: "our civilization has based its relationship to animals on the difference between creatures with and those without th[e] power of abstract knowledge and the ability to dominate nature that it confers. All our thoughts that follow in this pattern carry us further away from understanding any other constitution of identity, and have alienated us especially from the quality of a relationship with another based on the shared capacity to feel pain, privation, or joy and fullness of spontaneous vitality."[38]

Regarding the material/physical dimension (including even aesthetics), there is substantial truth in David Ehrenfeld's polemical critique of humanism's arrogance—namely, that the intellectual and social ideals of human dignity and power became so exclusively and exuberantly anthropocentric that they have grown to the cancerous extremity of endangering biospheric health and beauty.[39] Since this situation presents difficulties of epistemic and ethical import, it can be characterized as problematic in the Deweyan sense.[40] Environmental crisis and bioethical confusion are existential catalysts for further scientific and moral inquiry. At a very basic level of disposition, we worry about our own prospects and care about how we affect others.[41]

As a result, there has been a rising tide of moral theory that seeks to go beyond anthropocentrism. Unfortunately, the foremost transhuman ethics remain all-too-humanist in that they fixate on human-like mentation in other organisms. The crypto-speciesist flaw in this stratagem was noticed by critics even early on—according to renowned veterinarian and comparative psychologist Michael W. Fox: "In order to make a case for 'animal rights,' some philosophers, lawyers, ethologists, and others are eager to demonstrate that other nonhuman species have some degree of humanlike self-awareness. Such an approach in the final analysis is humanocentric and 'species-bound' since it assumes that only humanlike (or suprahuman) beings are worthy of being accorded rights."[42]

As Neil Evernden suspects, "the very idea of animal 'rights'—an idea that seems to presuppose a humanistic interpretation of justice and individuality —amounts to a kind of subterfuge to draw certain nonhumans into the protected circle of human self-definition."[43] Whether contingently or essentially, consequentialist appeals to sentience and deontological definitions of subjectivity function effectively as standards of moral significance (only?) by utilizing positive comparisons to human exemplars of consciousness.[44] Hence, accidentally or necessarily, they attract the derogative charge of personification from reactionary anthropocentrists. To avoid the still somewhat delegitimizing label of anthropomorphism, I propose that animal ethicists shed anthropocentric hierarchy altogether—even (the risk of) its appearance—and place their moral thinking behind the truly post-humanist task of reappreciating bodily animacy as such. Thus we may extend the range of our caring regard in the very gesture of recognizing our own vital status as animate zoomorphs.

So what is to be done to achieve as much? One tactic is critical (in the senses both of critique and of crisis): it consists of demonstrating the self-subversion of anthropocentrist assumptions—in Cary Wolfe's words, "showing how humanism must, if rigorously pursued, generate its own deconstruction once the 'defining' characteristics [of humanity] are found beyond the species barrier."[45] More than this is required, however. We need not only negative dialectics, but also some element of affirmation or reconstruction. I have sought such constructive positivity in the abstract principle and concrete experiences of ethically inflected symphysis. Whether symphysical or sympathetic in nature, a compassionate response to the problematic situation of post-humanism is attracting a growing number of influential advocates. Michael W. Fox uses it to restore a broadened banner of bioethics: "Bioethics is the key to finding alternatives and solutions. The trans-situational attitude of respect and reverence for all life comes from embracing the ethic of equal concern (equalitarianism) for animals, environment, and people alike. No one is first. What must come first from us is compassion. This is the essential ingredient of a viable life ethic."[46] Such a pronouncement harkens back to earlier exemplars of a broad-based bioethic (e.g., Albert Schweitzer and Van Rensselaer Potter),[47] and finds contemporary resonance in the field of postmodern theory. For example, Jacques Derrida became quite interested in the problematic of animality toward the end of his life and insisted on "the place that has to be accorded to the interpretation of this [transpecific] compassion, to the sharing of this suffering among the living, to the law, ethics, and politics that must be brought to bear upon this experience of compassion."[48]

Recently, Wolfe has urged that we take up this challenge "not by rushing toward the other, all the others, in some redemptive embrace, but precisely *by way of* theory."[49] What I would rather stress, regarding the ethos of corporal compassion charted in this book, is that it has at least as much to do with concrete, lived experience as with theoretical activity. Crafting a post-humanist agenda is not precisely or exclusively, nor even primarily, about the intellectual interruption of anthropocentrist ideology. Though it must include critical moments of counter-theorizing, if it is to refire latent yet abiding feelings of biophilia, post-humanism must engage with actual animals. Like ethicist and advocate Elisa Aaltola, I believe that "to respect the welfare of an animal we have to pay attention to it as something more than an abstraction: we have to see the content of its characteristics and understand its interests, instead of marveling from a distance at the form its [theoretically etherealized] 'difference' takes."[50] Such familiarity can and does occur, quite richly, on the level of what I have called symphysis.

The sort of symphysical awareness that I have illustrated via existential phenomenology and hermeneutics also demonstrates a distinctive contribution of Continental philosophy to animal ethics. This latter school of thought does not merely permit a translation of interspecies ethics into a different idiom of reflection—as mobilized herein, it shows a promising way toward a more positive vision of animal appreciation. Much, maybe most, of analytical animal rights theory and mainline animal liberation practice is given to a hands-off viewpoint—*let go!* or *lay off!* is the implicit (and often explicit) demand of the analysts and emancipators. As valuable as that exhortation is, it can only take us so far in the direction of recultivating an ethos in solidarity with other forms of life. Sociologist Adrian Franklin perhaps overstates the problem when he condemns the "puritanical, separatist orthodoxy" of animal rights/liberation, claiming that "it seeks to put an end to all contact and relationships with animals."[51] Yet he is surely right to notice that it "seems out of kilter with the general direction of change in recent years" toward a widespread feeling "not that we should live apart but that we should work out a moral and ethical way of living together. The point is not that people want less contact with animals but, if anything, more." It has been observed that "the [attitudinal] preconditions of moral capacity . . . are not 'given', are not a priori; rather they are a precious accomplishment of living with others."[52] We need, in other words, to work at nurturing and developing salutary and authentic modes of animal-affiliative *engagement*—and this is something corporal compassion is very well suited to enable or even engender. Our culture and we as individuals have much to gain anew on this front.

> With their parallel lives, animals offer man a companionship which is different from any offered by human exchange. Different because it is a companionship offered to the loneliness of man as a species.
>
> JOHN BERGER (1977)

> . . . in this moment of our present history, we have begun to formulate our relationship to animals differently than at all other times. This may have come about only because we can imagine a world without animals, now that our powers of destruction have grown so monstrously.
>
> MARCUS BULLOCK (2002)

Introduction: Somaesthetics and Animal Ethics

1. It is not, that is, a treatise of normative ethics. Here I take rhetorical inspiration from Yi-Fu Tuan, who has defended pluralism of genre in academe: "scholarly writing should make room for not only the architectonic monograph but also the exploratory essay that has the flavor of the beginnings of a dialogue." *Morality and Imagination* (Madison: University of Wisconsin Press, 1989), x.

2. Again, I am not entirely unique in following this general goal—compare, e.g., the groundbreaking work of Carleton Dallery, "Thinking and Being With Beasts," in *On the Fifth Day*, ed. R. K. Morris and M. W. Fox (Washington, DC: Acropolis, 1978). Compare T. L. S. Sprigge's admission on behalf of Anglophonic philosophy: "This is precisely what is required to solve detailed problems as to what is morally acceptable in the treatment of animals by man; one may call it the phenomenology of the life-worlds of other species." See "Metaphysics, Physicalism, and Animal Rights," *Inquiry* 22, no. 1–2 (1979): 121.

3. Compare, e.g., Richard Sorabji, *Animal Minds and Human Morals* (London: Duckworth, 1993). Sprigge, too, seems still wed to the idea that the moral considerability of animals rides on the question of their status as (noetic) centers of consciousness, the keys to locating such mentality being ethology, physiology, and empathy or imagination ("Metaphysics," 120f.).

4. See, e.g., S. Donnelley and K. Nolan, eds., "Animals, Science, Ethics," *Hastings Center Report* (May/June, 1990): supplement, and David Ehrenfeld, *The Arrogance of Humanism* (New York: Oxford University Press, 1978). Cf. "Does Humanism Encourage Human Chauvinism?" special issue of *Free Inquiry* (Spring 1993).

5. Compare, e.g., Tom Regan, *The Case for Animal Rights* (Berkeley: University of California Press, 1983) and Donald Griffin, *Animal Minds* (Chicago: University of Chicago Press, 1992).

6. The word 'associates' is used instead of the more conventional 'objects,' because the applicablility of the subject/object division itself is criticized in what follows. 'Associates' is meant broadly to refer to those who share space or spend time together.

7. Remarks on scope: insects present a challenging gray area for me; I am willing to listen more attentively now to people (such as theologian Martin Buber and poet Gary Snyder) who may want to include trees; affective attachment to artificially animated entities is confronted near the end of chapter 4.

8. Putatively supernatural entities—"spiritual bodies"—are not considered.

9. As explained in greater detail at a subsequent juncture of discussion, I refrain from using 'embodiment'—like 'incarnation,' such a word invites dualistic interpretations

I wish to avoid (e.g., metaphysical ensoulment). Exceptions occur either as indications of emphasis, that a phenomenon does operate *in* the body or flesh, or instances of writerly paleonymy.

10. I have not determined the appropriate position of plants in this scheme.

11. John Tambornino, *The Corporeal Turn* (Lanham: Rowman and Littlefield, 2002), 10.

12. *Ethos,* nicely enough given our subject, can also be heard with the Homeric overtones retrieved by late-Heideggerian thinking, according to which the term's root "was used to name the places where animals belong. The animal's *éthos* is the place to which it returns, its dwelling place." Charles Scott, *The Question of Ethics: Nietzsche, Foucault, Heidegger* (Bloomington: Indiana University Press, 1990), 143.

Chapter 1: Interspecies Ethics and Phenomenology of Body

The epigraph is from "Seeing the Animals," frontispoem, *Native American Animal Stories,* comp. J. Bruhac (Golden, CO: Fulcrum, 1992). Cf. E. Paci: "There is no zoology if we do not 'see' animals, or [phenomenologically] interpret the sight of them." From "The *Lebenswelt* as Ground and as *Leib* in Husserl," in *Patterns of the Life-World: Essays in Honor of John Wild,* ed. J. M. Edie et al. (Evanston: Northwestern University Press, 1970), 133. Also Cf. Carleton Dallery: "To see the animal moving in its environment is already to 'care' about the animal." From "Thinking and Being," 76.

1. See John D. Caputo, *Against Ethics: Contributions to a Poetics of Obligation with Constant Reference to Deconstruction* (Bloomington: Indiana University Press, 1993); and Richard Garner, *Beyond Morality* (Philadelphia: Temple University Press, 1994).

2. It may be thought that this move will be debilitating for animal ethics; I think on the contrary that it will prove helpful—in light, at least, of advocate Michael W. Fox's candid critique of the field/movement: "A major limitation of animal rights philosophy is that it tends to foster self-righteous moralizing, a sense of moral superiority, and a judgmental attitude toward opponents which only increases [any] existing polarization." *Bringing Life to Ethics: Global Bioethics for a Humane Society* (Albany: SUNY Press, 2001), 59. Perhaps it is not surprising that theoretical foundationalism should have a tendency to slide toward psychosocial fundamentalism in practice.

3. I would recommend Caputo to those who are enamored of approaches such as deconstructive criticism, and direct to Garner those who are devotees of linguistic philosophy in the mode of Anglophonic analysis.

4. Compare Michael Steinberg: "attempts to ground theories of ethics on reason have never proved to be as successful as advertised, and the character of our common experience itself provides a much more useful starting point." *The Fiction of a Thinkable World: Body, Meaning, and the Culture of Capitalism* (New York: Monthly Review, 2005), 51.

5. Even the rationalistic theory of Alan Gewirth, often cited as a contemporary justification of normative ethics, rests on the assumption of conative interests—which are themselves contingent phenomena of nature and/or culture, neither self-evident posits

nor generated purely by logic alone. Cf. *Reason and Morality* (Chicago: University of Chicago, 1978), and Evelyn Pluhar's usage of such for animal ethics in *Beyond Prejudice: The Moral Significance of Human and Nonhuman Animals* (Durham: Duke University Press, 1995), chap. 5, esp. pp. 240–68.

6. The *locus classicus* is Peter Singer, *Animal Liberation: A New Ethics for Our Treatment of Animals* (New York: New York Review and Avon, 1975). Also see Marjorie Spiegel, *The Dreaded Comparison: Human and Animal Slavery* (Philadelphia: New Society, 1988); Charles Patterson, *Eternal Treblinka: Our Treatment of Animals and the Holocaust* (New York: Lantern, 2002); and Carol Adams, *The Sexual Politics of Meat: A Feminist-Vegetarian Critical Theory* (New York: Continuum, 1991).

7. Mark Johnson, *Moral Imagination: Implications of Cognitive Science for Ethics* (Chicago: University of Chicago Press, 1993), 80. This point is also clarified by contrast: "moral deliberation is better described as imaginative exploration and transformation of experience, instead of the pigeonholing of cases under a fixed set of rules," 80. For details, see chap. 9 of the same work, esp. p. 242.

8. A paradigm example is David DeGrazia's landmark treatise, *Taking Animals Seriously: Mental Life and Moral Status* (Cambridge: Cambridge University Press, 1996).

9. Dr. Andrew Brown at the University of Puerto Rico–Mayagüez, with whom and others I shared many provocative and fruitful discussions during a National Endowment for the Humanities institute on environmental ethics and ecophilosophy at the University of Alaska–Anchorage in the summer of 2001. My apologies to him for utilizing his remark as a foil here (though that maneuver is also a gesture of respect).

10. Cf. Lawrence Hatab: "research suggests that empathy is in some sense natural, not in the sense of being invariant and universal, but in the sense of being indigenous, that is to say, *not* artificial or culturally constructed." *Ethics and Finitude: Heideggerian Contributions to Moral Philosophy* (Lanham: Rowman and Littlefield, 2000), 147.

11. Two examples of such criticism directed at animal ethics: John Rodman's essay, "Four Forms of Ecological Consciousness Reconsidered," in *Ethics and the Environment*, ed. D. Scherer and T. Thomas (Englewood Cliffs: Prentice-Hall, 1983), takes issue with its theoretical means; its end is contested by Tibor Machan in *Putting Humans First: Why We Are Nature's Favorites* (Lanham: Rowman and Littlefield, 2004).

12. Compare Hatab, for whom "the existential 'draw' of the Other" makes us "notice disengagement as a deviation." *Ethics and Finitude*, 150, 144.

13. David Michael Levin, *The Body's Recollection of Being: Phenomenological Psychology and the Deconstruction of Nihilism* (London: Routledge and Kegan Paul, 1985), 33. Many works and events could be cited to articulate the contours of such a turn in investigation and thought. A prime instance of the movement to which I allude is the interdisciplinary study, *Giving the Body Its Due* (SUNY Series: The Body in Culture, History, and Religion), ed. Maxine Sheets-Johnstone (Albany: SUNY Press, 1992). Other examples include several works published by the MIT Press: Michel Feher, Ramona Naddaff, and Nadia Tazi, eds., *Fragments for a History of the Body*, 3 vols (1989); Barbara Stafford, *Body Criticism: Imaging the Unseen in Enlightenment Art and Medicine* (1991); and Jonathan

Crary and Sanford Kwinter, eds., *Incorporations* (1992). See also Donn Welton's compendia, *Body and Flesh: A Philosophical Reader* (Oxford: Blackwell, 1998) and *The Body: Classic and Contemporary Readings* (Oxford: Blackwell, 1999).

14. Friedrich Nietzche, *Thus Spoke Zarathustra* (pt. 1), trans. W. Kaufmann, in *The Portable Nietzsche* (New York: Viking. 1954; Penguin, 1976), 146f.

15. For Bergson, see his *Matter and Memory*, trans. N. M. Paul and W. S. Palmer (Garden City: Doubleday, 1959); on Marcel's influence, see R. Zaner, *The Problem of Embodiment*, 2nd ed. (The Hague: Martinus Nijhoff, 1971); Merleau-Ponty's main work is the *Phenomenology of Perception*, trans. C. Smith (London: Routledge and Kegan Paul, 1962; New Jersey: Humanities Press, 1989); Sartre's chief reflection occurs in *Being and Nothingness*, trans. H. E. Barnes (New York: Washington Square/Simon and Schuster, 1966).

16. The italicized terms are mine, paraphrasing Sartre's central discourse on the body in *Being and Nothingness*, pt. 3, chap. 2, pp. 404–60; next reference is to pp. 460–70.

17. Sartre does hint at a putative synthesis, but his "third ontological dimension of the body" is neither convincing nor, ultimately, necessary.

18. Jacques Derrida, *Of Spirit: Heidegger and the Question*, trans. G. Bennington and R. Bowlby (Chicago: University of Chicago Press, 1989).

19. Readers who smell a proof surrogate here are advised that this terse claim is elaborated and defended over the course of subsequent chapters (esp. chap. 2).

20. Paul Shepard, *Thinking Animals* (New York: Viking, 1978).

21. Erazim Kohak, *The Embers and the Stars: A Philosophical Inquiry into the Moral Sense of Nature* (Chicago: University of Chicago, 1984), 75.

22. Didier Franck, "Being and the Living," trans. P. T. Connor, in *Who Comes After the Subject?* ed. E. Cadava et al. (New York: Routledge, 1991), 146.

23. Martin Heidegger, "Letter on Humanism," in *Basic Writings*, ed. D. F. Krell (San Francisco: HarperCollins, 1993), 228. In the same vein, he speaks of "our scarcely conceivable, abysmal bodily kinship with the beast" (230).

24. Compare Franck: "An animal [for Heidegger] is not *Dasein*, and is thus not primordially constituted by being-with [*Mitsein*]." From "Being and the Living," 137.

25. Martin Heidegger, *Die Grundbegriffe der Metaphysik*, in *Gesamtausgabe*, vol. 29/30 (Frankfurt am Main: V. Klostermann, 1982). Translated by W. McNeill and N. Walker as *The Fundamental Concepts of Metaphysics: World, Finitude, Solitude* (Bloomington: Indiana University Press, 1995). See, in particular, sections 42–63 (which together comprise chapters 2–5 of pt. II).

26. Ibid, 179, italics original.

27. Jacques Derrida, "The Animal That Therefore I Am (More to Follow)," trans. D. Wills, *Critical Inquiry* 28, no. 2 (Winter 2002): 408.

28. Ibid., 409. What is the alternative? According to Derrida "we have to envisage the existence of 'living creatures' whose plurality cannot be assembled within the single figure of an animality that is simply opposed to humanity" (415). Or, "that means refraining from reducing [life-forms'] differentiated and multiple difference in a similarly massive

and homogenizing manner." See "And Say the Animal Responded?" trans. D. Wills, in *Zoontologies: The Question of the Animal,* ed. C. Wolfe (Minneapolis: University of Minnesota Press, 2003), 128.

29. Heidegger, *Fundamental Concepts,* 192ff. Next quotation from 194.

30. Friedrich Nietzsche, *The Anti-Christ(ian),* §14. In *Twilight of the Idols; The Anti-Christ(ian),* trans. R. J. Hollingdale (New York: Penguin, 1968).

31. Heidegger, *Fundamental Concepts,* 195.

32. Michael Haar, *The Song of the Earth,* trans. R. Lilly (Bloomington: Indiana University Press, 1993), 29; italics original.

33. Hans Albert, *Treatise on Critical Reason,* trans. M. V. Rorty (Princeton: Princeton University Press, 1985), 171ff.

34. David Farrell Krell, *Daimon Life: Heidegger and Life-Philosophy* (Bloomington: Indiana University Press, 1992), 105.

35. Nietzsche, *Thus Spoke Zarathustra,* 126.

36. Compare Krell, *Daimon Life,* 118: "Are dog and god, viewed metaphysically, or ultrametaphysically, the primordial reversible?"

37. See ibid., "is this [superhumanimal] being in-between . . . something shared by god, dog, and Da-, something one might call *daimon life*?" Next two quotations from page 114.

38. Agnes Heller, "World, Things, Life and Home" (typescript, 1992), 6; later published as "On the Railway Station" in *A Philosophy of History in Fragments* (Oxford: Blackwell, 1993). Heller's Kantian-Husserlian argument is that *the* world is properly an object of cognitive command or epistemic enquiry—not of ontological possession.

39. Cf. Wolfe, *Zoontologies,* 5: "not *the* world but simply *a* world emerges from building a shared form of life,"

40. Heller, "World, Things, Life and Home," 29.

41. Cf. the following remarks: Krell, *Daimon Life,* 134: "Freud says that in mourning the *human* world suddenly becomes impoverished, the *human* being poor in world"; Heidegger's admission (as in *Fundamental Concepts,* sec. 47) that the *animal* is poor—not bankrupt—in world.

42. See Anthony Weston, *Back to Earth: Tomorrow's Environmentalism* (Philadelphia: Temple University Press, 1994), especially his discussion of "self-validating inclusion vs. reduction," 93ff.

43. Again, note how Heidegger stresses the temporalizing historicity of *Dasein.* Then cf. Japanese philosopher Watsuji Tetsuro's insistence on adding to Heideggerian *Daseinsanalyse* an ontologically spatial dimension of "climaticity." *Climate and Culture: A Philosophical Study,* trans. G. Bownas (Japan: The Hokuseido Press, 1961). Cf. also Carol Bigwood's notion of "be[com]ing in the world-earth-home." *Earth Muse: Feminism, Nature, and Art* (Philadelphia: Temple University Press, 1993), chap. 8.

44. Compare Heidegger's own comment that Kantian "time as pure self-affection forms the essential structure of subjectivity." From *Kant and the Problem of Metaphysics,* 4th ed., trans. R. Taft (Bloomington: Indiana University Press, 1990), sec. 34, p. 129.

45. Is this sort of being ever *born*? Does it develop and grow as a *living* being amongst other forms of life? Cf. Krell's life-philosophical treatment of "Dasein natal / Dasein fatal." *Daimon Life,* pt. 1, "Advanced Za-ology."

46. Cf. Levin, *Body's Recollection.*

47. See esp. Mary Midgley, *Beast and Man: The Roots of Human Nature* (Ithaca: Cornell University Press, 1978); and Midgley, *Animals and Why They Matter* (Harmondsworth: Penguin, 1983).

48. Cf. Kant's notorious lack of direct concern for non-persons, whereby we have only derivative duties toward animals. *Lectures on Ethics,* trans. L. Infield (London: Methuen and Co., 1963), 239ff.

49. Franck, "Being and the Living," 145.

50. Using Bruce Foltz, *Inhabiting the Earth: Heidegger, Environmental Ethics, and the Metaphysics of Nature* (Atlantic Highlands: Humanities Press, 1995), I must in good faith note that my criticism over the past several pages applies "proximally and for the most part" to the earlier Heidegger. Foltz shows that a later Heidegger is able to treat more subtly the questions of human animality and life as such, by interpreting the latter as "intensified self-emergence" (*zoe* qua *phusis/psuche*) (130–34). Still, Foltz may have overstated his charitable case, which needs to be cross-examined by exposure to the crucible of Krell's critique (149n34).

51. Franck, "Being and the Living," 145. Cf. Maxine Sheets-Johnstone, *The Roots of Thinking* (Philadelphia: Temple University Press, 1990), which inaugurates a "paleo-anthropological hermeneutics."

52. Maurice Merleau-Ponty, "Husserl at the Limits of Phenomenology," in *In Praise of Philosophy and Other Essays,* trans. J. O'Neill (Evanston: Northwestern University Press, 1988), 190.

53. Maurice Merleau-Ponty, "The Concept of Nature, II: Animality, the Human Body, Transition to Culture," *In Praise of Philosophy,* 163. On the former concept, cf. Adolf Portmann, *Animal Forms and Patterns,* trans. H. Czech (New York.: Schocken, 1967) and Sheets-Johnstone's usage of "animate form," *Roots of Power,* esp. pp. 70–72.

54. Gary Madison, *The Phenomenology of Merleau-Ponty* (Athens: Ohio University Press, 1981), 6.

55. Merleau-Ponty, *The Structure of Behavior,* trans. A. L. Fisher (Boston: Beacon, 1963), 159.

56. See also John Banaan, *The Philosophy of Merleau-Ponty* (New York: Harcourt, Brace and World, 1967), vii.

57. Merleau-Ponty, "Intertwining-Chiasm," in *The Visible and the Invisible,* trans. A. Lingis (Evanston: Northwestern University Press, 1969), 142. Next quotation from 143.

58. Cf. Danne Polk, "Un-Cartesian Nature: Merleau-Ponty and Postmodern Ecology," in *Skepteon* 1 (1993): 27–52.

59. Edmund Husserl, *Ideas Pertaining to a Pure Phenomenology and to a Phenomenological Philosophy,* book III: *Phenomenology and the Foundations of the Sciences,* trans. T. Klein and W. Pohl, vol. 1 of *Edmund Husserl: Collected Works* (The Hague: Martinus Nijhoff, 1980), p. 7, par. 2b. Same cite for next quotation.

60. Edmund Husserl, *Ideas Pertaining to a Pure Phenomenology and to a Phenomeno-logical Philosophy,* book II: *Studies in the Phenomenology of Constitution,* trans. R. Rojcewicz and A. Schuwer, vol. 3 of *Edmund Husserl: Collected Works* (Dordrecht: Kluwer, 1989), p. 170, par. 42. Next quotation is from p. 171, par. 45.

61. Husserl, *Ideas III,* p. 6, par. 2a

62. See, e.g., Husserl, *Ideas III,* supp. ii's turn to "personal ego and animate organism" (119) and *Ideas II* par. 46's focus on "the constitution of the reality 'I as man'" (175ff.).

63. Again, cf. Sartre and Heidegger with Midgley on homo- vs. heterogeneous con-stitution of the existential lifescape. Also, note that Enzo Paci, commenting on the place and method of somatology, persists in abiding by the Husserlian dogma of solipsism-as-starting-point: he states, "somatic life is grasped by subjective processes," and claims, "one must acknowledge as valid only the first-person experience of a subject." See "*Lebenswelt* as Ground and as *Leib*," 133, 124.

64. Edmund Husserl, *Cartesian Meditations* 5.55, trans. D. Cairns (The Hague: Mar-tinus Nijhoff, 1960), 126.

65. I take the notions of "related other" and "deviant similar" (as biocentric and ho-mocentric, respectively) from Shepard, *Thinking Animals.*

66. See, for instance, Anthony Steinbock, "The Phenomenological Concepts of Normality and Abnormality," *Man and World,* 28, no. 3 (1995): 241–60.

67. Those interested in defending Husserl might compare the conclusion of my main text with the Husserlian treatment of phenomenological communitarianism in H. P. Steeves, "The Boundaries of the Phenomenological Community: Non-Human Life and the Extent of Our Moral Enmeshment," paper delivered to the Society for Phe-nomenology and Existential Philosophy, New Orleans, 1993; later published as part of *Founding Community: A Phenomenological-Ethical Inquiry* (Dordrecht: Kluwer, 1998).

68. Historically, there exists a curious litany of confessions undertaken by phenom-enologists as they passed the buck along or aside on the issue of biotic animation. After Husserl (and the Heidegger of *Being and Time*), Michel Henry continues the confessional tradition: "with regard to the relationships between the living body and the human body, their study depends upon a comparative phenomenology, about how we [humans] per-ceive animals and about how we perceive other men [*sic*]." *Philosophy and Phenomenol-ogy of the Body,* trans. G. Etzkorn (The Hague: Martinus Nijhoff, 1975), 6. Typically in such acknowledgments, the existence, if not the importance, of animality is duly admit-ted and then promptly ignored or dismissed as irrelevant to the author's anthropic dis-cussion. Fortunately, a minority countermovement has grown up within the ranks of phenomenologically and hermeneutically inclined philosophers. See, for instance, the early efforts of Hans Jonas, *The Phenomenon of Life: Toward a Philosophical Biology* (New York: Harper and Row, 1966) and Marjorie Grene, *The Understanding of Nature: Essays in the Philosophy of Biology,* vol. 23 of Boston Studies in the Philosophy of Science (Dordrecht: D. Reidel, 1974). Somewhat later, Krell's *Daimon Life* is a remarkable act of reconcilia-tion with life-philosophy; and most recently, see the latest collections edited for SUNY Press by H. P. Steeves (*Animal Others: On Ethics, Ontology, and Animal Life,* 1999) and by C. Brown and T. Toadvine (*Eco-Phenomenology: Back to the Earth Itself,* 2003).

69. Merleau-Ponty, *Structure of Behavior,* 145–60.

70. Maurice Merleau-Ponty, *Nature: Course Notes from the College de France,* trans. R. Vallier and ed. D. Segland (Evanston: Northwestern University Press, 2003), 183. What Merleau-Ponty is getting at here is a hermeneutic of organismal existence not reducible to mechanistic explanation—he is interested, in other words, in the latter of two approaches distinguished this way: "we can either analyze the processes of the animal under a micro-scope, or see a totality [of meaning] in the animal" (187).

71. Merleau-Ponty, *Visible and Invisible,* 274. Carleton Dallery and David Abram approvingly refer to passages such as these in the context of their own work on develop-ing humane and ecologically sound phenomenologies. Cf., respectively, "Thinking and Being with Beasts" and "Merleau-Ponty and the Voice of the Earth," *Environmental Ethics* 10, no. 2 (Summer 1988): 101–20.

72. Most of the text presented here is taken nearly verbatim from my essay, "Human and Nonhuman Lifeworlds," *Environmental and Architectural Phenomenology* 3, no. 2 (1992): 10.

73. Cf. Adolf Portmann, "The Orientation and World-Relation of Animals": "we have decisively settled upon world-relation, effected through inwardness and self-representation, as the highest characterization of the living being." In *Essays in Philo-sophical Zoology,* trans. R. B. Carter (Lewiston, NY: Edwin Mellen, 1990), 15.

74. On a broad enough construal of life (as highly organized matter/energy) and orientation (as any array or growth), certain crystals, clays, stars, planets, etc. might con-ceivably confuse the distinction between vegetal and mineral being. Botanic or biotic bor-der disputes, however, are beside the point for the purposes of my thesis. Admittedly there persist taxonomic grey zones across the spectrum of entities, making ontological classifica-tion somewhat vague or fuzzy—yet without thereby rendering it incoherent or unhelpful.

75. Kenneth Shapiro, "The Death of the Animal: Ontological Vulnerability," *Be-tween the Species* 5 (Fall 1989): 183–93. Cf. Franck's critique of Heidegger's attempt to phe-nomenologize animal being by descriptively employing the concept of "captivation." See "Being and the Living," 141ff. Again, also cf. Krell, *Daimon Life,* pt. 1.

76. Cf. Merleau-Ponty: "we must understand [animal] life as the opening of a field of action," *Nature,* 173.

77. In his endorsement of Dionysian cultural therapies, Nietzsche was an almost shamanic champion of similar ecstatic pursuits. Cf. my "Nietzsche's Feral Philosophy: Thinking Through An Animal Imaginary," in *A Nietzschean Bestiary: Becoming Ani-mal Beyond Docile and Brutal,* ed. C. D. Acampora and R. R. Acampora (Lanham: Rowman and Littlefield, 2004). See also H. P. Duerr, *Dreamtime: Concerning the Bound-ary Between Wilderness and Civilization,* trans. F. Goodman (Oxford: Basil Blackwell, 1985).

78. Above, I hope to have evaded an essentializing determination of that criterion —and thus, in light of my proposed ontology of organisms, I believe it acceptable to demonstrate transpecificity of bodily worldhood on the basis of "family resemblance" in existential residence. Since we are discussing forms of life-world, I trust that my gloss here on terminology derived from the later Wittgenstein is not misplaced.

79. This is not a questioning of biological kinship, which I regard as positively established by evolutionary ecology. Philosophically, <u>my primary subject of inquiry is not the scientized but rather the phenomenal (live/felt) body,</u> and taking this as an object of phenomenological elucidation will also require a certain poetics, since we lack a vocabulary for much of what I seek to describe.

80. Carleton Dallery, "Thinking and Being with Beasts," 77.

81. Bill Neidjie, *Story about Feeling,* ed. K. Taylor (Broome, W. Australia: Magabala, 1989), 18ff. Note that in Aboriginal English "e" is a pronoun indicating "he or she."

82. Elsewhere (in the same work) Neidjie extends this testimony beyond the animalic boundary, to include even trees. Cf. Martin Buber: "I contemplate a tree. . . . I can feel it as movement: the flowing veins around the sturdy, striving core, the sucking of the roots, the breathing of the leaves. . . . The tree is no impression, no play of my imagination, no aspect of a mood; it confronts me bodily [*leibt mir gegenüber*] and has to deal with me as I must deal with it—only differently." *I and Thou,* trans. W. Kaufmann (New York: Charles Scribner's Sons, 1970), 57f.

83. Cf. Gilles Deleuze and Felix Guattari on the value of "minor" works/traditions; see, e.g., *Kafka,* trans. D. Polan (Minneapolis: University of Minnesota Press, 1986).

84. Jakob von Uexküll, "A Stroll Through the Worlds of Animals and Men," in *Instinctive Behavior: The Development of a Modern Concept,* trans. and ed. C. H. Schiller (New York: International Universities Press, 1957), quoted in B. E. Rollin, *The Unheeded Cry: Animal Consciousness, Animal Pain, and Science,* (Oxford: Oxford University, 1981), 227, italics added.

85. But compare Uexküll's crypto-spiritual "operator" ("built into" an organism) and Sheets-Johnstone's critique of "em-bodiment" and "in-carnation" talk (as discursive repository of residual dualism). Panel on *Roots of Thinking* (Society for Phenomenology and Existential Philosophy, New Orleans, 1993). For elaboration of this issue, refer to the introduction to this book.

86. Frederik Jacobus Johannes Buytendijk, *Prolegomena to an Anthropological Physiology,* trans. A. Giorgi et al. (Pittsburgh: Duquesne University Press, 1974), 17, italics original.

87. *Prolegomena,* 21, italics added. On this very issue, compare Heidegger's relevant stand taken in the "Letter on Humanism" (mentioned before) and Michael Polanyi's perspective in his essay "Understanding Ourselves": "our own [human] body has a special place in the universe" because it is intellectively infused with a pragmatico-linguistically acculturated "mental life by which we surpass the [nonhuman] animals." *The Study of Man* (London: Routledge and Kegan Paul, 1959), 31.

88. *Prolegomena,* 18, 20, 21, all italics original. Cf. the second quotation with Merleau-Ponty's claim in *Nature:* "the animal must be considered as a field; that is, it is both physical being and a meaning" (150). The Aristotelian soul-talk in the last quotation is not (supernaturally) spiritual in meaning; it merely attributes to the animal a self-moving, live body (*Leib*), as opposed to an inertly material one (*Körper*).

89. Read charitably, Buytendijk could escape self-contradiction—by reinscribing *speciated* difference within *generic* unity (and thus conceiving the human body as radi-

cally specific though not entirely distinctive in kind). This move would slow, but not reverse, his anthropocentrist backslide (since humanity would still be "unique").

90. See, e.g., Gernot Böhme's eco-aesthetic essay, "Die Mensch-Natur-Beziehung am Beispiel Stadt," in his *Fur eine okologische Naturasthetik* (Frankfurt am Main: Suhrkamp, 1989); for the case of the forest, as it were, cf. Kohak, *Embers and the Stars*. Other illustrations are included in Donna Haraway's biohistorical work, *Primate Visions: Gender, Race and Nature in the World of Modern Science* (New York: Routledge, 1989), as well as her *The Companion Species Manifesto: Dogs, People, and Significant Otherness* (Chicago: Prickly Paradigm, 2003). In addition, cf. E. O. Wilson's arguments for sociobiology, e.g., in *On Human Nature* (Cambridge, MA: Harvard University Press, 1978), and Barbara Noske's argumentation for what might be called "zoo-sociology" in her *Humans and Other Animals: Beyond the Boundaries of Anthropology* (London: Pluto Press, 1989). Finally, Kate Soper, *What is Nature?* (Oxford: Blackwell, 1995) works out a nondualistic distinction from culture worth retaining.

91. Carol Bigwood, "Renaturalizing the Body (With the Help of Merleau-Ponty)," *Hypatia* 6, no. 3 (1991): 60.

92. Not only is the dilemma itself false, but each of its alternatives is untenable. The scientized or romantic return has received commonly recognized criticism; against the reduction to textual analysis, see e.g., Susan Bordo, "Feminism, Postmodernism, and Gender-Skepticism," in *Feminism/Postmodernism,* ed. L. J. Nicholson (New York: Routledge, 1990).

93. See, e.g., Diane Dutton and Carl Williams, "A View from the Bridge," *Anthrozoös* 17, no. 3 (2004): 210–24; Mark Johnson, *The Body in the Mind* (Chicago: University of Chicago Press, 1987); and Rom Harré's "corporeal psychology" in his *Physical Being* (Oxford: Blackwell, 1991).

94. Luce Irigaray, "Animal Compassion," in *Animal Philosophy: Ethics and Identity,* ed. P. Atterton and M. Calarco (London: Continuum, 2004), 195.

95. See, e.g., Josephine Donovan and Carol Adams, eds., *Beyond Animal Rights: A Feminist Caring Ethic for the Treatment of Animals* (New York: Continuum, 1996).

96. Sympathy is still too tied to the discourse of intellective empathy and also invites association with pity's connotation of condescending sentimentality.

97. For relevant exemplars of these fields' respective contributions, see Martin Hoffman's *Empathy and Moral Development* (Cambridge: Cambridge University Press, 2000) and Frans de Waal's *Good Natured: The Origins of Right and Wrong in Humans and Other Animals* (Cambridge, MA: Harvard University Press, 1996).

98. A growing movement of subversive somatology now has a manifesto, George Lakoff and Mark Johnson's *Philosophy in the Flesh: The Embodied Mind and Its Challenge to Western Thought* (New York: Basic/Perseus, 1999), esp. chap. 14.

Chapter 2: Flesh-and-Blood Being-in-a-World

1. Thomas Nagel, "What Is It Like to Be a Bat?" *Philosophical Review* 83 (October 1974): 435–50. Quotes in this and the next paragraph are from this source on the following pages: 436, 440, 442n, 449.

2. Paul Taylor, *Respect for Nature: A Theory of Environmental Ethics* (Princeton: Princeton University Press, 1986), 127f. For a concretely detailed illustration of a method like Taylor's—one that concentrates more on speciation than on individuation of worldhood —see Uexküll, "Stroll Through the Worlds." Cf. Kenneth Joel Shapiro, "Understanding Dogs Through Kinesthetic Empathy, Social Construction, and History," *Anthrozoös* 3, no. 3: 184–95, for an example of the empathic route.

3. Yi-Fu Tuan, *Topophilia: A Study of Environmental Perception, Attitudes, and Values* (Englewood Cliffs: Prentice-Hall, 1974), 5.

4. What is sought is something like what Heidegger calls "self-transposition." About that idea, Heidegger writes, "self-transposition does not mean the factical transference of one existing human being into the interior of another being. [. . .] Nor does it mean the factical substitution of oneself for another being so as to take its place." *Fundamental Concepts of Metaphysics,* sec. 49, p. 202.

5. Here I borrow the term "subject-of-a-life" from Tom Regan, *Case for Animal Rights,* 243.

6. Notice that, from this perspective, objections such as Tuan's above become less of an impediment.

7. This term is borrowed from—but not used exactly as in—Ivan Illich, *Tools for Conviviality* (New York: Harper and Row, 1973).

8. Michael Steinberg, *The Fiction of a Thinkable World: Body, Meaning, and the Culture of Capitalism* (New York: Monthly Review, 2005), 24.

9. Heidegger, *Die Grundbegriffe,* sec. 50, p. 210.

10. Alasdair MacIntyre, *Dependent Rational Animals: Why Human Beings Need the Virtues* (Chicago: Open Court, 1999), 14.

11. Andrew Fuller, *Insight into Value* (Albany: SUNY Press, 1990), 50.

12. McIntyre, *Dependent Rational Animals,* 14.

13. Heidegger, *Die Grundbegriffe,* sec. 62, p. 269, italics original; sec. 50, p. 210. "Comportment" for Heidegger refers to a pre-theoretical recognition of a possibility for "taking as." Thus, bound up in the meaning of the table, for example, is its being "taken as" a possible place for eating, etc. More on deprivation, and the associated condition of "captivation," follows later in this chapter.

14. Alasdair MacIntyre, from his Carus lecture "How Impoverished is the World of the Nonhuman Animal?" in *Dependent Rational Animals,* 46.

15. Here, personhood is internal to the scope of *Homo sapiens* and mind is Cartesianly presumed to be something separate or separable from "the body."

16. Dutton and Williams, "View from the Bridge," 216f.; last page quotes Eileen Crist, *Images of Animals* (Philadelphia: Temple University Press, 1999), 217.

17. Dutton and Williams, "View from the Bridge," 218f. For supporting research in cognitive science, linguistics, neurology, and philosophy of mind and language, see Lakoff and Johnson, *Philosophy in the Flesh.*

18. Dutton and Williams, "View from the Bridge," 219. Note that the claim is about much, not most, bodily experience (the latter would be going too far, in view of varying sensorimotor modalities).

19. Cf. Alphonso Lingis, *The Community of Those Who Have Nothing in Common* (Bloomington: Indiana University Press, 1994) and Peter Sloterdijk, *Critique of Cynical Reason*, trans. M. Eldred (Minneapolis: University of Minnesota, 1987).

20. Cf. Shane Phelan, "Intimate Distance," in *In the Nature of Things: Language, Politics, and the Environment*, ed. J. Bennett and W. Chaloupka (Minneapolis: University of Minnesota Press, 1993).

21. Paul Taylor stipulates a definition of 'bioculture' as "that aspect of any human culture in which humans create and regulate the environment of living things and systematically exploit them for human benefit." *Respect for Nature*, 53. Curiously, this definition deconstructs the very possibility of (Tayloresque) ethics of bioculture (insofar as Taylor himself elsewhere institutes a radical proto-ethical split between the moral attitude of respect and the anti- or non-moral attitude of exploitation). Hence I am inclined to define 'bioculture' more broadly, simply as "that dimension of culture in which humans and other living beings exist together (materially or symbolically)."

22. Vicki Hearne, *Adam's Task: Calling Animals by Name* (New York: Random/Vintage, 1987); and Shapiro, "Understanding Dogs."

23. Abram, "Merleau-Ponty"; Polk, "Un-Cartesian Nature."

24. Toward one end of this bipolarity of lifeworld, "bioculture" dwindles in organic diversity to nearly homo-exclusive technotopes (e.g., shopping malls); toward the other end, "the wild" is never pristinely pure of cultural processes' material traces and conceptual constructions (e.g., even Antarctic ice bears the artificial marks of both physical pollution and juridical/scientific sectoring).

25. F. G. Asenjo, *In-Between: An Essay on Categories* (Washington, DC: University Press of America, 1988), 52.

26. In phrasing the question this way, I am grafting into our discussion modern ecology's term for botanically mixed community (ecotone), recontextualizing it, and thereby transforming its meaning to describe lived space that is biotically hybrid between cultivation and wilderness, a place where artificial and natural aspects of being-in-a-world tend to merge. Cf. Richard T. T. Forman's *Land Mosaics: The Ecology of Landscapes and Regions* (New York: Cambridge University Press, 1995).

27. Edward Casey, *Getting Back into Place: Toward a Renewed Understanding of the Place-World* (Bloomington: Indiana University Press, 1993), 255f., italics added.

28. Neil Evernden, *The Natural Alien: Humankind and Environment*, 2nd ed. (Toronto: University of Toronto Press, 1993), 152. 'Collage' might be a better term than 'mosaic.'

29. Watsuji Tetsuro, *Climate and Culture: A Philosophical Study*, trans. G. Bownas (Japan: Hokuseido Press, 1961), v.

30. Ibid., 9. Watsuji argues a biogeographic case against the crypto-Hegelian conception of history still lurking in Heidegger's text: "climate is . . . quite inseparable from history. For it is from the union of climate with history that the latter gets its flesh and bones. In terms of the contrast between spirit and matter, history can never be merely

spiritual self-development. . . . History and climate in isolation from each other are mere abstractions" (10).

31. Compare historian Fernando Braudel's *The Mediterranean and the Mediterranean World in the Age of Philip II,* vol. 1, trans. Sian Reynolds (New York: Harper and Row, 1972), pt. 1; Johann Gottfried von Herder's climatic study of the human spirit, *Reflections on the Philosophy of the History of Mankind,* ed. F. Manuel (Chicago: University of Chicago Press, 1968), 13–20; and Jose Ortega y Gasset's "Historia Geographia," in *Kant. Hegel. Dilthey,* 2nd ed. (Madrid: Revista de Occidente, 1961), 109–14.

32. Watsuji, *Climate and Culture,* 4f.

33. Ibid., 11, 12.

34. Eliot Deutsch, "The Concept of the Body," in *Self as Body,* ed. T. Kasulis et al. (Albany: SUNY Press, 1993), 19n24. Deutsch follows Merleau-Ponty's demonstration that "having a body is, for a living creature, to be intervolved in a definite environment" (quoted by Deutsch at p. 14).

35. Sven Dijkgraaf, "An Excursion through the Sensory World of Animals," in *Man and Animal,* trans. M. Nawiasky (London: MacGibbon and Kee, 1972), 58.

36. Craig Holdrege, "How Does a Mole View the World?" *In Context* (Spring 2003): 16.

37. In *The Flexible Giant: Seeing the Elephant Whole* (Ghent, NY: Nature Institute, 2003), Holdrege describes the touchstone of the method thus: "The idea of the coherent organism, framed as a question, becomes the guiding light of inquiry" (3). For more applications to, and illustrations of, other animal species (e.g., cow, horse, lion, sloth), refer to http://www.natureinstitute.org/txt/ch/index.htm.

38. Holdrege, "How Does a Mole," 18. Next two quotations from same source, pages 18 and 17, respectively.

39. Daniel Stern, *Diary of a Baby* (New York: Basic, 1998). For Stern's methodology, see the introductory "The Unfolding Worlds of a Baby's Life," 1–10.

40. Merlau-Ponty, *Visible and the Invisible.*

41. Quoted in Abram, "Voice of the Earth," 112n39. Cf. Casey: "another name for th[e naturo-cultural] region is 'flesh,' or, more exactly, 'the flesh of the world.'" *Back into Place,* 255.

42. This is true even beyond Merleau-Ponty's own focus on sensorimotor surfaces. Drew Leder argues that blood, bones, guts, and other innards "constitute their own circuitry of vibrant, pulsing life which precedes the perceptual in fetal life, outruns it in sleep, sustains it from beneath at all moments" and, hence, "it is through visceral, not just perceptual, exchange that the total interpenetration of body and world is realized." See "Flesh and Blood: A Proposed Supplement to Merleau-Ponty," in *The Body,* ed. D. Welton (Oxford: Blackwell, 1999), 203, 205.

43. Abram, "Voice of Earth," 112.

44. Ibid., 114f. For poetic resonance, see Novalis: "nature is a community of marvels into which we are introduced through the medium of our body." *The Novices of Sais*

(New York: Curt Valentin, 1949). For scientific analogue, see Tyler Volk, *Gaia's Body: Toward a Physiology of Earth* (Cambridge, MA: MIT Press, 2003).

45. Abram, "Voice of Earth," 113.

46. Merleau-Ponty, *Visible and Invisible,* 167, 274.

47. Abrams, "Voice of Earth," 119.

48. Jane Bennett, *Unthinking Faith and Enlightenment: Nature and the State in a Post-Hegelian Era* (New York: NYU Press, 1987).

49. Moreover, there does not appear to be any good analogue for the cook or chef—unless, of course, one subscribes to creationist cosmology or intelligent design. See Shannon Sullivan, *Living Across and Through Skins: Transactional Bodies, Pragmatism, and Feminism* (Bloomington: Indiana University Press, 2001), 14ff.

50. Ibid., 17f.

51. Ralph R. Acampora and Christa Davis Acampora, Introduction, in *A Nietzschean Bestiary: Becoming Animal Beyond Docile and Brutal,* ed. C. D. Acampora and R. R. Acampora (Lanham, MD: Rowman and Littlefield, 2004), xxi–xxxii.

52. Michéle Le Dœuff, *The Philosophical Imaginary,* trans. Colin Gordon (London: Athlone Press, 1988), 2.

53. Mark Johnson, *Moral Imagination: Implications of Cognitive Science for Ethics* (Chicago: University of Chicago Press, 1993), 193. On the same page, Johnson also spells out a pertinent implication: "When it comes to our moral deliberations, therefore, we are hardly ever engaged in applying literal, univocal concepts directly to states of affairs in the world."

54. See Angelika Fischer, "Bodies, Selves and Boundaries: A Look at the Social Construction of the Body in Western and Aboriginal Culture" (master's thesis, University of Western Australia, Nedlands, 1984). Cf. Holdrege, *Flexible Giant,* chap. 9, "The Sensitive Boundary" (esp. pp. 36f.).

55. Paul Shepard, "Introduction: Ecology and Man—A Viewpoint," in *The Subversive Science,* ed. P. Shepard and D. McKinley (Boston: Houghton Mifflin, 1969), 2; John Compton, "Reinventing the Philosophy of Nature," *Review of Metaphysics* 33 (September 1979), 24.

56. My terminology here borrows from, and builds upon, that of Douwe Tiemersma. See *Body Schema and Body Image: An Interdisciplinary and Philosophical Study* (Amsterdam: Swets and Zeitlinger, 1989). Cf. Evernden's suggestion that "embodied limits" make an animal species "the functionary of a particular 'place,'" *Natural Alien,* 151.

57. Bernd Jager, "Body, House and City," in *Dwelling, Place and Environment,* ed. D. Seamon and R. Mugerauer (New York: Columbia University Press, 1989), 215. Cf. Immanuel Kant, "What is Orientation in Thinking?" in *The Philosophy of the Body,* ed. Stuart Spicker (Chicago: Quadrangle Press, 1970).

58. Joseph Grange, "Place, Body and Situation," in *Dwelling, Place and Environment,* ed. Seamon and Mugerauer, 81f.

59. In this way my project retains a vaguely Heideggerian moment of "clearing," an "opening" in which there might emerge something like "strife between world and earth."

Martin Heidegger, "The Origin of the Work of Art," trans. A. Hofstadter. In *Poetry, Language, Thought* (New York: Harper and Row, 1971).

60. Here I break from Heidegger's prophylactic apprehension regarding the putative pollution of (primordial) phenomenology by any form of regional ontology. Indeed, I zooscopically explore "municipal" ontology.

61. Grange, "Place, Body and Situation," 82, italics added.

62. Through the Earth's tropical zones there is—as, for example, in Australia's Northern Territory—a binary to-and-fro between seasons referred to simply as "the Wet" and "the Dry."

63. Indeed, percussion such as this supplies a relatively rare mediation of the carnal surfaces and visceral depths of somatic experience; more typically, as Leder notes: "Visceral interoceptions tend to be qualitatively restricted, temporally intermittent, spatially indefinite and causally ambiguous compared to the world exteroception reveals." See "Flesh and Blood," 203.

64. David Michael Levin, *The Listening Self* (New York: Routledge, 1989), 272. Cf. Michel Haar, *The Song of the Earth,* trans. R. Lilly (Bloomington: Indiana University Press, 1993), esp. preface.

65. I am about to depart from the formal strictures of phenomenology as originally conceived, to the extent that I drop thoroughgoing "epoche" of science from my descriptive strategy. Phenomenological purists should attend to two points on this score: epoche is (to be) always only provisional; I incorporate into my method of description not science as such (i.e., as objectivist theory) but rather as significant for life-field perception.

66. The history brought into focus by my phenomenology is (a zoocentric version) of the quotidian, micro-variety that Spanish existentialist Miguel de Unamuno called "intra-history" in contradistinction to the mainstream macro-variety of "official history." See Michael Weinstein, *The Tragic Sense of Political Life* (Columbia: University of South Carolina Press, 1977).

67. Against the oculocentric bias of Western (intellectual) tradition, cf. Stafford, *Body Criticism,* for an eloquent effort at resurrecting the haptic dimension of aesthetically lived bodiment.

68. For a distinction between live environment (*Lebensumwelt*) and community of life (*Lebensmitwelt*), see Hiroshi Kojima, "Von der apriorischen Struktur der Lebenswelt," in *Phänomenologie der Praxis,* ed. H. Kojima (Würzburg: Königshausen and Neumann, 1989), 73–76 (sec. 1 and sec. 2).

69. The use of "merely" in quotation marks is meant to indicate that a purely representational account of (any) visual experience may (always) be anemic. Cf. Alva Noë's "enactive approach" to perception: "To model vision correctly, then, we must model it . . . as something that directly involves not only the brain but also the animate body and the world." *Action in Perception,* 30.

70. John Berger, "Why Look at Animals?" in *About Looking* (New York: Pantheon, 1980), 22f.

71. On the level of literary imagination, however, there are still divergent insights to

be gained from Gaston Bachelard—cf. his *The Poetics of Space,* trans. Jolas (Boston: Beacon Press, 1969), esp. chaps. 8 and 9.

72. Again, compare Noë: "perceiving is a way of acting. Perception is not something that happens to us, or in us. It is something we do. . . . To be a perceiver is to understand, implicitly, the effects of movement on sensory stimulation. . . . our ability to perceive not only depends on, but is constituted by, our possession of [certain] sensorimotor knowledge." *Action in Perception,* 1f. Cf. Fuller: "Our body, with its sensory and motor capacities, plays a crucial role in all perception." *Insight into Value,* 71.

73. Tiemersma, *Body Schema,* 337.

74. By comparison, the concept of *Leibesheim* would represent the former notion's further determination (under more specific hermeneutics of residence or territory).

75. Tiemersma, *Body Schema,* 348. Cf. Paci: "The animation of the lived body brings about a mingling of psychological experience with the experience of matter and of material bodies." From "The *Lebenswelt* as Ground and as *Leib* in Husserl," *Patterns of the Life-World,* 130.

76. Tiemersma, *Body Schema,* 350f.

77. Ibid., 351f.

78. Neil Evernden, *Natural Alien,* 42f. Next quotes from pages 44, 38, and 40, respectively.

79. Michael Weinstein, *Structure of Human Life: A Vitalist Ontology* (New York: NYU Press, 1979). An earlier champion was Hans Driesch; see his *The History and Theory of Vitalism,* trans. C. Ogden (London: Macmillan, 1914). By comparison to Weinstein's, Driesch's dated work seems now to be mostly of antiquarian interest for historians of natural philosophy or science.

80. Ibid., 39. The next quotation is from p. ix.

81. Weinstein's emphasis on organismic particularity might ultimately diverge from modes of doing phenomenology that include or stress transpecificity of *Leibesheim,* especially insofar as the latter receives Merleau-Pontyan thematization under a global aspect of world-flesh.

82. Heidegger, *Fundamental Concepts,* sec. 58a, p. 237, italics original. The next full-sentence quotation is from sec 58b, p. 239, italics original.

83. Indeed, it is questionable whether the concept of instinct ever actually "explains" anything. Often deployed to the point nearly of vacuity, it ends up serving as little more than a cipher indicative of ignorance (used, that is, precisely when we do not know what's going on or how to explain a certain behavior).

84. Sullivan, *Living Across and Through Skins,* 30ff. Here are echoes of Merleau-Ponty's "styles" of bodily address to lived worlds.

85. Heidegger, *Fundamental Concepts,* sec. 58b, p. 239.

86. Cf. Heidegger, in one of his better moments of hermeneutic sensitivity to animal lives, on the ontological "housing" of snailhood: "One might say that the snail [in its manner of movement] occasionally quits its lodgings while holding onto them. . . . The snail is not in its house [= shell] as water is in a glass. Rather, it has the interiority of

its house as world , which it bumps against, palpates [or touches], in which it stays warm, and so on." Translated by Krell, *Daimon Life,* 90, from *Prolegomena zur Geschichte des Zeitbegriffs* (Marburg lecture, Summer 1925).

Chapter 3: Appreciation of Animal Nature under the Aspect of Bodiment

1. Georges Bataille, *Visions of Excess: Selected Writings, 1927–1939* (Minneapolis: University of Minnesota Press, 1985). See also D. Hollier, *Against Architecture: The Writings of Georges Bataille,* trans. B. Wing (Cambridge, MA: MIT Press, 1989).

2. Compare Risieri Frondizi's observation: "The creative and lofty sense of life is based fundamentally on the drive for a positive value, as opposed to the negative, of a superior value as opposed to the inferior." *What is Value? An Introduction to Axiology,* 2nd ed. (LaSalle: Open Court, 1971), 11.

3. For the primacy of conflictual appreciation in lived experience, see Weinstein, *Structure of Human Life,* esp. chap. 4, and *Tragic Sense,* esp. chap. 7.

4. The designations "deviant similitude" and "related otherness" are Paul Shepard's. See his *Thinking Animals: Animals and the Development of Human Intelligence* (New York: Viking, 1978).

5. Michel Foucault, *Discipline and Punish: The Birth of the Prison,* trans. A. Sheridan (New York: Random, 1979), 174–88. Cf. Bennett, *Unthinking Faith,* 146.

6. J. N. Findlay, *Axiological Ethics* (London: Macmillan/St. Martin's Press, 1970), 83.

7. James Hart, "Value Theory and Phenomenology," in *Phenomenology of Values and Valuing,* ed. J. Hart and L. Embree (Dordrecht: Kluwer, 1997), 6f.

8. Frondizi, *What is Value?* 133f. Next quotes are from this source, pages 133 and 134, italics original.

9. Compare Aristotle's warning against logicizing morality in *Nicomachean Ethics,* trans. T. Irwin (Indianapolis: Hackett, 1985), ll. 1094b24f.

10. Frondizi, *What is Value?* 130.

11. Cf. Findlay: "The world of our normal experience is not the neutral world of the impartial scientist: it is painted with as many axiological tinges as men have sentiments." *Axiological Ethics,* 11.

12. For relational axiology articulated via *Gestalt,* see Frondizi, *What is Value?* chap.5, sec. 5. Cf. Fuller's definition, in *Insight into Value,* 136: "Value is a whole of meaning that is positively or negatively required in its place within a lifeworld context."

13. Frondizi, *What is Value?* 151, 153.

14. Don Marietta, "The Concept of Objective Value," in Hart and Embree, *Phenomenology of Values,* 19.

15. The pattern of appreciation sketched here is thus parallel in form to the noetic-noematic structure of cognition that Husserlian epistemology posits.

16. J. N. Findlay, *Values and Intentions* (New York: Macmillan, 1961), 74–92. Cf. J. Baird Callicott: "Value, like any other natural property, [is] a potentiality actualized by a

[properly] situated observer/valuer." See "Intrinsic Value in Nature," *Electronic Journal of Analytic Philosophy* 3 (Spring 1995): art. 4, par. 73.

17. Here, I am glossing a fairly famous dictum of J. S. Mill, for whom the semantic content of *object* or *body* was the "permanent possibility of sensation."

18. Idiotic and even mass delusions do happen, appearing so against the weight of wider or more profound values; conceptually, however, "universal illusion" is impossible. That would constitute its own valuational reality, on my view—i.e., absent any transcendent or higher-order metaphysics of value.

19. Levin, *Body's Recollection,* 243.

20. Compare John Dewey, *Theory of Valuation* (Chicago: University of Chicago Press, 1939/1966), which argues the pragmatist case for a biosocial account. (Dewey exhibits a Humean-Darwinian naturalism. There should be no fear of eliminative reductionism here—for even if today's naturalism, say, sociobiology or evolutionary psychology, seems bent on reducing culture to nature "without remainder," still Dewey's "biosociological" treatment of moral, religious, and artistic phenomena shows that he is interested rather in uplifting physical sciences into the philosophic enterprise of wisely crafting cultural ideals. His emphasis is thus edifying.)

21. My anti-anesthetic phrasing here borrows from terminology of South American existentialism, especially that of Uruguayan skeptic Carlos Vaz Ferreira as redeployed by Weinstein. See *Tragic Sense,* 171.

22. In respect, at least, to ethical axiology, cf. Thomas Nagel's admission in *The Possibility of Altruism* (Oxford: Clarendon Press, 1970) that "something beyond justification is required" (4) and Nel Noddings's claim in *Caring: A Feminine Approach to Ethics and Moral Education* (Berkeley: University of California Press, 1984) that "the moral viewpoint is prior to any notion of justification" (95).

23. Marietta, "Concept of Objective Value," 27f., 26.

24. Frondizi, *What is Value?* 123, 157.

25. Questions concerning the genesis and grooming of such instincts require metaphilosophical treatment attuned to the history and sociology of rationality; accordingly, they fall beyond the appropriate range of my study's focus.

26. Recent developments in the natural sciences may also be applicable here; specifically, new physics and contemporary ecology are relevant to comprehending (the force of) the "likelihood" or "probability" at stake. In "Intrinsic Value, Quantum Theory, and Environmental Ethics," J. Baird Callicott argues that these fields (can be construed so as to) contribute a view of value as virtual—potentiality vivified by the interaction of certain life-forms that have undergone conducive evolution: "nature affords a range of potential value . . . actualized in relationship to us or to other similarly constituted organisms." *Environmental Ethics* 7, no. 3 (Fall 1985): 271.

27. Classical philosophy's custom of incessantly asking why-questions bespeaks an exuberant sense of enquiry as well as a childlike lack of self-limitation. As contemplative drive, this habit begets speculation. Cf. Lipman et al. (1977), quoted by J. White in his "The Roots of Philosophy," in *The Impulse to Philosophise,* ed. A. P. Griffiths (Cambridge:

Cambridge University Press, 1992): "Children begin to think philosophically when they begin to ask why" (73). Perhaps they become full-fledged philosophers as they refuse to withdraw that query . . .

28. Frondizi, *What Is Value?* 9.

29. David Michael Levin, *Body's Recollection,* chap. 3.

30. Levin, *Body's Recollection,* 235, 233.

31. Levin, *Body's Recollection,* 253, 249. The next three quotes come from this source, pages 257 and 256.

32. Levin, *Listening Self,* 177.

33. Kate Rigby, "Beyond the Frame: Art, Ecology, and the Aesthetics of Nature," *Thesis Eleven* 32 (1992): 119.

34. Gernot Böhme, *Fur eine ökologische Naturasthetik,* quoted and translated by Rigby, "Beyond the Frame," 121.

35. Ibid. Cf. Arnold Berleant, *The Aesthetics of Environment* (Philadelphia: Temple University Press, 1992).

36. Ben-Ami Scharfstein, *Of Birds, Beasts, and Other Artists: An Essay on the Universality of Art* (New York: NYU Press, 1988).

37. Ibid., 38–63.

38. Richard Shusterman, "Somaesthetics: A Disciplinary Proposal," *Journal of Aesthetics and Art Criticism* 57, no. 3 (Summer 1999): 302. I will not explore this field in depth, but readers should be advised that it constitutes a rich resource for somatological aesthetics and hence opens possibilities for valuing or prizing the body.

39. Deane Curtin provides an interesting discussion of this example and numerous others in his "Recipes for Values" in *Cooking, Eating, Thinking Transformative Philosophies of Food,* ed. D. Curtin and L. Heldke (Bloomington: Indiana University Press, 1992), 123–44. See also his "Food/Body/Person" in the same volume.

40. Embree, "Value of Nature," in Hart and Embree, *Phenomenology of Values,* 57.

41. This last instance is phenomenologically dissonant: the buyer seeks interaction with *Leib,* but the prostitute sells usage of *Körper.* Confusing these agents' intentions is the transaction's atmosphere of mutually bad faith: the buyer must recognize that one purchases something asymptotically approaching mere meat, while the provider must be acutely aware of the existentially infinitesimal space between corporeal finance and live bodiment. Thus, prostitution typically involves inauthentic pursuits—of encountering a body that (for the most part) allows only contact, and of temporarily commodifying a body that has always to be lived as one's own.

42. Nietzsche, *Ecce Homo,* "Why I am so clever." An interesting discussion of Nietzsche's concern for the "small things" is found in Sullivan, *Living Across and Through Skins,* 115ff. Another work that focuses on Nietzsche's own "small things" in terms of "place, climate, and recreation" is David Farrell Krell and Donald L. Bates, *The Good European: Nietzsche's Work Sites in Word and Image* (Chicago: University of Chicago Press, 1997).

43. From this point onward in the chapter, Nietzsche's works will be cited parenthetically in the text. Abbreviated titles will be followed by section numbers or, when rel-

evant, part (Roman) and section (Arabic) numbers. Publication information is listed in the bibliography. The following abbreviations will be used for titles:

BGE: Beyond Good and Evil

GS: The Gay Science

GM: On the Genealogy of Morals

Z: Thus Spoke Zarathustra (included in *The Portable Nietzsche*)

TI: Twilight of the Idols

WP: The Will to Power

44. I have modified Kaufmann's translation here.

45. An interesting account of this idea, described in terms of Nietzsche's quasi-Humean "bundle theory of the self" can be found in Steven D. Hales and Rex Welshon's *Nietzsche's Perspectivism* (Urbana: University of Illinois Press, 2000): 157–82.

46. Sullivan, *Living Across and Through Skins,* chap. 1 (on the notion of bodying specifically) and p. 116 (on her discussion of Nietzsche).

47. In the words of another contemporary body-critic, Michael Steinberg, "we are linked with our fellow creatures and with the environment which transforms with our acts. . . . Our acts literally incorporate personal, social, and genetic history; all are present in the body that in hearing, seeing, and responding is continually transformed." *Fiction of a Thinkable World,* 40.

48. The most significant discussion of these ideas appears in Gregory Moore, *Nietzsche, Biology, and Metaphor* (New York: Cambridge University Press, 2002).

49. Recently, John Richardson has argued extensively that Nietzsche's critiques of Darwin actually expose his agreement with him, and that on the point of Darwin's conservatism and lack of accounting for creativity, Nietzsche was particularly off the mark as Darwin anticipated some of the very ideas Nietzsche proposed as counters. Richardson's work is very interesting and is impressive in its scope. But I am not satisfied that he has adequately addressed the differences between Darwin and Rolph or assessed Nietzsche's embrace of the latter. See John Richardson, *Nietzsche's New Darwinism* (Oxford: Oxford University Press, 2005).

50. This passage can be usefully compared with *Twilight of the Idols,* "Expeditions," in which Nietzsche conveys the idea that great beings expend rather than conserve themselves.

51. Prominent discussions of Nietzsche and Roux are found in Wolfgang Müller-Lauter, *Nietzsche: His Philosophy of Contradictions and the Contradictions of His Philosophy* (Urbana: University of Illinois Press, 1999), 161–82; and Moore, *Nietzsche, Biology, and Metaphor,* chap. 1.

52. Cf. Bernd Magnus, "The Uses and Abuses of *The Will to Power,*" in *Reading Nietzsche,* ed. Robert C. Solomon and K. Higgins (Oxford: Oxford University Press, 1988).

53. Compare these citations with *BGE* 14 and with *BGE* 22, in which Nietzsche discusses the fact that physics is "interpretation, not text" and imagines that someone could view the same phenomena and interpret it as "will to power"; see also *GS* 374, in which Nietzsche wonders whether "all existence is not essentially engaged in *interpretation.*"

54. These ideas bear some similarities to how Nietzsche discusses the relation be-

tween first and second natures in "On the Use and Disadvantage of History for Life," section 3, *Unmodern Observations.*

55. See my "Nietzsche's Feral Philosophy," 1–13, from which some material in the following pages is drawn.

56. Adrian Del Caro, *Grounding the Nietzsche Rhetoric of Earth* (Berlin: Walter de Gruyter, 2004), 430. Del Caro translates *Übermensch* as "superhuman."

57. Graham Parkes, "Staying Loyal to the Earth: Nietzsche as an Ecological Thinker" in *Nietzsche's Futures,* ed. John Lippitt (London: Macmillan, 1999): 167–86.

58. This is not to say that such goods are intuitive, immediately obvious, or transparent. Part of Nietzsche's insistence that "we are unknown to ourselves" (e.g., *GM* P: 1) is that the physiological processes that constitute us are complex and involve multiple processes of subduing, appropriating, and overcoming—such that much that we are remains unfamiliar, or at least requires a great deal of interpretation.

59. For examples, see *BGE* 44 and *GM* I: 13.

60. Other (wild) animals significant to Nietzsche's Zarathustran persona are the serpent and the eagle, symbols of ("evil") wisdom and pride respectively. See *Z*:1 P:10 and *Z*:4 "The Song of Melancholy" 1. For commentary, see Heidegger's *Nietzsche, Volume II: The Eternal Recurrence of the Same,* trans. D. F. Krell (San Francisco: HarperCollins, 1984/1991), pt. 1, chap. 7. See also essays on the blond beast, serpent, camel, and lion, in Acampora and Acampora, *Nietzschean Bestiary.*

61. Del Caro, *Grounding the Nietzsche Rhetoric of Earth,* 405.

62. On another hybrid animal in Nietzsche's works, see Lawrence J. Hatab, "The Satyr and Human-Animality in Nietzsche" in Acampora and Acampora, *Nietzschean Bestiary.*

63. Indeed, "the 'wild animal' has not been exterminated at all; it lives, it thrives, it has only become—deified." From *BGE,* quoted and translated by Margot Norris, *Beasts of the Modern Imagination* (Baltimore: The Johns Hopkins University Press, 1985), 10.

64. Del Caro, *Grounding the Nietzsche Rhetoric,* 409.

65. See *WP* 1045: "the splendid 'animal' must be given first—what could any 'humanization' matter otherwise!" Compare this transvaluatory rescue with W. Kaufmann's tendency to treat animality as a condition of cultural bankruptcy (of, at most, merely marginal worth).

66. One finds these ideas introduced in T. J. Reed, "Nietzsche's Animals: Idea, Image and Influence," in *Nietzsche: Imagery and Thought,* ed. M. Pasley (Berkeley: University of California Press, 1978), sec. 1, esp. pp. 160f., and Margot Norris characterizes Nietzsche's enterprise as a "recuperation" of zootic principles, *Beasts of the Modern Imagination,* 22.

67. As Del Caro puts it, "Nietzsche makes it clear that we are never far from the animal and we in fact do injustice to ourselves and to animals when we accentuate the distance between animal and human." *Grounding the Nietzsche Rhetoric,* 410.

68. In agreeing that Nietzsche "does not express a romantic desire to return, in literal fashion, to a natural state or condition of humanity," Wayne Klein explicates that because

translation requires at least two languages and a translator, it "can be no more certain and make no more claims to correctness and decidability than interpretation can." *Nietzsche and the Promise of Philosophy* (Albany: SUNY Press, 1997), 178, 176.

69. Jennifer Ham, "Taming the Beast: Animality in Wedekind and Nietzsche," in *Animal Acts: Configuring the Human in Western History*, ed. J. Ham and M. Senior (New York: Routledge, 1997), 159. Cf. the post-Nietzschean, tripartite typology of Oedipal animals, State animals, and demonic animals in Gilles Deleuze and Felix Guattari, *A Thousand Plateaus: Capitalism and Schizophrenia*, vol. 2, trans. Brian Massumi (Minneapolis: University of Minnesota Press, 1987), 240f.

70. Think, for examples, of trickster figures such as the edge-dwelling coyote or of escape artists such as stray dogs and alley cats. These sorts of animals can make their way in (i.e., have behavioral repertoires capable of negotiating) a variety of environments, natural and built, across territories diversified in degrees of cultural modification. Cf. also rats, roaches, and other "weedy species" in David Quammen, "Planet of Weeds," *Harper's* 297, no. 1781 (October 1998): 57–69 (esp. 66ff.). Nietzsche's own illustration (the philosopher) is a human subspecies, so to speak.

71. According to Del Caro, "even the highest conceptions of humanity [for Nietzsche] cannot afford to stray beyond the principle of solidarity with animals." *Grounding the Nietzsche Rhetoric*, 413.

72. See *GM* III:7 and *TI* "Maxims" 3. Cf. *WP* 1027.

73. More extensive discussion of liminal nature of human animality is found in Christa Davis Acampora, "Paws, Claws, Jaws, and Such: Interpretation and Metaphoric Modalities" in Acampora and Acampora, *A Nietzschean Bestiary*.

74. This phrase is from the work of Graham Parkes, to whom I am indebted for provoking me into consideration of the present theme. See his *Composing the Soul* (Chicago: University of Chicago, 1994), 357.

75. See Parkes, *Composing the Soul*, esp. pt. 2.

76. Del Caro states, "Nietzsche's post-humanism is . . . biocentric in the sense that it places the highest values on vitality per se." *Grounding the Nietzsche Rhetoric*, 417.

77. Cf. Noddings, *Caring*.

78. José Ortega y Gasset, *Meditations on Hunting*, trans. H. B. Wescott (New York: Scribner, 1972). Note that the activity of philosophically valorizing the venatory is not limited to European intellectuals—besides Teutonic and Iberian machismo, there is that of the American thinker Paul Shepard, who writes in his preface to Ortega's work: "the glory of man [*ecce*] is a hunting heritage" and "domesticated animals [*ipso facto*] are degenerate" (13).

79. Clarissa Pinkola Estes, *Women Who Run With the Wolves: Myths and Stories of the Wild Woman Archetype* (New York: Ballantine, 1992). Cf. Robert Bly, *Iron John: A Book about Men* (Reading: Addison-Wesley, 1990).

80. For an interspecific rehabilitation of virtue-talk in an unabashed context of animal-as-citizen, see Hearne, *Adam's Task*.

81. Note the call for a hermeneutic of humanity that can elucidate "what it means to be human, to stand uncertainly between the wilderness of beast and prey and the peace-

able kingdom" of domesticity. Matt Cartmill, *A View to Death in the Morning: Hunting and Nature through History* (Cambridge, MA: Harvard University Press, 1993), quoted in the 1994 newsletter of the International Society for Environmental Ethics.

82. That term could be rescued from axiological denigration on the basis of fruitful work being done in the growing field of architectural phenomenology—see, e.g., the SUNY series *Dwelling, Seeing and Designing.*

83. See, e.g., Ted Polhemus, ed., *The Body Reader: Social Aspects of the Human Body* (New York: Random/Pantheon, 1978); cf. Constance Classen, *Worlds of Sense: Exploring the Senses in History and across Cultures* (London: Routledge, 1993). See also Foucauldian and (especially Francophile) feminist literatures, e.g., Rosalyn Diprose and Robyn Ferrell, eds., *Cartographies: Poststructuralism and the Mapping of Bodies and Spaces* (North Sydney: Allen and Unwin, 1991).

84. Even the biological body is deprivileged and seen to be shaped at the hands of science's theoretical and technical "frameworking"—and is thus deemed a historical product. Henry, *Philosophy and Phenomenology,* 4.

85. Donna Haraway was an early exemplar of such indeterminacy—her model of "cyborg politics" is displayed in *Primate Visions* and in *Simians, Cyborgs, and Women* (London: Free Association, 1991). See also Judith Butler, *Bodies That Matter* (New York: Routledge, 1993); Elizabeth Grosz, *Volatile Bodies* (Bloomington: Indiana University Press, 1994); Alphonso Lingis, *Foreign Bodies* (New York: Routledge, 1994); and Olivier Dyens, *Metal and Flesh,* trans. Evan J. Bibbee (Cambridge, MA: MIT Press, 2001).

86. For an early exemplar of such universality see D. M. Levin—his ontological model is well developed in *Body's Recollection, Listening Self,* and *The Opening of Vision: Nihilism and the Postmodern Situation* (London: Routledge and Kegan Paul, 1988). See also Johnson, *Body in the Mind;* Drew Leder, *The Absent Body* (Chicago: University of Chicago Press, 1990); Sue Cataldi, *Emotion, Depth, and Flesh: A Study of Sensitive Space* (Albany: SUNY Press, 1993); and especially a set of impressive works by Maxine Sheets-Johnstone: *The Roots of Thinking; The Roots of Power* (LaSalle: Open Court, 1994); and *The Primacy of Movement* (Amsterdam: John Benjamins, 1999).

87. As contemporary body-theorist John Tambornino puts it, "much of the discussion of the body . . . focuses almost exclusively on *representations* of the body. This focus, conceptually and substantively, tends to emphasize language, belief, and symbolic systems while overlooking affect, disposition, and disciplinary practices." *Corporeal Turn,* 2.

88. Helen Chadwick, *Enfleshings* (New York: Aperture, 1989), 97.

89. Martin Dillon, *Merleau-Ponty's Ontology* (Bloomington: Indiana University Press, 1988), xi. Instead of "grounding," I would prefer to talk in terms of "navigating"; not foundationalism, but *flotationalism.*

90. Consider Susan Bordo's rhetorical query: "Let's agree we cannot 'get outside' the (historically sedimented) discourses and representations that shape our reality. Does this mean that all we are legitimately permitted to talk about is our reality *as* discourse and representation?" See "Bringing Body to Theory," in *Body and Flesh,* ed. D. Welton (Oxford: Blackwell, 1998), 89.

91. Sullivan, *Living Across and Through Skins,* 61. Cf. Bordo: "The body's material-

ity is . . . first and foremost about concreteness, and concrete (and limiting) location." See "Bringing Body to Theory," 92.

92. Compare Henry: "it will be objected that the human body presents itself to man with characteristics which have varied throughout the course of history. . . . However, this is not the original body, but various ways in which man represents this body to himself and behaves toward it. . . . But the ontological basis which founds both objects and attitudes is indifferent to this evolution; the latter always presupposes the ontological foundation." *Philosophy and Phenomenology*, n4. For subtler treatment, and feminist contrast, cf. Bigwood, *Earth Muse*, esp. chaps. 4 and 8; the phrase quoted in the main text above is from p. 44.

93. Daniel Guerriere, "Foundations for an Axiology of Life," *Journal of Value Inquiry* 18 (1984): 203.

Chapter 4: *Ethos* and *Leib*

1. Levin, *Body's Recollection*, 239.

2. Dallery, "Thinking and Being with Beasts," 74–76. Cf. Martin Buber's botanical limit-case: "As I contemplate [lit. 'look at'] the tree I am drawn into a relation. . . . One should not try to dilute the meaning of the relation: relation is reciprocity." *I and Thou*, 8.

3. Levin, *Body's Recollection*, 233, italics original.

4. Cf. Francis Hutcheson: "When we call this [moral] determination a *sense* or *instinct*, we are not supposing it of that low kind dependent on bodily organs, such as even the brutes have. It may be a constant setled [*sic*] determination in the [human] soul itself, as much as our powers of judging and reasoning." From *A System of Moral Philosophy* (1755), as excerpted in *The Enlightenment*, ed. F. E. Manuel (Englewood: Prentice-Hall, 1965), 69.

5. I have in mind the Hutcheson-Hume-Smith lineage (of which Shaftesbury may be considered the source). See David Daiches Raphael, *The Moral Sense* (London: Geoffrey Cumberlege, 1947).

6. Arne J. Vetlesen, *Perception, Empathy, and Judgment: An Inquiry into the Preconditions of Moral Performance* (State College: Pennsylvania State University Press, 1994), 210, 216.

7. Josephine Donovan, "Attention to Suffering," in Donovan and Adams, *Beyond Animal Rights*, 158.

8. Levin, *Body's Recollection*, 247.

9. Still, those interested in exploring the promise and pitfalls of further explication of criteria should consult Kenneth Shapiro, *Bodily Reflective Modes: A Phenomenological Method for Psychology* (Durham: Duke University Press, 1985), esp. chap. 6 (167–209). Shapiro develops a somatic methodology for addressing experiential phenomenology of lifestyles and existential problems (applied, e.g., to the lived experience of ambivalence and its plausibly dialectical resolution).

10. Maurice Mandelbaum, *Phenomenology of Moral Experience* (Baltimore: The

Johns Hopkins University Press, 1969) 67. The next reference to Mandelbaum in this paragraph is to the same source, p. 61.

11. Cf. Mary Wiseman, "Empathetic Identification," *American Philosophical Quarterly* 15, no. 2 (1978) and Taylor, *Respect for Nature*, wherein the moral attitude of respect for (wild) living things is held to "cohere" with a biocentric outlook or metaphysic.

12. I do not want to give the impression of having interpretively collapsed two historically and theoretically distinct intellectual developments, namely the eighteenth-century theory of moral sentiments and the twentieth-century model of empathetic identification. (Richard Holton brought the risk of such a conflation to my attention [personal communication].) To clarify: I think that since the former theory leaves the origination of moral sentimentality mysterious, the latter model can come to function as an attempt to ground it in a "psycho-ethics" of projective imagination—and it is this sort of move I find wanting.

13. In "Moral Considerability and Universal Consideration," Thomas H. Birch defines "deontic experience" as a proto-ethically primitive "experience, in response to something or someone, that one *must* do something, that one is called upon to do something . . . it is the experiential source and the inspiration of our obligations." From *Environmental Ethics* 15, no.4 (1993): 322.

14. David Seamon uses the word 'symphysis' in "Different Worlds Coming Together," in *Dwelling, Seeing and Designing* (Albany: SUNY Press, 1993). He notes that it originated in medical usage and means in ancient Greek, "the state of growing together" (230).

15. Commenting on the experience of artwork, Christopher Perricone is on the way toward such a conception when he asserts, "It is important to emphasize that 'feel' and 'imaginative' are bodily. . . . One imaginatively identifies with the life of others through one's own bodily experience." From "Bugged Out," *Journal of Aesthetic Education* 37, no. 2 (Summer 2003): 25.

16. I do not deny that there may be important links connecting ethos, eros, and earth; exploring their possibility or actuality will not, however, be my present focus; for guidance on such an investigation, cf. S. Cataldi's *Emotion, Depth, and Flesh* (Albany: SUNY Press, 1993) and M. Daly's *Pure Lust* (Boston: Beacon, 1984).

17. Putatively, the functional "core" or structural "seat" of these processes need not be anatomically reified into a biologically scientized apparatus—buried neurologically, for example, somewhere in the cranial and/or spinal tissue. As I conceive it, an ethical sensorium operates on a phenomenally physical plane—not necessarily on a materially physiological level.

18. Greco-Germanic philosophy from Aristotle to Hegel and Marx has evolved a tradition of philosophical anthropology on the premise of studying merely the human animal's pure species-being; the post-humanist task before us now is to go beyond that tradition's homo-exclusive bounds to consider broader animal types by submitting particular experiences of interspecific encounter to phenomenological investigation.

19. Husserl, *Ideas III*, par. 2b, p. 7.

20. Donovan, "Attention to Suffering," 149–58.

21. Edith Stein, *On the Problem of Empathy*, trans. W. Stein, *The Collected Works of Edith Stein,* vol. 3, 3rd ed. (Washington, DC: ICS Publications, 1989), sec. 3.5b, p. 59. Same citation for next quotation.

22. Ibid. In "Kinaestheic Empathy," Jaana Parviainen also indicates Stein's ambivalence on this point—see *Dialogue and Universalism* 13, no. 11/12 (2003): 156.

23. Shapiro, "Understanding Dogs."

24. Conspecifically, within humanity that is, Scheler's theory of the common psychic field is appropriate. See *Nature of Sympathy,* trans. Peter Heath (Hamden: Archon, 1970).

25. Stein, *Empathy,* sec. 3.5b, p. 58. Cf. Shapiro's appeal to "*kinesthetic* empathy" ("Understanding Dogs"), which focuses even further onto a finer modification of empathic sensuality.

26. Midgley, *Animals,* chap. 10.

27. Here I take issue with an earlier phenomenology of bodily empathy and sympathy offered by Edith Wyschogrod, according to whom we "can be said to empathize largely with [human] persons and only rarely with [nonhuman] animals, while it is even more difficult to imagine a [sympathetic] community of feeling with animals over some shared object." From "Empathy and Sympathy as Tactile Encounter," *Journal of Medicine and Philosophy* 6 (1981): 28. Against such anthropocentrism, see also my discussion of Vicki Hearne's work (which provides testimony of cross-species partnership mediated by somatic phenomena).

28. Kuang-Ming Wu, *On the "Logic" of Togetherness: A Cultural Hermeneutic* (Leiden: Brill, 1998), 17.

29. Michael A. Weinstein, *Finite Perfection: Reflections on Virtue* (Amherst: University of Massachusetts Press, 1985).

30. See Stephan Grätzel, *Die philosophische Entdeckung des Leibes* (Stuttgart: Franz Steiner, 1989), esp. sec. 2.1.2 for reference to Fichte (pp. 61ff.). It might be thought that Emmanuel Levinas's philosophy of primordial alterity would be therapeutic precisely with reference to this challenge. Probably so, but later in this chapter I will argue that the moral metaphysics of Levinas is not nearly so serviceable for animal ethics as is sometimes supposed.

31. Compare Michel Henry, "The Critique of the Subject," trans. P. Connor, in *Who Comes After the Subject?* ed. E. Cadava et al. (New York: Routledge, 1991). Cf. Lauren Wispé, *The Psychology of Sympathy,* Perspectives in Social Psychology (New York: Plenum, 1991), chap. 7.

32. The generally moral and specifically bioethical salience of these conditions—susceptibility to disability/death and enmeshment in social/relational webs—is underscored and well articulated by Alasdair MacIntyre in "Vulnerability, Dependence, Animality," chap. 1 of his Carus lectures, *Dependent Rational Animals: Why Human Beings Need the Virtues* (Chicago: Open Court, 1999).

33. In *Physical Being,* Rom Harré claims that "the meaning and defensibility of a bodily obligation has hinged on the fact that it is or was or will be a person who is thus embodied" (138). I am introducing the intelligibility of morally charged symphysis beyond this limitation of scope to the class of persons.

34. Edith Wyschogrod, "Towards a Postmodern Ethics: Corporeality and Alterity," in *The Ethical*, ed. Edith Wyschogrod and G. McKenny (Oxford: Blackwell, 2003), 155. The next quote is from p. 163.

35. Hans Reiner, "On the Adaptation of the Phenomenological Method to, and Its Refinement as a Method of, Ethics," in *Duty and Inclination: The Fundamentals of Morality* (The Hague: Martinus Nijhoff, 1983), 254, italics original. The next quotation is from pp. 257f., italics original.

36. Why ought one accept such an invitation? I do not believe one must, of course (since that would constitute instead an imperative), but I should think most people (certainly those already reading this book) will find the proposal interesting and worthwhile —and in this conviction I am relying not so much on authorial suasion as on innate tendencies of curiosity and sociability that are central to being a human animal.

37. In treating this case some will prefer simply to fall back on adoption of the maxim, "Never inflict needless pain." But that would leave uninterpreted the moral crux of the matter, namely the range of what is [to be] deemed "needful." On this issue the rival account I am discussing is comparatively unhelpful—because it is not obvious how to see or read necessity off the surfaces of things, even with the mind's eye. By contrast, my treatment of the situation (below) is useful for sorting out *vital* needs—because it appeals precisely to the felt vitality of the entire body (the basis or nexus, that is, of one's very livelihood).

38. Hatab, *Ethics and Finitude*, 143, italics original.

39. The parenthetical proviso is meant to bracket issues having to do with extraordinary varieties of religious experience (e.g., shamanic visions) or with psychosomatically altered states of pathology (e.g., sympathy pains)—concerns beyond the scope of my study.

40. Compare Robert Goodin: "What gives rise to our special duties to protect animals from pain and suffering is their peculiar vulnerability to us." *Protecting the Vulnerable: A Reanalysis of Our Social Responsibilities* (Chicago: University of Chicago, 1985), 181. Although my illustrations highlight injury and illness, vulnerability can also connote susceptibility to death and decay. For the moral upshot, cf. Werner Marx, *Towards a Phenomenological Ethics: Ethos and the Life World*, trans. S. Heyvaert (Albany: SUNY Press, 1992), esp. chap. 2.

41. Selecting a stereotypically benign species can appear to prejudice the moral accounting at stake in this illustration. Instead of squirrels, for instance, is (deontically protectionist) symphysis possible with sharks? The degree to which it is *not* measures how alien their aquatic *Leibesheim* is to us land-dwellers; the mor(t)al terror that sharks strike in us is (partially) a refraction of our terrestriality rather than an index of their "evil nature." Of course, some sharks actually become homicidal—in such cases our nonaltruistic intuitions regarding them reflect biological instincts for self-preservation, and our ethical judgments sanctioning violence against them underscore social conventions permitting deeds done out of self-defense.

42. Caputo, *Against Ethics*, 213.

43. Caputo's "sarxography" buttresses the somaesthetic framework of morals I have been tracing. Cf. Hiroshi Kojima's attention to the mediation of *Lebensmitwelt* by *Körper-*

lichkeit in *Phänomenologie der Praxis,* 75ff.) and Irving Singer's suggestion that a sense of solidarity might "occur in the material dimension alone" (letter to author, February 6, 1995).

44. I do not, however, think that it needs justification—despite the fact that much of mainstream Anglophonic philosophy has become the handmaiden of science, I believe philosophers nevertheless retain certain literary rights peculiar to their creatively truth-seeking craft.

45. Reiner, *Duty and Inclination,* 260.

46. Though it might disappoint traditional philosophers of ethical theory, I make no apologies for this result; it befits the primarily descriptive status of phenomenology itself, methodologically speaking. This study offers not so much "new norms" as rather "moral somatology" (on analogy to the more familiar and established field of moral psychology).

47. Compare Hutcheson, who suggests that we define *sense* as a "Determination of our Minds." See *An Essay on the Nature and Conduct of the Passions and Affections,* 3rd ed. (Gainesville: Scholars' Facsimilies and Reprints, 1969 [1742]), sec. 1, art. 1; cf. Johnson, *Body in the Mind,* esp. chaps. 1 and 6.

48. Wu, *On the "Logic,"* 5.

49. Elisa Aaltola's summation of Deleuze and Guattari's influence on posthumanist morality; from her "'Other Animal Ethics' and the Demand for Difference," *Environmental Values* 11, no. 2 (2002): 203. The quote in the next paragraph is from 206f.

50. Most of this paragraph is indebted to commentaries by, among others, Mary Midgley, *Animals and Why They Matter;* Randall Lockwood, "Anthropomorphism Is Not a Four-Letter Word" (paper presented at the Conference on the Perception of Animals in American Culture, Washington, DC, 1983); and Vicki Hearne, *Animal Happiness* (New York: HarperCollins, 1994).

51. See L. Daston and G. Mitman, eds., *Thinking With Animals: New Perspectives on Anthropomorphism* (New York: Columbia University Press, 2005).

52. Aaltola, "Demand for Difference," 204. Cf. Tom Tyler's Heideggerian rendition of this point in his "If Horses Had Hands . . ." *Society and Animals* 11, no. 3 (2003).

53. Such a view changes the ethical landscape. Donna Haraway has lately commented on the import of Hearne's position: "The question turns out not be what are animal rights, as if they existed preformed to be uncovered, but how may a human enter into a rights relationship with an animal?" *Companion Species Manifesto,* 53.

54. Hearne, *Adam's Task,* 38. Cf. John Berger: "Animals offer [us] a companionship which is . . . offered to the loneliness of man as a species." *About Looking,* 4.

55. Hearne, *Adam's Task,* 79f; next quotation is from p. 81. On the phenomenological differentiation of species, compare Nagel, *Possibility of Altruism,* and Tuan, *Topophilia,* with Dijkgraaf, "Excursion through the Sensory World of Animals."

56. Hearne, *Adam's Task,* 105 (example starts at pp. 97f.); next phrase quoted is from pp. 108ff. A projectively imaginal interpretation of the tracking scenario would be interrupted on this account.

57. Hearne, *Adam's Task*, 111. Cf. the haptic audition of cicadas put forward in chapter 2, a distancing example of one-way somaesthesia that shows at once our sensory immersion in a wider world of (even insect) inhabitants as well as our relation at a remove with/from those bugs.

58. In referring to Hearne above, I do not mean to endorse the entirety of her animal-ethical discourse. I share the skepticism some have voiced about her (often polemical) rhetoric and its philosophic upshot: Ken Shapiro thinks "her [literary] work is an apology for her [training] work" (personal communication). Annabelle Sabloff characterizes *Adam's Task* as "a disquisition on the place of (some) animals in the human moral domain, rather than an inquiry into the moral position of human beings as animals sharing the world with other beings." *Reordering the Natural World* (Toronto: University of Toronto Press, 2001), 211n15.

59. Some points of discussion in the next several pages derive from my article, "*Oikos* and *Domus*: On Creative Co-Habitation With Other Creatures," *Philosophy and Geography* 7, no. 2 (August 2004).

60. The *locus classicus* is Aldo Leopold's moral meditation on a "land ethic" in *A Sand County Almanac* (New York: Oxford University Press, 1949); also, the model is latent in much animal rights advocacy.

61. As Diane Michelfelder claims, "Wildlife that inhabit and have found a home in urban settings are our nonhuman neighbors. As a result we have a moral obligation to respond to them accordingly and treat them as the neighbors that they are." From "Valuing Wildlife Populations in Urban Environments," *Journal of Social Philosophy* 34, no. 1 (Spring 2003): 86.

62. Compare St. Thomas Aquinas: "'neighbor' cannot be understood to include irrational creatures because they do not share man's rational life. Therefore charity does not extend to them." *Summa Theologiae* 2a2ae, quoted by John Llewelyn, *The Middle Voice of Ecological Conscience: A Chiasmic Reading of Responsibility in the Neighbourhood of Levinas, Heidegger, and Others* (New York: St. Martin's, 1991), 269.

63. Llewelyn, *Middle Voice*, 49, 65. Cf. Sartre's meditations on "Faces," *Essays in Phenomenology*, ed. M. Natanson (The Hague: Martinus Nijhoff, 1966), 157–63.

64. John Llewelyn, "Am I Obssessed by Bobby? (Humanism of the Other Animal)," in *Re-Reading Levinas*, ed. R. Bernasconi and S. Critchley (Bloomington: Indiana University Press, 1991), 240ff.

65. David Krell, "Cristy's Mortality," epilogue to *Daimon Life*, 318. Note that Cristy's eye "did not accuse," implying that it could have—which would presuppose an awareness of mor(t)ality, that the dog is capable of registering damage, attributing wrong, and anticipating demise; perhaps, then, Krell is suggesting that Cristy has met the Levinasian criterion identified by Llewelyn.

66. Wu, *On the "Logic,"* 25n20.

67. Peter Atterton, "Ethical Cynicism," in *Philosophy: Ethics and Identity*, ed. P. Atterton and M. Calarco (London: Continuum, 2004), 58; next quotation from p. 61.

68. See David Clark, "On Being the Last Kantian in Nazi Germany: Dwelling with

Animals after Levinas," in *Animal Acts: Configuring the Human in Western History,* ed. J. Ham and M. Senior (New York: Routledge, 1997), where Clark admits that in Levinas's thought "the animal both has and does not have a face; it is characterized in its essence by having (face) without having" (180). Note how redolent this is of Heidegger's double-speak about animal worldhood/deprivation. Compare Matthew Calarco's "Levinas' Dreaded Comparison," in *Radicalizing Levinas* (Albany: SUNY Press, forthcoming).

69. Barry Holstun Lopez, *Of Wolves and Men* (New York: Charles Scribner's Sons, 1978), 281.

70. Lopez, *Of Wolves and Men,* 280. Cf. Aristotle, *Nicomachean Ethics,* ll. 1171b32–1172a14.

71. Lopez, *Of Wolves and Men,* 284. Cf. L. Wispé, *Psychology of Sympathy,* chap. 8. The next two quotations from Lopez are from *Of Wolves and Men,* pp. 282 and 285, italics added. Cf. Shapiro's kinesthetic empathy in "Understanding Dogs."

72. Compare Richard Sorabji, who states that the Stoics thought we humans "can extend *oikeiosis* [= belonging] (and hence justice) only to other rational beings" as such; from *Animal Minds,* 124. But cf. Theophrastus, Aristotle's student and colleague, according to whom humans and other animals cohabitate a common moral space partly due to sharing "bodily origins" (e.g., flesh)—in Porphyry, *Abstinence* 3.25, cited by Sorabji, 178.

73. Steeves, *Founding Community,* 140.

74. Midgley, *Why Animals Matter,* chap. 10.

75. Compare Henry Beston's talk, echoing Amerindian notions, of animal species as "other nations." This politic phrasing puts our intercourse outside the intimacy of familial or even social ties, and yet preserves a place of parity for relationship among "peoples" that would be denied by the strictures of positive science and purely exploitive utility. See *The Outermost House: A Year of Life on the Great Beach of Cape Cod* (Garden City: Doubleday, 1928), 25. Also compare Ted Benton, *Natural Relations: Ecology, Animal Rights and Social Justice* (London: Verso, 1993), introduction.

76. For positive illustrations of animal companionship that supersede ordinary, ethically ambivalent forms of pet-keeping, see zoologist Barbara Smuts, "Reflection," in J. M. Coetzee, *The Lives of Animals,* ed. A. Gutmann (Princeton: Princeton University Press, 1999), 115ff. Cf. Haraway, *Companion Species Manifesto.*

77. For a nonhierarchical model of cross-species kinship, see Jim Mason's advocacy in *An Unnatural Order: Uncovering the Roots of Our Domination of Nature and Each Other* (New York: Simon and Schuster, 1993), esp. chap. 9.

78. Thus, though divergent in method from, they are not necessarily inimical in purpose to, phenomenological philosophy. In fact, as regards body inquiry itself, studies of *phenomenal* bodiment (somaticity) and of *material* bodiment (corporeality) can and do complement and encourage each other (examples include investigations of "phantom limbs" and of "fire-walking"). Hence, as somatologists in search of biotic/bodily conjunctions, let us not altogether shun the natural sciences and ethnographic approaches (a disavowal that would constitute misplacement of methodological purism).

79. The problem of non-interactive instances was cast poignantly by Richard Sorabji (in conversation, 1995).

80. Compare Yi-Fu Tuan, *Morality and Imagination,* chap. 9 (esp. pp. 169f.) and Johnson, *Moral Imagination,* chap. 8 (esp. pp. 199ff.).

81. The imagination's employment is important, too, in bridging *tenses* of experience—i.e., by memorial restoration and projective anticipation. Thus the moral life's temporal continuity is nourished by imaginative activity. Compare Mark Nepo, "The Bridge of Well-Being: The Stranger, The Fellow, The Completing Other," *Parabola* 22, no. 2 (May 1995): 17–20; also recall Berger's comment about humanity's species-alienation (note 54 to this chapter).

82. Compare Wispé's principle from *Psychology of Sympathy:* "we sympathize with sentient beings to whom we attribute the capacity to feel pain and the capacity to know they are feeling it" (71). Applying this principle to an insect case, she confesses that even if "the butterfly does not 'know' what is happening . . . if I think the butterfly is in pain, that is sufficient to arouse my sympathy" (71). The confusion can be dissolved, and the confession's content made more sensible, by using *symphysis* as a descriptor, without appeal to conditions of cognition or cogitation.

83. Lily-Marlene Russow, in "Why Do Species Matter?" *Environmental Ethics* 3, no. 2 (1981), argues for the worth of species as (visual/behavioral) character-types on the basis of aesthetic appeal, but this argument courts caprice insofar as it lies exposed to a subjectively anthropogenic axiology of beauty beheld. Another position would be to claim simply that species as (molecular/biological) genetic codes are themselves valuable, but such a stance is neither self-evident nor well-defended.

84. See chapter two, including references to David Abram's work. Beyond basic biomorality, an *environmental* ethic of embodiment would have to fix the range of the "flesh-of-the-world" according to a personalistic, bioregional, or Gaian scope. Cf. Casey's lococentric implacement of ecological morality, in *Getting Back into Place,* chap. 8: ". . . in the biotic community, place and occupant-of-place belong together indissolubly. As a result, both particular places and their natural denizens call for our respectful nurturance as entities valuable in their own right. Places em-body values; better yet, they *situate* them" (265).

85. The first example (that of artificial "*Mitsein*") illustrates a possible difficulty for the account of togetherness given above; the second one, in the next paragraph, threatens to unsettle my portrayal of vulnerability (if, that is, mere thinghood allows of natural "needs").

86. Rae Langton has cautioned me with this sort of puzzle (personal comment).

87. See Llewelyn's *Middle Voice,* postface.

88. Compare Charles Scott, *The Lives of Things* (Bloomington: Indiana University Press, 2002). Note that I also defer discussion of the relation(s) between transpecific and strictly human bodiment ethics, as well as of the emerging ethos or etiquette of cyberspatial "bodies." Cf. Freya Carkeek and Paul James, "This Abstract Body," *Arena* 99/100 (1992): 66–85.

89. The rest of this paragraph derives mostly from my essay, "The Problematic Situation of Post-Humanism and the Task of Recreating a Symphysical Ethos," *Between the Species: A Journal of Ethics* 11, no. 2 (Winter/Spring, 1995): 25–29.

90. Arne Naess, "Notes on the Politics of the Deep Ecology Movement," in *Sustaining Gaia: Contributions to Another World View,* ed. Frank Fisher (Melbourne: Monash University, 1987), 180.

91. See Stephen Kellert and E. O. Wilson, eds., *The Biophilia Hypothesis* (Washington, DC: Island Press, 1993), and Stephen Kellert, *Kinship to Mastery: Biophilia in Human Evolution and Development* (Washington, DC: Island Press, 1997).

92. See primatologist Frans de Waal, *Good Natured,* esp. chap. 2, and psychologist Martin Hoffman, *Empathy and Moral Development,* esp. pp. 22 and 282.

93. Olin Eugene Myers and Carol Saunders, "Animals as Links toward Developing Caring Relationships with the Natural World," in *Children and Nature: Psychological, Sociocultural, and Evolutionary Investigations,* ed. P. H. Kahn and S. R. Kellert (Cambridge, MA: MIT Press, 2002), 160; the next sentence paraphrases p. 156. To quell any incipient queasiness about naturalistic determinism, it would be helpful here to heed the interpretive advice of Lawrence Hatab: "Calling empathy natural is simply to say that it shows itself spontaneously in human experience, that it is in some sense intrinsic to human comportment, though dependent on environmental influences for its flourishing (analogous to the natural propensity for language that is nevertheless not automatic or self-generating)." *Ethics and Finitude,* 147.

94. On somatic origins, see also Eugene Myers, *Children and Animals: Social Development and Our Connections to Other Species* (Boulder: Westview, 1998), 42. The next sentence quotes from pp. 153f. (Myers cites Jerome Kagan in this passage).

95. See, e.g., Gail Eisnitz, *Slaughterhouse* (Amherst, NY: Prometheus, 1997).

96. Cf. Hatab: "If empathy is primal in human experience in some way, then to whatever extent empathic relations are indicative of an ethical sense (caring-about and caring-for), in this respect human beings do not 'become' [moral] as life proceeds, they are *already* ethical to a certain extent." *Ethics and Finitude,* 147.

Chapter 5: Body Bioethics in Realms of the Carnal and the Carceral

1. Here my advice echoes the metaphilosophical counsel of Aristotle, *Nicomachean Ethics,* ll. 1141b15f. Operating thus, the vocational task or eros of the finite philosopher remains forever incomplete—always only pursuit, at most virtually consummated.

2. John Haldane, "Philosophy and the Ethics of the Environment," in *Ethics and the Environment,* ed. C. C. W. Taylor (Oxford: Corpus Christi College, 1992), 76.

3. See Paul Komesaroff, "Bioethics and Nature: The Case of Animal Experimentation," *Thesis Eleven* 32 (1992): esp. 71ff.

4. Haldane, "Philosophy and the Ethics," Cf. Abraham Edel, Elizabeth Flower, and Finbarr W. O'Connor: "This separation of theory and practice is a holdover from early twentieth-century philosophy, which still haunts the [applied ethics] field." From *Critique of Applied Ethics: Reflections and Recommendations* (Philadelphia: Temple University Press, 1994), 7.

5. Cf. Edel, Flower, and O'Connor, *Critique,* chap. 1, "Practical Moral Problems in an Age of Rapid Technological and Social Change."

6. One of the more curious developments in the history of what Nietzsche termed "the ascetic ideal" is the way in which a certain configuration of Christianity conflates the carnal and the carceral, whereby we arrive at the body-as-prison (house) or flesh-as-jail (cell). Ironically, modern medicine—which prides itself on having dispelled religious metaphors from health science—perpetuates this figure of conflation when, in effect, it militarily biologizes the body as built of *cells* and *barriers* (rather than, say, flows and surfaces-of-contact).

7. Franck, "Being and the Living," 145.

8. Cf. Susan Bordo, *Unbearable Weight: Feminism, Western Culture, and the Body* (Berkeley: University of California Press, 1993) and E.-D. Schulze, *Flux Control in Biological Systems: From Enzymes to Populations and Ecosystems* (San Diego: Academic Press, 1994). The latter is especially intriguing in that it mediates the duality I have posited above: "Micro-instability (imbalance) is a requirement for regulation and it appears to be the basis for stability at the macro-scale" (484).

9. Compare expert advice on the art of animal handling: "The handler must be able to perceive the feelings of the animal and take appropriate steps to alleviate pain." Note that it is a matter of perception, not conception. Quoted from Murray Fowler's textbook, *Restraint and Handling of Wild and Domestic Animals,* 2nd ed. (Ames: Iowa State University Press, 1995), 5b.

10. Hank Davis and Dianne Balfour, "The Inevitable Bond," in *The Inevitable Bond: Examining Scientist-Animal Interactions,* ed. Davis and Balfour (Cambridge: Cambridge University Press, 1992), 4.

11. D. Estep and S. Hetts, "Interactions, Relationships, and Bonds: The Conceptual Basis for Scientist-Animal Relations," in Davis and Balfour, *Inevitable Bond,* 17.

12. B. J. F. Lonergan, *Insight: A Study of Human Understanding,* rev. ed. (San Francisco: Harper and Row, 1978), 184. The term *constitutive extroversion* is actually F. P. Braio's paraphrase from *Lonergan's Retrieval of the Notion of Human Being* (Lanham: University Press of America, 1988), 19.

13. Max Scheler, *Man's Place in Nature,* trans. H. Meyerhoff (Boston: Beacon, 1961), 39.

14. There is nothing paranormal about the incorporation to which I allude; perfectly ordinary illustrations abound. Two examples from human experience are the motile extension of arm into tennis racquet during play and the haptic expansion of skin onto car-shell while driving.

15. In addition to Lonergan and Scheler; see my account of animal worldhood in chapter 2 and D. F. Krell's argument for the compatibility of animality and appropriation. *Daimon Life,* 1992, esp. chaps. 3 and 6.

16. Cf. note 6, above.

17. Lynda Birke, "Who—or What—are the Rats (and Mice) in the Laboratory?" *Society and Animals* 11, no. 3 (2003): 213, 210.

18. Ken Shapiro has already suggested that ethical implications in this transformation, in his "Understanding Dogs," 187, 194.

19. M. R. Gamble, "The Design of Experiments," in *Laboratory Animals: An Intro-*

duction for New Experimenters, ed. A. A. Tuffery (Chichester: John Wiley and Sons, 1987), 56.

20. See, e.g., M. Rose and D. Adam, "Evidence for Pain and Suffering in Other Animals," in *Animal Experimentation: The Consensus Changes,* ed. G. Langley (New York: Chapman and Hall, 1989), esp. pp. 60ff.

21. Gamble, "Design," 57.

22. Compare the ethnic and gender "sensitivity workshops" staged in various institutional and organizational contexts.

23. This disruption of sociality can, most tragically, occur on a conspecific level.

24. Birke, "Who—or What," 215f.

25. For a graphic comparison, see David Lynch's film, *Blue Velvet.*

26. Derrida, "Animal That Therefore I Am," 382, italics original. In this neo-Cartesian view, animals merely react but do not really respond (see 377).

27. Birke, "Who—or What," 215.

28. See Shapiro, "Death of the Animal," 188b.

29. Birke, "Who—or What," 211. This and the next two paragraphs draw and quote from the same source, pages 220, 217, 218, and 210.

30. Perhaps, though, this challenge lends all the more weight to the iconography's redemptive upshot (from lowest to highest, that is).

31. Birke, "Who—or What," 214. Cf. Mary Midgley, *Science as Salvation: A Modern Myth and Its Meaning* (London: Routledge, 1992).

32. In altered forms/contexts, different parts of this section have variously appeared in other works of mine: "Extinction by Exhibition," *Human Ecology Review* 5, no. 1 (1998): 1–4; "Zoöpticon: Inspecting the Site of Live Animal Infotainment," in *Phenomenological Approaches to Popular Culture,* ed. Michael T. Carroll and Eddie Tafoya (Bowling Green University: Popular Press, 2000 [Copyright: University of Wisconsin Press]), 151–61; "Redemption from Extinction: Examining the Zoological Ark of Biotopia," *Between the Species: An Electronic Journal for the Study of Philosophy and Animals* (Spring 2002).

33. Shapiro, "Death Animal," 190b. Cf. Lyons (1989): "the flower is part of the bee's anatomy"—quoted in Shapiro, 190.

34. See Shapiro, "Death Animal," 191f.

35. See Terry Maple and E. Archibald, *Zoo Man* (Atlanta: Longstreet, 1993).

36. See Hal Markowitz, *Behavioral Enrichment in the Zoo* (New York: Van Nostrand Reinhold, 1982).

37. In fact, state-of-the-art reconstruction goes to the point where entire ecosystems have been assembled and stocked (e.g., Montreal's Biodome).

38. Markowitz, *Behavioral Enrichment,* 12. Remember, too, that "as far as wild animals are concerned, any captive situation involves some form of restraint." Quoted from Murray Fowler, *Restraint and Handling of Wild and Domestic Animals,* 2nd ed. (Ames: Iowa State University Press, 1995), p. 3b.

39. Compare Umberto Eco, *Travels in Hyper-Reality* (San Diego: Harcourt Brace Jovanovich, 1986) and Jean Baudrillard, *America,* trans. C. Turner (London: Verso, 1988).

40. Colin Tudge, *Last Animals at the Zoo: How Mass Extinction Can Be Stopped* (Washington, DC: Island Press, 1992), 256.

41. Neil Evernden, *The Natural Alien: Humankind and Environment* (Toronto: University of Toronto Press, 1993), 151.

42. Tudge, *Last Animals,* 255.

43. Ullrich Melle, "How Deep is Deep Enough? Ecological Modernization or Farewell to the World-City?" in *Environmental Philosophy and Environmental Activism*, ed. D. Marietta and L. Embree (Lanham: Rowman and Littlefield, 1995), 107.

44. Tudge, *Last Animals,* 170.

45. My caricature is not unlicensed, for zoo ideology has a tendency to wax Noachian: see philosopher Jacques Dufresne's Biodome encomium, in which he refers to "technology in the service of life" under a "Rainbow Covenant"—see "The Meaning of Biodome," *Quatre-Temps* 16, no. 2 (Summer 1992): 6–12.

46. As Tudge makes clear, training in wilderness survival skills will be necessary for successful reintroduction of future zoo animals. *Last Animals,* chap. 7, esp. pp. 233–40.

47. Compare Bob Mullan and Garry Marvin, *Zoo Culture* (London: Weidenfeld and Nicolson, 1987), xvii: "interpreting the presentation of wild animals in the zoo reveals much more about the variety of the cultural expression of human identity than it does about the zoological nuances of the animal universe." Quotes in this paragraph come from the same source, pages 45 and 37.

48. Weston, *Back to Earth* 13 (also see chap. 7). Cf. Heini Hediger's admission that "friendship between animal and man, in the sense of intimate positive relations, can only be achieved by unforced, voluntary approach on the part of the animal, and not through the irresistible force of contact." *Wild Animals in Captivity*, trans. G. Sircom (London: Butterworths Scientific Publications, 1950), 165.

49. Compare Mullan and Marvin, *Zoo Culture,* esp. pp. 31 and 43, and Shane Phelan's talk of a more congenial attitude. She calls this intermediate position, and her essay, "Intimate Distance." See pp. 44–62.

50. Berger, "Why Look at Animals?" in *About Looking,* 26.

51. Alexander Wilson, *The Culture of Nature: North American Landscape from Disney to the Exxon Valdez* (Cambridge: Blackwell, 1990), 248.

52. Foucault, *Discipline and Punish*, 297. Cf. Desmond Morris, *The Human Zoo* (New York: McGraw Hill, 1969).

53. Stephen Bostock, *Zoos and Animal Rights* (London: Routledge, 1993), 63.

54. Compare Foucault, *Discipline and Punish*, 135–69.

55. Michel Foucault, "How is Power Exercised?" trans. L. Sawyer, in *Beyond Structuralism and Hermeneutics*, ed. H. Dreyfus and P. Rabinow (Chicago: University of Chicago Press, 1983), 221. Lest one think that my application of Foucauldian power analysis is misplaced precisely because of this condition, I should note that freedom itself is not radical for Foucault (as against its instantiation in, say, Sartrean subjectivity): "by this [= freedom] we mean individual or collective subjects who are faced with a field of possibilities in which several ways of behaving, several reactions and diverse comportments may be realized" (221). Such a description is applicable to many (kinds of) nonhumans.

56. Heini Hediger, *Studies of the Psychology and Behavior of Captive Animals in Zoos and Circuses*, trans. G. Sircom (London: Butterworths Scientific Pub., 1955), 3, 18.

57. Peter Batten, with D. Stancil, *Living Trophies: A Shocking Look at the Conditions in America's Zoos* (New York: Thomas Y. Crowell, 1976).

58. Batten, *Living Trophies,* chap. 12.

59. Foucault, *Discipline and Punish*, 201.

60. Berger puts this anti-phenomenon starkly: "The zoo to which people go to meet animals, to observe them, to see them, is, in fact, a monument to the impossibility of such encounters." This is the pornographic moment of zooscopy. See "Why Do We Look," 19. Cf. Carol J. Adams, *Neither Man nor Beast: Feminism and the Defense of Animals* (New York: Continuum, 1994), esp. chap. 2.

61. Biological analogs are rare, but cf. Hediger: "A cage-like siliceous sponge, the Venus' Flower Basket often encloses crustaceans, which reach the lumen of the mesh-like cylinder of sponge, then grow up and can no longer get out. In this example the mesh acts not only in a negative way by restricting free movement, but also in a positive way: the mesh of the sponge provides protection to the small crustaceans against enemies—in much the same way as the iron bars or other fencing in a zoo provide security for the captive animals." *Man and Animal in the Zoo*, trans. G. Vevers and W. Reade (New York: Seymour Lawrence/Delacorte Press, 1969), 2.

62. This is the sort of fear evident in Thomas Birch, "The Incarceration of Wildness: Wilderness Areas as Prison," *Environmental Ethics* 12, no. 1 (Spring 1990), namely, the suspicion "that there is no wilderness [free otherness] anymore in the contemporary world, in the technological imperium"(10).

63. Hediger, *Wild Animals*, 3. Cf. Michel Foucault, *The Birth of the Clinic: An Archaeology of Medical Perception,* trans. A. M. Sheridan-Smith (New York: Vintage, 1973). On Hediger's program of systematic science, see *Wild Animals,* 169: "Every zoological garden is a part of the whole system and must fit into the picture with all other zoos."

64. Hediger, *Studies of the Psychology,* 148: "The [animal's] whole body is like an open book, to be read by those who know how."

65. Foucault, *Discipline and Punish*, 294.

66. Hediger, *Wild Animals in Captivity*, 157. Likewise, compare the worth of tutoring the animal body at p. 161: "Trained animals have more show value than raw [*sic*] animals." The next quotation is from the same source, p. 163.

67. Although he does not dwell on it as a definite danger, Hediger at least recognizes the reductive/restrictive tendency of scientific/technical practices (inc. the zoological). See *Man and Animal,* 111: "For the geneticist, some animals are virtually nothing more than mere carriers of chromosomes; the research worker on venoms sees his specimens only as walking phials of poison; to the brain specialist the external appearance of an animal is lost behind its brain structure. . . . Probably zoo people are also not exempt from corresponding professional distortions, they too suffer from a certain occupational blindness."

68. See Tudge, *Last Animals*, "The Whole Animal: Behaviour Conserved" (chap. 7).

69. Compare Koen Margodt, *The Welfare Ark: Suggestions for a Renewed Policy for Zoos* (Brussels: VUB Press, 2001).

70. Kellert, *Kinship to Mastery*, 98.

71. Edward O. Wilson, *Biophilia* (Cambridge, MA: Harvard University Press, 1984).

72. Marilyn Frye, *The Politics of Reality* (Trumansburg, NY: Crossing Press, 1983), 67. Quotations in the next two paragraphs come from the same source, pp. 67, 66, 74, and 76.

73. Regarding the awareness of predator and of prey, cf. Ortega y Gasset, *Meditations on Hunting*.

74. Compare Yi-Fu Tuan's conception of love in *Dominance and Affection: The Making of Pets* (New Haven: Yale University Press, 1984), x.

75. Alphonso Lingis, *Excesses: Eros and Culture* (Albany: SUNY Press, 1984), 8. The next quotation is from p. 13.

76. Ibid., 10f. This bears some resemblance to, and can be compared with, Mary Caputi's psychodynamic rehabilitation of obscenity as "that dimension of culture that allows us to cross boundaries, exceed limits . . . [and] allows for continuity, the sensation of merging and fusion with the world, a sense of communion." From *Voluptuous Yearnings: A Feminist Theory of the Obscene* (Lanham: Rowman and Littlefield, 1994), 6.

77. Frye, *Politics of Reality*, 75. The next two quotations are from pp. 75 and 73.

78. This point marks an example of how the approach of practical philosophy I have followed in this chapter differs from the standard method of applied ethics: by allowing new experiences to penetrate reflection, it encourages and enables self-critique and adjustment of outlook, rather than insisting on deductive extension of first principles (top-down theorizing).

79. The last few pages derive largely from my "Zoos and Eyes: Contesting Captivity and Seeking Successor Practices," *Society and Animals* 13, no. 1 (2005): 83–85; for concrete illustrations of actual post-zoo transformations, see 80–82. For reflections on broader conceptions of authentic animal encounter, cf. my "*Oikos* and *Domus:* On Constructive Co-Habitation with Other Creatures," *Philosophy and Geography* 7, no. 2 (2004).

Chapter 6: Contexts and Promise of Corporal Compassion

1. Although this sort of argumentive endeavor is often considered a matter of almost mechanical science, it actually approximates a magical art—for it attempts by cognitively conservative means (rules of logic preserving premises' truth) to arrive at epistemic enrichment (correct conclusion containing novel ideation). Maybe this appearance is just "sleight-of-mind," insofar as the alleged novelty of idea is merely a psychological phenomenon (already logically "latent" in the premises). Cf. Stephen Toulmin, *Human Understanding* (Princeton: Princeton University Press, 1972) and *The Place of Reason in Ethics* (Cambridge: Cambridge University Press, 1958).

2. Weinstein, *Structure of Human Life*, 40.

3. Cf. Warwick Fox's approach to ecosophy in "Proof, Moral Injunctions, and Experiential Invitations," *Toward a Transpersonal Ecology* (Boston: Shambhala, 1990), 242–47.

4. In my estimation, an especially promising direction for future development of such research would be to combine Rom Harré's theory of "corporeal psychology," from

Physical Being with Mark Johnson's body studies from *Moral* under the catalytic influence of Shannon Sullivan's pragmatist somaesthetics in *Living Across and Through Skins.*

5. See also Alice Ingerson, "Tracking and Testing the Nature/Culture Dichotomy," in *Historical Ecology: Cultural Knowledge and Changing Landscapes,* ed. C. L. Crumley (Santa Fe: School of American Research Press, 1994), 43–66.

6. Compare Bigwood's call to examine "earthly and skyly" world-involvement in *Earth Muse.*

7. For interdisciplinary examples, see M. Bennett and D. Teague, eds., *Nature of Cities: Ecocriticism and Urban Environments* (Tucson: University of Arizona Press, 1999) and Peter Brand, *Urban Environmentalism* (New York: Routledge, 2005).

8. This move tends to subsume culture within nature, whereas the more popular theory of postmodernity tends to circumscribe nature itself within cultural concepts. The latter account is implicitly committed to lending epistemology priority over ontology; for a critique of this stance, cf. Martin Dillon, *Semiological Reductionism: A Critique of the Deconstructionist Movement in Postmodern Thought* (Albany: SUNY Press, 1995).

9. It might also be relevant to multiculturalism—cf. Henry Beston, who speaks of different species as "other nations." *Outermost House,* 25.

10. The content of this feeling is of obvious importance for the transmission of relational axiology to moral philosophy. Recall Buber's warning: "One should not try to dilute the meaning of relation; relation is reciprocity." Quoted in Donald L. Berry, *Mutuality: The Vision of Martin Buber* (Albany: SUNY Press, 1985), 19.

11. For a more sympathetic treatment of moral sense theory, especially in relation to Hume, see Philip Mercer, *Sympathy and Ethics: A Study of the Relationship between Sympathy and Morality with Special Reference to Hume's* Treatise (Oxford: Clarendon Press, 1972).

12. This point diverges from the imaginative model of empathic identity, which structures explication of scenarios by appeal to sentimental projection.

13. Compare Henry S. Salt, *Animals' Rights: Considered in Relation to Social Progress* (1892; repr. Clarks Summit, PA: Society for Animal Rights, 1980) and Daniel Dombrowski, *Hartshorne and the Metaphysics of Animal Rights* (Albany: SUNY Press, 1988).

14. See Regan, *Case for Animal Rights;* note the Rawlsian methodology therein.

15. Julian Franklin, *Animal Rights and Moral Philosophy* (New York: Columbia University Press, 2005), 78, 80.

16. Compare Lawrence Hatab's observation in *Ethics and Finitude,* 149: "From a developmental standpoint, empathic affects emerge prior to cognizance of moral principles, and the affects seem to predispose people toward, and help activate, moral principles." Thus affective connection takes (at least temporal) precedence over discursive deliberation; that the former phenomenon is a necessary, not sufficient condition for ethics is also made clear by Hatab (at pp. 154–61).

17. See, e.g., Arne Naess, "The Shallow and the Deep, Long-Range Ecology Movement: A Summary," *Inquiry* 16, no. 1 (Spring 1973): 95–100.

18. Bigwood's *Earth Muse* might be a good place to begin answering these queries. Her work manages to avoid the twin dangers tempting postmodern feminism, that is, theoretical euphoria of radical constructionism and mystical nostalgia for goddess wor-

ship. Another useful source would be the work of Carol Adams—see *Sexual Politics of Meat* and *Neither Man nor Beast.*

19. See, e.g., E. McKenna and A. Light, eds., *Animal Pragmatism* (Bloomington: Indiana University Press, 2004), 9ff.

20. Philip McReynolds, "Overlapping Horizons of Meaning," in ibid., 75, 78. See also p. 74.

21. Sullivan, *Living Across and Through Skins.*

22. Dale Jamieson, "Against Zoos," *Reflecting on Nature: Readings in Environmental Philosophy,* ed. L. Gruen and D. Jamieson (Oxford: Oxford University Press, 1994), 291–99. The following quotes from Jamieson come from pages 292, 298, and 299.

23. Berger, *About Looking,* 26.

24. Edith Wyschogrod, "Does Continental Ethics Have a Future?" in *Ethics and Danger: Essays on Heidegger and Continental Thought,* ed. Arleen Dallery and Charles E. Scott with P. Holley Roberts (Albany: SUNY Press, 1992), 230.

25. Ibid., 235, 239.

26. Ibid., 239. See also Wyschogrod, "Towards a Postmodern Ethics." Cf. Hans Jonas, who fixes the locus of responsibility at the point of "continually critical vulnerability of being," in *The Imperative of Responsibility* (Chicago: University of Chicago Press, 1984), 135.

27. Werner Marx, *Towards a Phenomenological Ethics: Ethos and the Life-World,* trans. S. Heyvaert (Albany: SUNY Press, 1992).

28. Compare Krell, *Daimon Life,* and Elaine Scarry, *The Body in Pain: The Making and Unmaking of the World* (New York: Oxford University Press, 1985).

29. Marx, *Towards a Phenomenological Ethics,* 56. Again, compare Jonas: "only what is alive, in its constitutive indigence and fragility, *can* be an object of responsibility"— yet, according to him, "the primary objects of responsibility are other human subjects" (*Imperative,* 98).

30. Compare Krell's phenomenological contestation of Heidegger's dying/perishing distinction in *Daimon Life,* esp. at pp. 317–19 ("Cristy's Mortality").

31. See Holdrege, *Flexible Giant,* 37.

32. Joyce Poole, *Coming of Age with Elephants* (New York: Hyperion, 1996), 159f., as quoted by Holdrege, *Flexible Giant,* 38. Though this passage clearly invites mental attributions or projections, notice how its crucial cues are actually bodily behaviors that resonate with our own symphysical routines and memories.

33. Robert Goodin, *Protecting the Vulnerable: A Reanalysis of Our Social Responsibilities* (Chicago: University of Chicago Press, 1985), 181.

34. Mental factors (e.g., second-order consciousness of one another's mutual recognition) may also have to come into play for respect in this sense to emerge fully as an ethical phenomenon.

35. Dallery, "Thinking and Being," 85.

36. In *Against Ethics,* for example, John Caputo claims that obligation simply happens —without the rational(izing) justifications of philosophy. Perhaps the medicine for such skepsis must come, if at all, not as outright antidote but rather as vaccination; I admit to concocting the latter myself, in the manner of a Humean-style "skeptical (dis)solution."

Cf. David Hume, *An Enquiry Concerning Human Understanding,* in *The Empiricists* (Garden City: Anchor/Doubleday, 1974), sec. 5.

37. Donnelley and Nolan, "Animals, Science, and Ethics," 2.

38. Marcus Bullock, "Watching Eyes, Seeing Dreams, Knowing Lives," in *Representing Animals,* ed. N. Rothfels (Bloomington: Indiana University Press, 2002), 111.

39. Ehrenfeld attributes this malignancy to a hubristic faith in rational control. See *Arrogance of Humanism.* Cf. Carolyn Merchant, *The Death of Nature* (New York: Harper and Row, 1980) and the special issue of *Free Inquiry* entitled, "Does Humanism Encourage Human Chauvinism?"

40. For reference to Dewey's definition and dynamics of the "problematic situation," see John Dewey, *The Moral Writing of John Dewey,* ed. J. Gouinlock (New York: Hafner Press, 1976).

41. Cary Wolfe makes the noteworthy observation that this concern is not limited to zoophiles, because as long as rationalistic anthropocentrism is regnant, "the humanist discourse of species[ism] will always be available for use by some humans against other humans as well, to countenance violence against the social other of whatever species—or gender, or race, or class, or sexual difference." *Animal Rites: American Culture, the Discourse of Species, and Posthumanist Theory* (Chicago: University of Chicago Press, 2003), 8.

42. Michael W. Fox, "Species Identity and Self-Awareness," in *Species Identity and Attachment,* ed. M. Aaron Roy (New York: Garland, 1980).

43. Neil Evernden, *The Social Creation of Nature* (Baltimore: The Johns Hopkins University Press, 1992), 141n33. In his editorial introduction to *Zoontologies,* Cary Wolfe notes that "one of the central ironies of animal rights [and liberation] philosophy . . . is that its philosophical frame remains an essentially humanist one in its most important philosophers (utilitarianism in Peter Singer, neo-Kantianism in Tom Regan)" (xii).

44. Attend to the transmission of philosophic theories into political practices. Cf. Singer *Animal Liberation* and Regan, *Case for Animal Rights,* with sociohistorical accounts of movement-building in Susan Sperling, *Animal Liberators: Research and Morality* (Berkeley: University of California Press, 1988) and James Jasper and Dorothy Nelkin, *The Animal Rights Crusade: The Growth of a Moral Protest* (New York: Free Press, 1992).

45. Wolfe, *Animal Rites,* 42.

46. Michael W. Fox, *Bringing Life to Ethics: Global Bioethics for a Humane Society* (Albany: SUNY Press, 2001), 57.

47. For the former, see Albert Schweitzer, *The Animal World of Albert Schweitzer,* ed. C. R. Joy (Boston: Beacon Press, 1950) and *The Teaching of Reverence for Life,* ed. R. Winston and C. Winston (New York: Holt, Rinehart and Winston, 1965); for the latter see Van Rensselaer Potter, *Bioethics: Bridge to the Future* (Englewood Cliffs: Prentice-Hall, 1971) and *Global Bioethics* (East Lansing: Michigan State University Press, 1988).

48. Derrida, "Animal That Therefore I Am," 395, quoted by Wolfe, *Zoontologies,* 34.

49. Wolfe, *Zoontologies,* 207, italics original. A relevant example of hyper-theory run amok is Giorgio Agamben, *The Open: Man and Animal,* trans. K. Attell (Stanford: Stanford University Press, 2004); a better model for balancing high-flying reflection with grass-rootsy experience can be found in Haraway, *Companion Species Manifesto.*

50. Aaltola "Other Animal Ethics," 204.

51. Adrian Franklin, *Animals and Modern Cultures: A Sociology of Human-Animal Relations in Modernity* (London: Sage, 1999), 174. The next two quotations are from this source, pp. 174, 188.

52. Arne J. Vetlesen, "Why Does Proximity Make a Moral Difference?" *Praxis International* 12 (1993): 383.

BIBLIOGRAPHY

Aaltola, Elisa. "'Other Animal Ethics' and the Demand for Difference." *Environmental Values* 11, no. 2 (2002).

Abram, David. "Merleau-Ponty and the Voice of the Earth." *Environmental Ethics* 10, no. 2 (Summer 1988): 101–20.

Acampora, C. D., and R. R. Acampora, eds. *A Nietzschean Bestiary: Becoming Animal Beyond Docile and Brutal.* Lanham: Rowman and Littlefield, 2004.

Acampora, Ralph R. "Extinction by Exhibition." *Human Ecology Review* 5, no. 1 (1998: 1–4).

———. "Human and Nonhuman Lifeworlds." *Environmental and Architectural Phenomenology* 3, no. 2 (1992): 10.

———. "Nietzsche's Feral Philosophy: Thinking Through an Animal Imaginary." In *A Nietzschean Bestiary: Becoming Animal Beyond Docile and Brutal,* edited by C. D. Acampora and R. R. Acampora, 1–13. Lanham: Rowman and Littlefield, 2004.

———. "*Oikos* and *Domus*: On Creative Co-Habitation with Other Creatures." *Philosophy and Geography* 7, no. 2 (August 2004): 219–35.

———. "The Problematic Situation of Post-Humanism and the Task of Recreating a Symphysical Ethos." *Between the Species: A Journal of Ethics* 11, no. 2 (Winter/Spring 1995): 25–29.

———. "Redemption from Extinction: Examining the Zoological Ark of Biotopia." *Between the Species: An Electronic Journal for the Study of Philosophy and Animals* (Spring 2002). http://cla.calpoly.edu/~jlynch/index.html.

———. "Using and Abusing Nietzsche for Environmental Ethics." *Environmental Ethics* 16, no. 2 (1994): 187–94.

———. "Zoöpticon: Inspecting the Site of Live Animal Infotainment." In *Phenomenological Approaches to Popular Culture,* edited by Michael T. Carroll and Eddie Tafoya. Bowling Green: Popular Press, 2000 (copyright University of Wisconsin Press).

———. "Zoos and Eyes: Contesting Captivity and Seeking Successor Practices." *Society and Animals* 13, no. 1 (2005): 69–88.

Adams, Carol J. *Neither Man nor Beast: Feminism and the Defense of Animals.* New York: Continuum, 1994.

———. *The Sexual Politics of Meat: Feminist-Vegetarian Critical Theory.* Pbk. ed. New York: Continuum, 1991.

Agamben, Giorgio. *The Open: Man and Animal.* Translated by K. Attell. Stanford: Stanford University Press, 2004.

Albert, Hans. *Treatise on Critical Reason.* Translated by M. V. Rorty. Princeton: Princeton University Press, 1985.

Angier, Natalie. "Scientists Mull Role of Empathy in Man and Beast." *New York Times,* May 9, 1995, sec. C, pp. 1, 6.

Arehart-Treichel, Joan. "Animal Science from the Animals' Perspective." *Science News* 122 (July 24, 1982): 59–62.

Aristotle. *Nicomachean Ethics.* Translated by T. Irwin. Indianapolis: Hackett, 1985.

Aschoff, Jurgen. "Temporal Orientation: Circadian Clocks in Animals and Humans." *Animal Behaviour* 37 (June 1989): 881–97.

Asenjo, F. G. *In-Between: An Essay on Categories.* Washington, DC: Center for Advanced Research in Phenomenology and University Press of America, 1988.

Atterton, P. "Ethical Cynicism," in *Animal Philosophy: Ethics and Identity,* edited by P. Atterton and M. Calarco. London: Continuum, 2004.

Atterton, P., and M. Calarco, eds. *Animal Philosophy: Ethics and Identity.* London: Continuum, 2004.

Attfield, Robin. *The Ethics of Environmental Concern.* New York: Columbia University Press, 1983.

Bachelard, Gaston. *The Poetics of Space.* Translated by Maria Jolas. Boston: Beacon Press, 1969.

Banaan, John. *The Philosophy of Merleau-Ponty.* New York: Harcourt, Brace and World, 1967.

Bataille, Georges. *Visions of Excess: Selected Writings, 1927–1939.* Theory and History of Literature, vol. 14. Minneapolis: University of Minnesota Press, 1985.

Batten, Peter, with D. Stancil. *Living Trophies: A Shocking Look at the Conditions in America's Zoos.* New York: Thomas Y. Crowell, 1976.

Baudrillard, Jean. *America.* Translated by C. Turner. London: Verso, 1988.

Bennett, Jane. *Unthinking Faith and Enlightenment: Nature and the State in a Post-Hegelian Era.* New York: NYU Press, 1987.

Bennett, M., and D. Teague, eds. *Nature of Cities: Ecocriticism and Urban Environments.* Tucson: University of Arizona Press, 1999.

Benton, Ted. "Humanism = Speciesism? Marx on Humans and Animals." In *Socialism, Feminism and Philosophy: A Radical Philosophy Reader,* edited by Sean Sayers and Peter Osborne. New York: Routledge, 1990.

———. *Natural Relations: Ecology, Animal Rights and Social Justice.* London: Verso, 1993.

Berger, John. *About Looking.* New York: Pantheon, 1980.

Bergson, Henri. *Matter and Memory.* Translated by N. M. Paul and W. S. Palmer. Garden City: Doubleday, 1959.

Berleant, Arnold. *The Aesthetics of Environment.* Philadelphia: Temple University Press, 1992.

Berry, Donald L. *Mutuality: The Vision of Martin Buber.* Albany: SUNY Press, 1985.

Beston, Henry. *The Outermost House: A Year of Life on the Great Beach of Cape Cod.* Garden City: Doubleday, 1928.

Bigwood, Carol. *Earth Muse: Feminism, Nature, and Art.* Philadelphia: Temple University Press, 1993.

———. "Renaturalizing the Body (With the Help of Merleau-Ponty)." *Hypatia* 6, no. 3 (1991).

Birch, Thomas H. "The Incarceration of Wildness: Wilderness Areas as Prison." *Environmental Ethics* 12, no. 1 (Spring 1990): 3–26.

———. "Moral Considerability and Universal Consideration." *Environmental Ethics* 15, no. 4 (1993): 313–32.

Birke, Lynda. "Who—or What—Are the Rats (and Mice) in the Laboratory?" *Society and Animals* 11, no. 3 (2003): 207–24.

Bly, Robert. *Iron John: A Book about Men.* Reading: Addison-Wesley, 1990.

Böhme, Gernot. *Fur eine ökologische Naturasthetik.* Frankfurt am Main: Suhrkamp, 1989.

Boone, J. A. *Kinship with All Life.* New York: Harper and Row, 1954.

Bordo, Susan. "Bringing Body to Theory." In *Body and Flesh: A Philosophical Reader,* edited by Donn Welton, 84–97. Oxford: Blackwell, 1998.

———. "Feminism, Postmodernism, and Gender-Skepticism." In *Feminism/Postmodernism,* edited by L. J. Nicholson. New York: Routledge, 1990.

———. *Unbearable Weight: Feminism, Western Culture, and the Body.* Berkeley: University of California Press, 1993.

Bostock, Stephen St. C. *Zoos and Animal Rights: The Ethics of Keeping Animals.* London: Routledge, 1993.

Braio, F. P. *Lonergan's Retrieval of the Notion of Human Being.* Lanham: University Press of America, 1988.

Braithwaite, John, and V. Braithwaite. "Attitudes toward Animal Suffering: An Exploratory Study." *International Journal of the Study of Animals* 3 (1982): 42–49.

Brand, Peter. *Urban Environmentalism.* New York: Routledge, 2005.

Braudel, Fernand. *The Mediterranean and the Mediterranean World in the Age of Philip II.* Vol. 1. Translated by Sian Reynolds. New York: Harper and Row, 1972.

Brown, Charles, and Ted Toadvine, eds. *Eco-Phenomenology: Back to the Earth Itself.* Albany: SUNY Press, 2003.

Bruhac, Joseph, comp. *Native American Animal Stories.* Golden, CO: Fulcrum, 1992.

Brumbaugh, Robert S. "Of Man, Animals, and Morals: A Brief History." In *On the Fifth Day,* edited by R. K. Morris and M. W. Fox. Washington, DC: Acropolis, 1978.

Buber, Martin. *I and Thou.* Translated by W. Kaufmann. New York: Charles Scribner's Sons, 1970.

Bullock, Marcus. "Watching Eyes, Seeing Dreams, Knowing Lives." In *Representing Animals,* edited by N. Rothfels, 99–118. Bloomington: Indiana University Press, 2002.

Butler, Judith. *Bodies That Matter.* New York: Routledge, 1993.

Buytendijk, Frederik Jacobus Johannes. *Prolegomena to an Anthropological Physiology.* Translated by A. Giorgi et al. Pittsburgh: Duquesne University Press, 1974.

Cabanas, Pierre Jean George. *On the Relations Between the Physical and Moral Aspects of Man.* Translated by Margaret Duggan Saidaj, edited by George Mora. Baltimore: The Johns Hopkins University Press, 1981.

Calarco, Matthew. "Levinas' Dreaded Comparison," In *Radicalizing Levinas*. Albany: SUNY Press, forthcoming.

Callicott, J. Baird. *Earth's Insights: A Survey of Ecological Ethics from the Mediterranean Basin to the Australian Outback*. Berkeley: University of California Press, 1994.

———. *In Defense of the Land Ethic: Essays in Environmental Philosophy*. Albany: SUNY Press, 1989.

———. "Intrinsic Value in Nature." *Electronic Journal of Analytic Philosophy* 3 (Spring 1995): art. 4. http://ejap.louisiana.edu/archives.html.

———. "Intrinsic Value, Quantum Theory, and Environmental Ethics." *Environmental Ethics* 7, no. 3 (Fall 1985): 257–76.

Caputi, Mary. *Voluptuous Yearnings: A Feminist Theory of the Obscene*. Lanham: Rowman and Littlefield, 1994.

Caputo, John. *Against Ethics: Contributions to a Poetics of Obligation with Constant Reference to Deconstruction*. Bloomington: Indiana University Press, 1993.

Carkeek, Freya, and Paul James. "This Abstract Body." *Arena* 99/100 (1992): 66–85.

Carter, Richard B. "Political Animals and Social Animals as Biologically Meaningful Categories." *Human Studies* 11 (January 1988): 65–86.

Carter, William R. "Why Personal Identity Is Animal Identity." *Logos [USA]* 11 (1990): 71–81.

Cartmill, Matt. *A View to Death in the Morning: Hunting and Nature through History*. Cambridge, MA: Harvard University Press, 1993.

Casey, Edward. *Getting Back into Place: Toward a Renewed Understanding of the Place-World*. Bloomington: Indiana University Press, 1993.

Cataldi, Sue. *Emotion, Depth, and Flesh: A Study of Sensitive Space*. Albany: SUNY Press, 1993.

Cave, George P. "Animals, Heidegger, and the Right to Life." *Environmental Ethics* 4 (Fall 1982): 249–54.

Chadwick, Helen. *Enfleshings*. New York: Aperture, 1989.

Clark, David. "On Being the Last Kantian in Nazi Germany: Dwelling with Animals after Levinas." In *Animal Acts: Configuring the Human in Western History*, edited by Jennifer Ham and M. Senior, 165–93. New York: Routledge, 1997.

Classen, Constance. *Worlds of Sense: Exploring the Senses in History and across Cultures*. London: Routledge, 1993.

Cobb, John B., Jr. "Beyond Anthropocentrism in Ethics and Religion." In *On the Fifth Day*, edited by R. K. Morris and M. W. Fox. Washington, DC: Acropolis, 1978.

Coetzee, J. M. *The Lives of Animals*. Edited by A. Gutmann. Princeton: Princeton University Press, 1999.

Collard, Andree, and Joyce Contrucci. *Rape of the Wild: Man's Violence Against Animals and the Earth*. Bloomington and Indianapolis: Indiana University Press, 1989.

Collingwood, R. G. *The Idea of Nature*. 1945. Reprint. New York: Oxford University Press, Galaxy, 1960.

Compton, John. "Reinventing the Philosophy of Nature." *Review of Metaphysics* 33 (September 1979).

Crary, Jonathan, and Sanford Kwinter. *Incorporations*. Zone Series. Cambridge, MA: MIT Press, 1992.

Curtin, Deane, and L. Heldke, eds. *Cooking, Eating, Thinking: Transformative Philosophies of Food*. Bloomington: Indiana University Press, 1992.

Dallery, Carleton. "Thinking and Being with Beasts." In *On the Fifth Day*, edited by R. K. Morris and M. W. Fox. Washington, DC: Acropolis, 1978.

Daly, Mary. *Pure Lust*. Boston: Beacon, 1984.

Daston, L., and G. Mitman eds. *Thinking With Animals: New Perspectives on Anthropomorphism*. New York: Columbia University Press, 2005.

Davis, Hank, and Dianne Balfour, eds. *The Inevitable Bond: Examining Scientist-Animal Interactions*. Cambridge: Cambridge University Press, 1992.

Davis, Karen. "The Otherness of Animals." *Between the Species: A Journal of Ethics* 4 (Fall 1988): 261–62.

DeGrazia, David. *Taking Animals Seriously: Mental Life and Moral Status*. Cambridge: Cambridge University Press, 1996.

Del Caro, Adrian. *Grounding the Nietzsche Rhetoric of Earth*. Berlin: Walter de Gruyter, 2004.

Deleuze, Gilles, and Felix Guattari. *Kafka: Toward a Minor Literature*. Translated by D. Polan. Minneapolis: University of Minnesota Press, 1986.

———. *A Thousand Plateaus: Capitalism and Schizophrenia*. Vol. 2. Translated by Brian Massumi. Minneapolis: University of Minnesota Press, 1987.

Derrida, Jacques. "And Say the Animal Responded?" Translated by D. Wills. In *Zoontologies*, edited by C. Wolfe, 121–46. Minneapolis: University of Minnesota Press, 2003.

———. "The Animal That Therefore I Am (More to Follow)." Translated by D. Wills. *Critical Inquiry* 28, no. 2 (Winter 2002): 369–418.

———. *Of Spirit: Heidegger and the Question*. Translated by G. Bennington and R. Bowlby. Chicago: University of Chicago Press, 1989.

Deutsch, Eliot. "The Concept of the Body." In *Self as Body in Asian Theory and Practice*, edited by T. Kasulis et al. Albany: SUNY Press, 1993.

Devall, Bill, and George Sessions. *Deep Ecology: Living as if Nature Mattered*. Salt Lake City: Peregrine Smith, 1985.

de Waal, Frans. *Good Natured: The Origins of Right and Wrong in Humans and Other Animals*. Cambridge, MA: Harvard University Press, 1996.

Dewey, John. *The Moral Writing of John Dewey*, edited by J. Gouinlock. New York: Hafner Press, 1976.

———. *Theory of Valuation*. Vol. 2, no. 4 of the *International Encyclopedia of Unified Science*. Chicago: University of Chicago Press, 1939 and 1966.

Diamond, Irene, and Gloria Feman Orenstein. *Reweaving the World: The Emergence of Ecofeminism*. San Francisco: Sierra Club, 1990.

Dijkgraaf, Sven. "An Excursion through the Sensory World of Animals." In *Man and Animal*, translated by M. Nawiasky. London: MacGibbon and Kee, 1972.

Dillon, Martin C. *Merleau-Ponty's Ontology*. Bloomington: Indiana University Press, 1988.

————. *Semiological Reductionism: A Critique of the Deconstructionist Movement in Postmodern Thought.* Albany: SUNY Press, 1995.

Diprose, Rosalyn, and Robyn Ferrell, eds. *Cartographies: Poststructuralism and the Mapping of Bodies and Spaces.* North Sydney: Allen and Unwin, 1991.

"Does Humanism Encourage Human Chauvinism?" special issue of *Free Inquiry* (Spring 1993).

Dombrowski, Daniel. *Hartshorne and the Metaphysics of Animal Rights.* Albany: SUNY Press, 1988.

Donnelley, S., and K. Nolan, eds. "Animals, Science, Ethics." *Hastings Center Report* (May/June 1990): supplement.

Donovan, Josephine. "Attention to Suffering." In *Beyond Animal Rights: A Feminist Caring Ethic for the Treatment of Animals,* edited by Josephine Donovan and Carol Adams, 147–69. New York: Continuum, 1996.

Donovan, Josephine, and Carol Adams, eds. *Beyond Animal Rights: A Feminist Caring Ethic for the Treatment of Animals.* New York: Continuum, 1996.

Dreyfus, Hubert L., and Paul Rabinow. *Michel Foucault: Beyond Structuralism and Hermeneutics.* 2nd ed. Chicago: University of Chicago Press, 1983.

Driesch, Hans. *The History and Theory of Vitalism.* Translated by C. Ogden. London: Macmillan, 1914.

Duerr, Hans Peter. *Dreamtime: Concerning the Boundary Between Wilderness and Civilization.* Translated by Felicitas Goodman. Oxford: Blackwell, 1985.

Dufresne, Jacques. "The Meaning of Biodome." *Quatre-Temps* 16, no. 2 (Summer 1992): 6–12.

Dutton, Diane, and Carl Williams. "A View from the Bridge: Subjectivity, Embodiment, and Animal Minds." *Anthrozoös* 17, no. 3 (2004): 210–24.

Dyens, Olivier. *Metal and Flesh.* Translated by Evan J. Bibbee. Cambridge, MA: MIT Press, 2001.

Eco, Umberto. *Travels in Hyper-Reality.* San Diego: Harcourt Brace Jovanovich, 1986.

Edel, Abraham, Elizabeth Flower, and Finbarr W. O'Connor. *Critique of Applied Ethics: Reflections and Recommendations.* Philadelphia: Temple University Press, 1994.

Ehrenfeld, David. *The Arrogance of Humanism.* New York: Oxford University Press, 1978.

Eisnitz, Gail. *Slaughterhouse.* Amherst, NY: Prometheus, 1997.

Estep, D., and S. Hetts. "Interactions, Relationships, and Bonds: The Conceptual Basis for Scientist-Animal Relations." In *The Inevitable Bond: Examining Scientist-Animal Interactions,* edited by Hank Davis and Dianne Balfour. Cambridge: Cambridge University Press, 1992.

Estes, Clarissa Pinkola. *Women Who Run With the Wolves: Myths and Stories of the Wild Woman Archetype.* New York: Ballantine, 1992.

Evernden, Neil. *The Natural Alien: Humankind and Environment.* Toronto: University of Toronto Press, 1985. 2nd ed., 1993.

————. *The Social Creation of Nature.* Baltimore: The Johns Hopkins University Press, 1992.

Feher, Michel, Ramona Naddaff, and Nadia Tazi, eds. *Fragments for a History of the Human Body.* 3 vols. Zone Series. Cambridge, MA: MIT Press, 1989.

Findlay, J. N. *Axiological Ethics.* London: Macmillan/St. Martin's, 1970.

———. *Values and Intentions.* New York: Macmillan, 1961.

Fischer, Angelika. "Bodies, Selves, and Boundaries: A Look at the Social Construction of the Body in Western and Aboriginal Culture." Master's thesis, University of Western Australia (Nedlands), 1984.

Foltz, Bruce V. *Inhabiting the Earth: Heidegger, Environmental Ethics, and the Metaphysics of Nature.* Atlantic Highlands: Humanities Press, 1995.

———. "On Heidegger and the Interpretation of Environmental Crisis." *Environmental Ethics* 6 (Winter 1984): 323–38.

Forman, Richard T. T. *Land Mosaics: The Ecology of Landscapes and Regions.* New York: Cambridge University Press, 1995.

Foucault, Michel. *The Birth of the Clinic: An Archaeology of Medical Perception.* Translated by A. M. Sheridan-Smith. New York: Pantheon, 1973.

———. *Discipline and Punish: The Birth of the Prison.* Translated by Alan Sheridan. New York: Random House, 1977.

———. "How is Power Exercised?" Translated by L. Sawyer. In *Michel Foucault: Beyond Structuralism and Hermeneutics*, edited by H. Dreyfus and P. Rabinow. Chicago: University of Chicago Press, 1983.

Fowler, Murray. *Restraint and Handling of Wild and Domestic Animals.* 2nd ed. Ames: Iowa State University Press, 1995.

Fox, Michael Allen. "Animal Experimentation: A Philosopher's Changing Views." *Between the Species: A Journal of Ethics* 3 (Spring 1987): 55–60.

Fox, Michael W. *Bringing Life to Ethics: Global Bioethics for a Humane Society.* Albany: SUNY Press, 2001.

———. "Relationships between the Human and Nonhuman Animals." In *Interrelationships between People and Pets,* edited by B. Fogle. Springfield, IL: Charles C. Thomas, 1981.

———. "Species Identity and Self-Awareness." In *Species Identity and Attachment*, edited by M. Aaron Roy. New York: Garland Press, 1980.

Fox, Warwick. *Toward a Transpersonal Ecology: Developing New Foundations for Environmentalism.* Boston: Shambhala, 1990.

Franck, Didier. "Being and the Living." Translated by P. T. Connor. In *Who Comes After the Subject?* edited by E. Cadava et al. New York: Routledge, 1991.

Franklin, Adrian. *Animals and Modern Cultures: A Sociology of Human-Animal Relations in Modernity.* London: Sage, 1999.

Franklin, Julian. *Animal Rights and Moral Philosophy.* New York: Columbia University Press, 2005.

Frondizi, Risieri. *What is Value? An Introduction to Axiology.* 2nd ed. LaSalle: Open Court, 1971.

Frye, Marilyn. *The Politics of Reality.* Trumanburg, NY: Crossing Press, 1983.

Fuller, Andrew. *Insight into Value: An Exploration of the Premises of a Phenomenological Psychology.* Albany: SUNY Press, 1990.

Gamble, M. R. "The Design of Experiments." In *Laboratory Animals: An Introduction for New Experimenters,* edited by A. A. Tuffery. Chichester: John Wiley and Sons, 1987.

Gardiner, Robert W. "Between Two Worlds: Humans in Nature and Culture." *Environmental Ethics* 12 (Winter 1990): 33–52.

Garner, Richard. *Beyond Morality.* Philadelphia: Temple University Press, 1994.

Gewirth, Alan. *Reason and Morality.* Chicago: University of Chicago Press, 1978.

Giles, James. "Bodily Theory and Theory of the Body." *Philosophy: The Journal of the Royal Institute of Philosophy* 66 (July 1991): 339–47.

Gilligan, Carol. *In a Different Voice: Psychological Theory and Women's Development.* Cambridge, MA: Harvard University Press, 1982.

Giraud, Raymond. "Rousseau and Voltaire: The Enlightenment and Animal Rights." *Between the Species: A Journal of Ethics* 1 (Winter 1984–85): 4–9.

Glacken, Clarence J. *Traces on the Rhodian Shore: Nature and Culture in Western Thought from Ancient Times to the End of the Eighteenth Century.* Berkeley: University of California Press, 1967.

Godlovitch, Stanley, R. Godlovitch, and J. Harris. *Animals, Men and Morals: An Enquiry into the Maltreatment of Nonhumans.* New York: Taplinger, 1972.

Goodin, Robert. *Protecting the Vulnerable: A Reanalysis of Our Social Responsibilities.* Chicago: University of Chicago Press, 1985.

Grange, Joseph. "Being, Feeling, and Environment." *Environmental Ethics* 7 (Winter 1985): 351–64.

———. "Place, Body and Situation." In *Dwelling, Place and Environment,* edited by D. Seamon and R. Mugerauer. New York: Columbia University Press, 1989.

Grätzel, Stephan. *Die philosophische Entdeckung des Leibes.* Stuttgart: Franz Steiner, 1989.

Grene, Marjorie. *The Understanding of Nature: Essays in the Philosophy of Biology.* Vol. 23 of Boston Studies in the Philosophy of Science; Vol. 66 of Synthese Library. Dordrecht: D. Reidel, 1974.

Griffin, Donald. *Animal Minds.* Chicago: University of Chicago Press, 1992.

Griffiths, A. P., ed. *The Impulse to Philosophise.* Cambridge: Cambridge University Press, 1992.

Grosz, Elizabeth. *Volatile Bodies.* Bloomington: Indiana University Press, 1994.

Guerriere, Daniel. "Foundations for an Axiology of Life." *Journal of Value Inquiry* 18 (1984): 195–206.

Gutting, Gary. *Michel Foucault's Archaeology of Scientific Reason.* Modern European Philosophy. Cambridge: Cambridge University Press, 1989.

Haar, Michel. *The Song of the Earth.* Translated by R. Lilly. Bloomington: Indiana University Press, 1993.

Haldane, John. "Philosophy and the Ethics of the Environment." In *Ethics and the Environment,* edited by C. C. W. Taylor. Oxford: Corpus Christi College, 1992.

Hales, Steven, and Rex Welshon. *Nietzsche's Perspectivism.* Urbana: University of Illinois Press, 2000.

Hallman, Max O. "Nietzsche's Environmental Ethics." *Environmental Ethics* 13 (Summer 1991): 99–125.

Ham, Jennifer, and M. Senior, eds. *Animal Acts: Configuring the Human in Western History.* New York: Routledge, 1997.

Hanna, Thomas. *Bodies in Revolt: A Primer in Somatic Thinking.* New York: Holt, Rinehart and Winston, 1970.

Haraway, Donna J. *The Companion Species Manifesto: Dogs, People, and Significant Otherness.* Chicago: Prickly Paradigm Press, 2003

———. *Primate Visions: Gender, Race and Nature in the World of Modern Science.* New York and London: Routledge, 1989.

———. *Simians, Cyborgs, and Women: The Reinvention of Nature.* New York: Routledge, 1991.

Harré, Rom. *Physical Being: A Theory for a Corporeal Psychology.* Oxford: Blackwell, 1991.

Hart, J., and L. Embree, eds. *Phenomenology of Values and Valuing.* Dordrecht: Kluwer, 1997.

Hatab, Lawrence. *Ethics and Finitude: Heideggerian Contributions to Moral Philosophy.* Lanham: Rowman and Littlefield, 2000.

Hearne, Vicki. *Adam's Task: Calling Animals by Name.* New York: Random House, Vintage, 1987.

———. *Animal Happiness.* New York: HarperCollins, 1994.

Hediger, Heini. *Man and Animal in the Zoo.* Translated by G. Vevers and W. Reade. New York: Seymour Lawrence/Delacorte Press, 1969.

———. *Studies of the Psychology and Behavior of Captive Animals in Zoos and Circuses.* Translated by G. Sircom. London: Butterworths Scientific Publications, 1955.

———. *Wild Animals in Captivity.* Translated by G. Sircom. London: Butterworths Scientific Publications, 1950.

Heidegger, Martin. *Basic Writings.* Translated by David Farrell Krell. New York: Harper and Row, 1977.

———. *Being and Time.* Translated by John Macquarrie and Edward Robinson. New York: Harper and Row, 1962.

———. *Die Grundbegriffe der Metaphysik.* Vol. 29/30 of *Gesamtausgabe.* Frankfurt am Main: V. Klostermann, 1982. Translated by W. McNeill and N. Walker as *The Fundamental Concepts of Metaphysics: World, Finitude, Solitude.* Bloomington: Indiana University Press, 1995.

———. *Kant and the Problem of Metaphysics.* 4th ed. Translated by R. Taft. Bloomington: Indiana University Press, 1990.

———. *Nietzsche, Volume II: The Eternal Recurrence of the Same.* Translated by D. F. Krell. San Francisco: HarperCollins, 1984/1991.

———. *Poetry, Language, Thought.* Translations by A. Hofstadter. New York: Harper and Row, 1971.

————. *The Question Concerning Technology and Other Essays.* Translated by William Lovitt. New York: Harper, Torchbooks, 1977.

Heller, Agnes. *A Philosophy of History in Fragments.* Oxford: Blackwell, 1993.

Henry, Michel. "The Critique of the Subject." Translated by P. T. Connor. In *Who Comes After the Subject?* edited by E. Cadava et al. New York: Routledge, 1991.

————. *Philosophy and Phenomenology of the Body.* Translated by G. Etzkorn. The Hague: Martinus Nijoff, 1975.

Herder, Johann Gottfried von. *Reflections on the Philosophy of the History of Mankind,* edited by F. E. Manuel. Chicago: University of Chicago Press, 1968.

Hoffman, Martin. *Empathy and Moral Development.* Cambridge: Cambridge University Press, 2000.

Holdrege, Craig. *The Flexible Giant: Seeing the Elephant Whole.* Ghent, NY: Nature Institute, 2003.

————. "How Does a Mole View the World?" *In Context* (Spring 2003).

Hollier, Denis. *Against Architecture: The Writings of Georges Bataille.* Translated by B. Wing. Cambridge, MA: MIT Press, 1989.

Hoy, David Couzens, ed. *Foucault: A Critical Reader.* Oxford: Blackwell, 1986.

Hume, David. *An Enquiry Concerning Human Understanding.* In *The Empiricists.* Garden City: Anchor/Doubleday, 1974.

Husserl, Edmund. *Cartesian Meditations.* Translated by D. Cairns. The Hague: Martinus Nijhoff, 1960.

————. *Ideas Pertaining to a Pure Phenomenology and to a Phenomenological Philosophy.* Book II: *Studies in the Phenomenology of Constitution.* Translated by R. Rojcewicz and A. Schuwer. Vol. 3 of *Edmund Husserl: Collected Works.* Dordrecht: Kluwer, 1989.

————. *Ideas Pertaining to a Pure Phenomenology and to a Phenomenological Philosophy.* Book III: *Phenomenology and the Foundations of the Sciences.* Translated by T. Klein and W. Pohl. Vol. 1 of *Edmund Husserl: Collected Works.* The Hague: Martinus Nijhoff, 1980.

Hutcheson, Francis. *An Essay on the Nature and Conduct of the Passions and Affections.* 3rd ed. Gainesville: Scholars' Facsimilies and Reprints, 1969 [1742].

Illich, Ivan. *Tools for Conviviality.* New York: Harper and Row, 1973.

Ingerson, Alice E. "Tracking and Testing the Nature-Culture Dichotomy." In *Historical Ecology: Cultural Knowledge and Changing Landscapes,* edited by C. L. Crumley, 43–66. Santa Fe: School of American Research Press, 1994.

Jager, Bernd. "Body, House and City." In *Dwelling, Place and Environment,* edited by D. Seamon and R. Mugerauer, 215–25. New York: Columbia University Press, 1989.

Jamieson, Dale. "Against Zoos." In *Reflecting on Nature: Readings in Environmental Philosophy,* edited by L. Gruen and D. Jamieson. Oxford: Oxford University Press, 1994.

Jasper, James, and Dorothy Nelkin. *The Animal Rights Crusade: The Growth of a Moral Protest.* New York: Free Press, 1992.

Johnson, Mark. *The Body in the Mind.* Chicago: University of Chicago Press, 1987.

————. *Moral Imagination: Implications of Cognitive Science for Ethics.* Chicago: University of Chicago Press, 1993.

Jonas, Hans. *The Imperative of Responsibility.* Chicago: University of Chicago Press, 1984.

————. *The Phenomenon of Life: Toward a Philosophical Biology.* New York: Harper and Row, 1966.

Kahn, P. H., and S. R. Kellert, eds. *Children and Nature: Psychological, Sociocultural, and Evolutionary Investigations.* Cambridge, MA: MIT Press, 2002.

Kant, Immanuel. *Lectures on Ethics.* Translated by L. Infield. London: Methuen and Co., 1963.

————. "What is Orientation in Thinking?" In *The Philosophy of the Body*, edited by Stuart Spicker. Chicago: Quadrangle Press, 1970.

Kasulis, T., et al., eds. *Self as Body in Asian Theory and Practice.* Albany: SUNY Press, 1993.

Katcher, Aaron Honori. "People and Companion Animal Dialogue: Style and Physiological Response." *National Forum: Phi Kappa Phi Journal* 66 (Winter 1986): 7–11.

Kaufmann, Walter. *Nietzsche: Philosopher, Psychologist, Antichrist.* Princeton: Princeton University Press, 1975/80.

Kellert, Stephen. *Kinship to Mastery: Biophilia in Human Evolution and Development.* Washington, DC: Island Press, 1997.

Kellert, Stephen, and E. O. Wilson, eds. *The Biophilia Hypothesis.* Washington, DC: Island Press, 1993.

Klein, Wayne. *Nietzsche and the Promise of Philosophy.* Albany: SUNY Press, 1997.

Kohak, Erazim. *The Embers and the Stars: A Philosophical Inquiry into the Moral Sense of Nature.* Chicago: University of Chicago Press, 1984.

Kojima, Hiroshi, ed. *Phanomenologie der Praxis im Dialog zwischen Japan und dem Westen.* Wurzburg: Konigshausen and Neumann, 1989.

Komesaroff, Paul. "Bioethics and Nature: The Case of Animal Experimentation." *Thesis Eleven* 32 (1992): 56–75.

Krell, David Farrell. *Daimon Life: Heidegger and Life-Philosophy.* Bloomington: Indiana University Press, 1992.

Krell, David Farrell, and Donald Bates. *The Good European: Nietzsche's Work Sites in Word and Image.* Chicago: University of Chicago Press, 1997.

Lakoff, George, and Mark Johnson. *Philosophy in the Flesh: The Embodied Mind and Its Challenge to Western Thought.* New York: Perseus/Basic, 1999.

Langer, Susanne K. *Mind: An Essay on Human Feeling.* Abridged by Gary Van Den Heuvel. Baltimore: Johns Hopkins Press, 1988.

Lawrence, Elizabeth A. "Relationships with Animals; The Impact of Human Culture." *National Forum: Phi Kappa Phi Journal* 66 (Winter 1986): 14–19.

Leder, Drew. *The Absent Body.* Chicago: University of Chicago Press, 1990.

————. "Flesh and Blood: A Proposed Supplement to Merleau-Ponty." In *The Body: Classic and Contemporary Readings*, edited by Donn Welton, 200–210. Oxford: Blackwell, 1999.

Le Dœuff, Michéle. *The Philosophical Imaginary.* Translated by Colin Gordon. London: Athlone Press, 1988.

Leopold, Aldo. *A Sand County Almanac.* New York: Oxford University Press, 1949.

Levin, David Michael. *The Body's Recollection of Being: Phenomenological Psychology and the Deconstruction of Nihilism.* London: Routledge and Kegan Paul, 1985.

———. "The Embodiment of Thinking: Heidegger's Approach to Language." In *Phenomenology: Dialogues and Bridges,* edited by Ronald Bruzina and Bruce Wilshire. Albany: SUNY Press, 1982.

———. *The Listening Self: Personal Growth, Social Change and the Closure of Metapysics.* New York: Routledge, 1989.

———. *The Opening of Vision: Nihilism and the Postmodern Situation.* London: Routledge and Kegan Paul, 1988.

Lingis, Alphonso. *The Community of Those Who Have Nothing in Common.* Bloomington: Indiana University Press, 1994.

———. *Excesses: Eros and Culture.* Albany: SUNY Press, 1984.

———. *Foreign Bodies.* New York: Routledge, 1994.

Lippitt, John, ed. *Nietzsche's Futures.* London: Macmillan, 1999.

Llewelyn, John. "Am I Obssessed by Bobby? (Humanism of the Other Animal)." In *Re-Reading Levinas,* edited by R. Bernasconi and S. Critchley. Bloomington: Indiana University Press, 1991.

———. *The Middle Voice of Ecological Conscience: A Chiasmic Reading of Responsibility in the Neighbourhood of Levinas, Heidegger, and Others.* New York: St. Martin's, 1991.

Lockwood, Randall. "Anthropomorphism Is Not a Four-Letter Word." Paper presented at the Conference on the Perception of Animals in American Culture, Washington, DC, 1983.

Lonergan, B. J. F. *Insight: A Study of Human Understanding.* Rev. ed. San Francisco: Harper and Row, 1978.

Lopez, Barry Holstun. *Of Wolves and Men.* New York: Charles Scribner's Sons, 1978.

Lovejoy, Arthur O. *The Great Chain of Being: A Study of the History of an Idea.* Cambridge, MA: Harvard University Press, 1978.

Machan, Tibor. *Putting Humans First: Why We Are Nature's Favorites.* Lanham: Rowman and Littlefield, 2004.

MacIntyre, Alasdair. *Dependent Rational Animals: Why Human Beings Need the Virtues.* Chicago: Open Court, 1999.

Madison, Gary. *The Phenomenology of Merleau-Ponty.* Athens: Ohio University Press, 1981.

Magnus, Bernd. "The Uses and Abuses of *The Will to Power.*" In *Reading Nietzsche,* edited by Robert C. Solomon and K. Higgins. Oxford: Oxford University Press, 1988.

Mandelbaum, Maurice. *The Phenomenology of Moral Experience.* Baltimore: Johns Hopkins University Press, 1969.

Manuel, F. E., ed. *The Enlightenment.* Englewood: Prentice-Hall, 1965.

Maple, Terry, and E. Archibald. *Zoo Man.* Atlanta: Longstreet, 1993.

Margodt, Koen. *The Welfare Ark: Suggestions for a Renewed Policy for Zoos.* Brussels: V.U.B. Press, 2001.

Marietta, Don E., Jr. "Knowledge and Obligation in Environmental Ethics: A Phenomenological Analysis." *Environmental Ethics* 4 (Summer 1982): 153–62.

Markowitz, Hal. *Behavioral Enrichment in the Zoo.* New York: Van Nostrand Reinhold, 1982.

Marx, Werner. *Towards a Phenomenological Ethics: Ethos and the Life World.* Translated by S. Heyvaert. Albany: SUNY Press, 1992.

Mason, Jim. *An Unnatural Order: Uncovering the Roots of Our Domination of Nature and Each Other.* New York: Simon and Schuster, 1993.

Mazis, Glen. *Earthbodies: Rediscovering Our Planetary Senses.* Albany: SUNY Press, 2002.

McKenna, E., and A. Light, eds. *Animal Pragmatism.* Bloomington: Indiana University Press, 2004.

McReynolds, Philip. "Overlapping Horizons of Meaning." in *Animal Pragmatism,* edited by E. McKenna and A. Light, 63–85. Bloomington: Indiana University Press, 2004.

Melle, Ullrich. "How Deep is Deep Enough? Ecological Modernization or Farewell to the World-City?" In *Environmental Philosophy and Environmental Activism,* D. Marietta and L. Embree, eds. Lanham: Rowman and Littlefield, 1995.

Mercer, Philip. *Sympathy and Ethics: A Study of the Relationship between Sympathy and Morality with Special Reference to Hume's* Treatise. Oxford: Clarendon Press, 1972.

Merchant, Carolyn. *The Death of Nature.* New York: Harper and Row, 1980.

Merleau-Ponty, Maurice. *In Praise of Philosophy and Other Essays.* Translated by J. O'Neill. Evanston: Northwestern University Press, 1988.

———. *Nature: Course Notes from the College de France.* Translated by R. Vallier and edited by D. Segland. Evanston: Northwestern University Press, 2003.

———. *Phenomenology of Perception.* Translated by C. Smith. London: Routledge and Kegan Paul, 1962; New Jersey: Humanities Press, 1989.

———. *The Primacy of Perception and Other Essays.* Edited by J. M. Edie. Evanston: Northwestern University Press, 1964.

———. *The Structure of Behavior.* Translated by A. L. Fisher. Boston: Beacon Press, 1963.

———. *The Visible and the Invisible.* Translated by A. Lingis. Evanston: Northwestern University Press, 1969.

Michelfelder, Diane. "Valuing Wildlife Populations in Urban Environments." *Journal of Social Philosophy* 34, no. 1 (Spring 2003).

Midgley, Mary. *Animals and Why They Matter.* Harmondsworth: Penguin, 1983.

———. *Beast and Man: The Roots of Human Nature.* Ithaca: Cornell University Press, 1978.

———. *Science as Salvation: A Modern Myth and Its Meaning.* London: Routledge, 1992.

Minson, Jeffrey. *Genealogies of Morals: Nietzsche, Foucault, Donzelot and the Eccentricity of Ethics.* New York: St. Martin's Press, 1985.

Moore, Gregory. *Nietzsche, Biology, and Metaphor.* Oxford: Oxford University Press, 2002.

Morris, David B. *The Culture of Pain.* Berkeley and Los Angeles: University of California Press, 1991.

Morris, Desmond. *The Human Zoo.* New York: McGraw Hill, 1969.

Mullan, Bob, and Garry Marvin. *Zoo Culture.* London: Weidenfeld and Nicolson, 1987.

Müller-Lauter, Wolfgang. *Nietzsche: His Philosophy of Contradictions and the Contradictions of His Philosophy.* Urbana: University of Illinois Press, 1999.

Myers, Olin Eugene. *Children and Animals: Social Development and Our Connections to Other Species.* Boulder: Westview, 1998.

Myers, Olin Eugene, and Carol Saunders. "Animal as Links toward Developing Caring Relationships with the Natural World." In *Children and Nature: Psychological, Sociocultural, and Evolutionary Investigations,* edited by P. H. Kahn and S. R. Kellert. Cambridge, MA: MIT Press, 2002.

Naess, Arne. *Ecology, Community, and Lifestyle: Outline of an Ecosophy.* Translated and revised by D. Rothenberg. Cambridge: Cambridge University Press, 1989.

———. "Notes on the Politics of the Deep Ecology Movement." In *Sustaining Gaia: Contributions to Another World View,* edited by Frank Fisher. Melbourne: Monash University (G.S.E.S.), 1987.

———. "The Shallow and the Deep, Long-Range Ecology Movement: A Summary." *Inquiry* 16, no. 1 (Spring 1973): 95–100.

Nagel, Thomas. *The Possibility of Altruism.* Oxford: Clarendon Press, 1970.

———. "What Is It Like to Be a Bat?" *Philosophical Review* 83 (October 1974): 435–50.

Naragon, Steven Scott. "Reason and Animals: Descartes, Kant, and Mead on the Place of Humans in Nature." Ph.D. diss., University of Notre Dame, 1987.

Neidjie, Bill. *Story about Feeling.* Edited by K. Taylor. Broome, W. Australia: Magabala, 1989.

Nepo, Mark. "The Bridge of Well-Being: The Stranger, The Fellow, The Completing Other." *Parabola* 22, no. 2 (May 1995): 17–20.

Nietzsche, Friedrich. *Beyond Good and Evil: Prelude to a Philosophy of the Future.* Translated by Walter Kaufmann. New York: Random House, Vintage, 1966.

———. *The Gay Science, with a Prelude in Rhymes and an Appendix of Songs.* Translated by Walter Kaufmann. New York: Random House, Vintage, 1974.

———. *Human, All-Too-Human.* Translated by M. Faber. Lincoln: University of Nebraska Press, 1984.

———. *On the Genealogy of Morals; Ecce Homo.* Translated by Walter Kaufmann (*Genealogy* with R. J. Hollingdale). New York: Random House, 1967; Vintage, 1969.

———. *The Portable Nietzsche* (including *Thus Spoke Zarathustra*). Edited and translated by Walter Kaufmann. New York: Viking, 1954; Penguin, 1976.

———. *Twilight of the Idols; The Anti-Christ(ian).* Translated by R. J. Hollingdale. New York: Penguin, 1968.

———. *Unmodern Observations.* Edited by W. Arrowsmith. New Haven: Yale University Press, 1990.

———. *The Will to Power.* Translated by Walter Kaufmann and R. J. Hollingdale; edited by Walter Kaufmann. New York: Random House, Vintage, 1968.

Noddings, Nel. *Caring: A Feminine Approach to Ethics and Moral Education.* Berkeley and Los Angeles: University of California Press, 1984.

Noë, Alva. *Action in Perception.* Cambridge, MA: MIT Press, 2005.

Norris, Margot. *Beasts of the Modern Imagination: Darwin, Nietzsche, Kafka, and Lawrence.* Baltimore: Johns Hopkins University Press, 1985.

Noske, Barbara. *Humans and Other Animals: Beyond the Boundaries of Anthropology.* London: Pluto Press, 1989.

Novalis. *The Novices of Sais.* New York: Curt Valentin, 1949.

Oliver, Mary. "Wild Geese." In *Dream Work.* Boston: Atlantic Monthly Press, 1986.

Ortega y Gasset, Jose. *Kant. Hegel. Dilthey.* 2nd ed. Madrid: Revista de Occidente, 1961.

———. *Meditations on Hunting.* Translated by H. B. Wescott. 1942. Reprint, New York: Charles Scribner's Sons, 1972.

Paci, Enzo. "The *Lebenswelt* as Ground and as *Leib* in Husserl." In *Patterns of the Life-World: Essays in Honor of John Wild,* edited by J. M. Edie et al. Evanston: Northwestern University Press, 1970.

Parkes, Graham. *Composing the Soul.* Chicago: University of Chicago Press, 1994.

———. "Staying Loyal to the Earth: Nietzsche as an Ecological Thinker." In *Nietzsche's Futures,* edited by John Lippitt, 167–86. London: Macmillan, 1999.

Parviainen, Jaana. "Kinaesthetic Empathy." *Dialogue and Universalism* 13 no. 11/12 (2003): 151–62.

Patterson, Charles. *Eternal Treblinka: Our Treatment of Animals and the Holocaust.* New York: Lantern, 2002.

Perricone, Christopher. "Bugged Out: A Reflection on Art Experience." *Journal of Aesthetic Education* 37, no. 2 (Summer 2003): 19–30.

Phelan, Shane. "Intimate Distance: The Dislocation of Nature in Modernity." In *In the Nature of Things: Language, Politics, and the Environment,* edited by J. Bennett and W. Chaloupka, 44–62. Minneapolis: University of Minnesota Press, 1993.

Pluhar, Evelyn. *Beyond Prejudice: The Moral Significance of Human and Nonhuman Animals.* Durham: Duke University Press, 1995.

Polanyi, Michael. *The Study of Man.* London: Routledge and Kegan Paul, 1959.

Polhemus, Ted, ed. *The Body Reader: Social Aspects of the Human Body.* New York: Pantheon, 1978.

Polk, Danne. "Un-Cartesian Nature: Merleau-Ponty and Postmodern Ecology." *Skepteon* 1 (1993): 27–52.

Poole, Joyce. *Coming of Age With Elephants.* New York: Hyperion, 1996.

Portmann, Adolf. *Animal Forms and Patterns.* Translated by H. Czech. New York: Schocken, 1967.

———. *Essays in Philosophical Zoology: The Living Form and the Seeing Eye.* Translated by Richard B. Carter. Lewiston, NY: Edwin Mellen Press, 1990.

Potter, Van Rensselaer. *Bioethics: Bridge to the Future.* Englewood Cliffs: Prentice-Hall, 1971.

———. *Global Bioethics.* East Lansing: Michigan State University Press, 1988.

Quammen, David. "Planet of Weeds." *Harper's* 297, no. 1781 (1998): 57–69.

Raphael, David Daiches. *The Moral Sense.* London: Geoffrey Cumberlege, 1947.

Redner, Harry. *In the Beginning Was the Deed: Reflections on the Passage of Faust.* Berkeley: University of California Press, 1982.

Reed, T. J. "Nietzsche's Animals: Idea, Image and Influence." In *Nietzsche: Image and Thought: A Collection of Essays,* edited by Malcolm Pasley. Berkeley: University of California Press, 1978.

Regan, Tom. *The Case for Animal Rights.* Berkeley and Los Angeles: University of California Press, 1983.

Reiner, Hans. *Duty and Inclination: The Fundamentals of Morality.* The Hague: Martinus Nijhoff, 1983.

Richardson, John. *Nietzsche's New Darwinism.* Oxford: Oxford University Press, 2005.

Rigby, Kate. "Beyond the Frame: Art, Ecology, and the Aesthetics of Nature." *Thesis Eleven* 32 (1992): 114–28.

Rilke, Rainer Maria. "The Panther." In *The Selected Poetry of Rainer Maria Rilke,* translated by S. Mitchell. New York: Random House, Vintage, 1989.

Ritvo, Harriet *The Animal Estate: The English and Other Creatures in the Victorian Age.* Cambridge, MA: Harvard University Press, 1982.

Rodman, John R. "Four Forms of Ecological Consciousness Reconsidered." In *Ethics and the Environment,* edited by D. Scherer and T. Attig. Englewood Cliffs: Prentice-Hall, 1983.

Rollin, B. E. *The Unheeded Cry: Animal Consciousness, Animal Pain, and Science.* New York: Oxford University Press, 1981.

Rose, M., and D. Adam. "Evidence for Pain and Suffering in Other Animals." In *Animal Experimentation: The Consensus Changes,* edited by G. Langley. New York: Chapman and Hall, 1989.

Rowan, Andrew, et al. "Animal Research, For and Against: Philosophical, Social and Historical Perspective." *Biological Medicine* 27 (1983): 1–7.

Roy, M. Aaron. *Species Identity and Attachment.* New York: Garland, 1980.

Rue, Loyal D. "Philosophy and the Natural History of Culture." *Contemporary Philosophy: Philosophic Research, Analysis, and Resolution* 12 (January 1988): 12–16.

Russow, Lily-Marlene. "Why Do Species Matter?" *Environmental Ethics* 3, no. 2 (1981).

Sabloff, Annabelle. *Reordering the Natural World.* Toronto: University of Toronto Press, 2001.

Salt, Henry S. *Animals' Rights: Considered in Relation to Social Progress.* 1892. Reprint. Clarks Summit, PA: Society for Animal Rights, 1980.

Sartre, Jean-Paul. *Being and Nothingness: A Phenomenological Essay on Ontology.* Translated by H. E. Barnes. New York: Washington Square Press/Simon and Schuster, 1966.

———. *Critique of Dialectical Reason.* Translated by A. Sheridan Smith. London and Atlantic Highlands: Humanities Press, 1976.

———. "Faces." In *Essays in Phenomenology,* edited by M. Natanson. The Hague: Martinus Nijhoff, 1966.

Scarry, Elaine. *The Body in Pain: The Making and Unmaking of the World.* New York: Oxford University Press, 1985.

Scharfstein, Ben-Ami. *Of Birds, Beasts, and Other Artists: An Essay on the Universality of Art.* New York: NYU Press, 1988.

Scheler, Max. *Formalism in Ethics and Non-Formal Ethics of Values: A New Attempt toward the Foundation of an Ethical Personalism.* Translated by Mannfred S. Frings and Roger L. Funk. Evanston: Northwestern University Press, 1973.

———. *Man's Place in Nature.* Translated by Hans Meyerhoff. Boston: Beacon, 1961.

———. *The Nature of Sympathy.* Translated by Peter Heath. Hamden: Archon, 1970.

Schulze, E.-D., ed. *Flux Control in Biological Systems: From Enzymes to Populations and Ecosystems.* San Diego: Harcourt Brace, Academic Press, 1994.

Schweitzer, Albert. *Albert Schweitzer: An Anthology.* Enlarged by Charles R. Joy, ed. Boston: Beacon Press, 1956.

———. *The Animal World of Albert Schweitzer,* edited by C. R. Joy. Boston: Beacon Press, 1950.

———. *The Philosophy of Civilization.* Translated by C. T. Campion. Buffalo, NY: Prometheus, 1987.

———. *The Teaching of Reverence for Life,* edited by R. Winston and C. Winston. New York: Holt, Rinehart and Winston, 1965.

Scott, Charles E. *The Lives of Things.* Bloomington: Indiana University Press, 2002.

———. *The Question of Ethics: Nietzsche, Foucault, Heidegger.* Bloomington: Indiana University Press, 1990.

Seamon, David. "Different Worlds Coming Together." In *Dwelling, Seeing, and Designing: Toward a Phenomenological Ecology,* edited by David Seamon. Albany: SUNY Press, 1993.

Seamon, David, and Robert Mugerauer, eds. *Dwelling, Place and Environment: Towards a Phenomenology of Person and World.* 1985. Reprint. New York: Columbia University Press, Morningside, 1989.

Serpell, James. *In the Company of Animals: A History of Human-Animal Relationships.* Oxford: Blackwell, 1986.

Shapiro, Kenneth Joel. *Bodily Reflective Modes: A Phenomenological Method for Psychology.* Durham: Duke University Press, 1985.

———. "The Death of the Animal: Ontological Vulnerability." *Between the Species: A Journal of Ethics* 5 (Fall 1989): 183–93.

———. "Understanding Dogs Through Kinesthetic Empathy, Social Construction, and History." *Anthrozoös* 3, no. 3: 184–95.

Sheets-Johnstone, Maxine. *Giving the Body Its Due.* SUNY Series: The Body in Culture, History, and Religion. Albany: SUNY Press, 1992.

————. *The Primacy of Movement.* Amsterdam: John Benjamins, 1999.

————. *The Roots of Power.* LaSalle: Open Court, 1994.

————. *The Roots of Thinking.* Philadelphia: Temple University Press, 1990.

Shepard, Paul. "Introduction: Ecology and Man—A Viewpoint." In *The Subversive Science,* edited by P. Shepard and D. McKinley. Boston: Houghton Mifflin, 1969.

————. *Thinking Animals: Animals and the Development of Human Intelligence.* New York: Viking, 1978.

Shusterman, Richard. "Somaesthetics: A Disciplinary Proposal." *Journal of Aesthetics and Art Criticism* 57, no. 3 (Summer 1999): 299–313.

Silberstein, Moshe, and P. Tamir. "Factors which Affect Student's Attitudes towards the Use of Living Animals in Learning Biology." *Science Education* 65 (1981): 119–30.

Singer, Peter. *Animal Liberation: A New Ethics for Our Treatment of Animals.* New York: New York Review and Avon, 1975.

Sloterdijk, Peter. *Critique of Cynical Reason.* Translated by M. Eldred. Minneapolis: University of Minnesota Press, 1987.

Smuts, Barbara. "Reflection." In *The Lives of Animals,* by J. M. Coetzee, edited by A. Gutmann, 107–20. Princeton: Princeton University Press, 1999.

Solomon, Robert C. *History and Human Nature: A Philosophic Review of European Philosophy and Culture, 1750–1850.* New York: Harcourt Brace Jovanovich, 1979.

Solomon, Robert C., and K. Higgins, eds. *Reading Nietzsche.* Oxford: Oxford University Press, 1988.

Soper, Kate. *What Is Nature?* Oxford: Blackwell, 1995.

Sorabji, Richard. *Animal Minds and Human Morals.* London: Duckworth, 1993.

Sperling, Susan. *Animal Liberators: Research and Morality* (Berkeley: University of California Press, 1988)

Sperlinger, David. "Natural Relations: Contemporary Views of the Relationship Between Humans and Other Animals." In *Animals in Research.* N.p.: John Wiley and Sons, 1981.

Spicker, Stuart F., ed. *The Philosophy of the Body: Rejections of Cartesian Dualism.* Chicago: Quadrangle Press, 1970.

Spiegel, Marjorie. *The Dreaded Comparison: Human and Animal Slavery.* Philadelphia and London: New Society and Heretic, 1988.

Sprigge, T. L. S. "Metaphysics, Physicalism and Animals Rights." *Inquiry* 22, no. 1–2 (1978): 101–43.

Stafford, Barbara. *Body Criticism: Imaging the Unseen in Enlightenment Art and Medicine.* Cambridge, MA: MIT Press, 1991.

Steeves, H. Peter, ed. *Animal Others: On Ethics, Ontology, and Animal Life.* Albany: SUNY Press, 1999.

————. *Founding Community: A Phenomenological-Ethical Inquiry.* Dordrecht: Kluwer, 1998.

Stein, Edith. *On the Problem of Empathy.* Translated by W. Stein. Vol. 3 of *The Collected Works of Edith Stein.* 3rd ed. Washington, DC: ICS Publications, 1989.

Steinberg, Michael. *The Fiction of a Thinkable World: Body, Meaning, and the Culture of Capitalism.* New York: Monthly Review Press, 2005.

Steinbock, Anthony. "The Phenomenological Concepts of Normality and Abnormality." *Man and World,* 28, no. 3 (1995): 241–60.

Steiner, George. *Martin Heidegger.* New York: Viking, 1979; Chicago: University of Chicago Press, 1987.

Stern, Daniel N. *Diary of a Baby: What Your Child Sees, Feels, and Experiences.* New York: Basic, 1998.

Stone, Christopher D. *Earth and Other Ethics: The Case for Moral Pluralism.* New York: Harper and Row, 1987; Perennial, 1988.

Sullivan, Shannon. *Living Across and Through Skins: Transactional Bodies, Pragmatism, and Feminism.* Bloomington: Indiana University Press, 2001.

Tambornino, John. *The Corporeal Turn: Passion, Necessity, Politics.* Lanham: Rowman and Littlefield, 2002.

Taylor, Paul W. *Respect for Nature: A Theory of Environmental Ethics.* Princeton: Princeton University Press, 1986.

Thomas, Keith. *Man and the Natural World: A History of the Modern Sensibility.* New York: Pantheon, 1983.

Tiemersma, Douwe. *Body Schema and Body Image: An Interdisciplinary and Philosophical Study.* Amsterdam: Swets and Zeitlinger, 1989.

Tilghman, B. R. "What Is It Like to Be an Aardvark?" *Philosophy: The Journal of the Royal Institute of Philosophy* 66 (July 1991): 325–38.

Toulmin, Stephen. *Human Understanding.* Princeton: Princeton University Press, 1972.

———. *The Place of Reason in Ethics.* Cambridge: Cambridge University Press, 1958.

Tuan, Yi-Fu. *Dominance and Affection: The Making of Pets.* New Haven: Yale University Press, 1984.

———. *Morality and Imagination: Paradoxes of Progress.* Madison: University of Wisconsin Press, 1989.

———. *Topophilia: A Study of Environmental Perception, Attitudes, and Values.* Englewood Cliffs: Prentice-Hall, 1974.

Tudge, Colin. *Last Animals at the Zoo: How Mass Extinction Can Be Stopped.* Washington, DC: Island Press, 1992.

Tyler, Tom. "If Horses Had Hands . . ." *Society and Animals* 11, no. 3 (2003): 267–81.

Uexküll, Jakob von. "A Stroll Through the Worlds of Animals and Men: A Picture Book of Invisible Worlds." In *Instinctive Behavior: The Development of a Modern Concept,* translated and edited by C. H. Schiller. New York: International Universities Press, 1957.

VanDeVeer, Donald, and Christine Pierce, eds. *People, Penguins, and Plastic Trees: Basic Issues in Environmental Ethics.* Belmont, CA: Wadsworth, 1986.

Vetlesen, Arne J. *Perception, Empathy, and Judgment: An Inquiry into the Preconditions of Moral Performance.* State College: The Pennsylvania State University Press, 1994.

———. "Why Does Proximity Make a Moral Difference?" *Praxis International* 12, no. 4 (1993): 371–86.

Vockell, Edward L., and F. Hodal. "Humane Education: The Status of Current Research and Knowledge." Special Report. National Association for the Advancement of Humane Education. East Haddam, Conn.: n.d.

Volk, Tyler. *Gaia's Body: Toward a Physiology of Earth.* Cambridge, MA: MIT Press, 2003.

Warren, Karen J., ed. "Ecological Feminism," special issue of *Hypatia: A Journal of Feminist Philosophy* 6.1 (Spring 1991).

Watsuji, Tetsuro. *Climate and Culture: A Philosophical Study.* Translated by G. Bownas. Japan: The Hokuseido Press, 1961.

Weinstein, Michael A. *Finite Perfection: Reflections on Virtue.* Amherst: University of Massachusetts Press, 1985.

————. *Structure of Human Life: A Vitalist Ontology.* New York: NYU Press, 1979.

————. *The Tragic Sense of Political Life.* Columbia: University of South Carolina Press, 1977.

Wellford, Harrison. "The Politics of Meat." In *Sowing the Wind.* New York: Bantam, 1973.

Welton, Donn, ed. *The Body: Classic and Contemporary Readings.* Oxford: Blackwell, 1999.

————. *Body and Flesh: A Philosophical Reader.* Oxford: Blackwell, 1998.

Weston, Anthony. *Back to Earth: Tomorrow's Environmentalism.* Philadelphia: Temple University Press, 1994.

Westra, Laura. "Ecology and Animals: Is There a Joint Ethic of Respect?" *Environmental Ethics* 11 (Fall 1989): 215–30.

Wilson, Alexander. *The Culture of Nature: North American Landscape from Disney to the Exxon Valdez.* Cambridge: Blackwell, 1990.

Wilson, Edward O. *Biophilia.* Cambridge, MA: Harvard University Press, 1984.

————. *On Human Nature.* Cambridge, MA: Harvard University Press, 1978.

Wiseman, Mary Bittner. "Empathetic Identification." *American Philosophical Quarterly* 15, no. 2 (1978): 107–13.

Wispé, Lauren. *The Psychology of Sympathy.* Perspectives in Social Psychology. New York: Plenum, 1991.

Wolfe, Cary. *Animal Rites: American Culture, the Discourse of Species, and Posthumanist Theory.* Chicago: University of Chicago Press, 2003.

————, ed. *Zoontologies: The Question of the Animal.* Minneapolis: University of Minnesota Press, 2003.

Wu, Kuang-Ming. *On the "Logic" of Togetherness: A Cultural Hermeneutic.* Leiden: Brill, 1998.

Wyschogrod, Edith. "Does Continental Ethics Have a Future?" In *Ethics and Danger: Essays on Heidegger and Continental Thought,* edited by Arleen Dallery and Charles E. Scott with P. Holley Roberts. Albany: SUNY Press, 1992.

————. "Empathy and Sympathy as Tactile Encounter." *Journal of Medicine and Philosophy* 6 (1981): 24–43.

————. "Towards a Postmodern Ethics: Corporeality and Alterity." In *The Ethical,* edited by Edith Wyschogrod and G. McKenny, 54–65. Oxford: Blackwell, 2003.

Wyschogrod, Edith, and G. McKenny, eds. *The Ethical.* Oxford: Blackwell, 2003.

Zaner, Richard. *The Problem of Embodiment.* 2nd ed. The Hague: Martinus Nijhoff, 1971.

Zimmerman, Michael E. *Heidegger's Confrontation with Modernity: Technology, Politics, and Art.* Bloomington: Indiana University Press, 1990.

———. "Toward a Heideggerian *Ethos* for Radical Environmentalism." *Environmental Ethics* (Summer 1983): 99–131.

Zwart, Hub. "What Is an Animal? A Philosophical Reflection on the Possibility of a Moral Relationship with Animals." *Environmental Values* 6, no. 4 (1997): 377–92.

INDEX

Abram, David, 31, 147n43, 148n45, 148n47, 165n84
animality/animalness, 14–15, 21–23, 45–46, 63–69, 84, 88, 104–5, 118–19, 121–22, 133, 138n28, 141n68, 155n65, 156n73, 160n32, 167n15; alien, 6; essence of, 11; human, 37, 140n50, 156n73; non-human, 7, 16–17, 106; phenomenology of, 9
appreciation: animal, 71, 80, 93, 117, 122–23, 133; of body, 5, 49; and cognition, 151n15; conflictual, 151n3; and the process of valuing, 53–54; sensory-aesthetic, 56
axiology, 6, 23, 49, 52, 55, 95, 108, 152n22, 165n83; relational, 91, 121, 123–25, 151n12, 172n10; somatic, 53, 75

being-with, 8, 27, 36, 120, 125, 138n24
Berger, John, 43, 44, 108, 127, 162n54, 165n81, 170n60
Bigwood, Carol, 22, 36, 120, 139n43, 158n92, 172n6, 172n18
biocentric, 18, 33, 91, 94, 141n65, 156n76, 159n11
bodiment, 8, 18, 21–22, 30–31, 38, 42, 49, 55, 57–60, 69–71, 74, 76, 93, 103–4, 119, 120, 164n78; animality and, 121; ethic of, 6, 125; ethos of, 84, 91, 97, 117, 123; human, 165n88; live, 14, 36, 40, 83, 124, 130; lived, 45, 105, 149n67, 153n41
body, 4–11, 13–14, 16–17, 20–21, 23, 30, 34–38, 41, 44–47, 55–61, 63, 65, 69, 70–74, 76, 80, 82, 89, 93, 97–100, 110, 118–20, 136n9, 143nn87–88, 145n15, 147n34, 147n42, 150n75, 152n17, 153nn38–39, 153n41, 157n87, 161n37; animal, 101, 105, 170n66; biological, 157n84; live/living, 77, 143n79; phenomenology of, 22, 40, 107, 111
bodying, 47, 60, 126, 154n46

Buytendijk, Frederik, 21–22, 119, 143n86, 143n89

captivation, 46, 142n75, 145n13
Caputo, John, 1–2, 82, 136n1, 136n3, 161nn42–43, 173n36
carceral, the, 67, 97–101, 103, 107–11, 123, 127, 167n6
care, 7, 44, 51, 69, 73, 107, 127
carnal, the, 34, 41, 111, 130, 149n63; and the carceral, 99–100, 103, 109, 123, 167n6; dialectic of, 97
climaticity, 33–34, 41, 43, 58, 80, 120, 139n43
considerability, 4, 85, 91, 135n3, 159n13
conviviality, 34, 73, 76, 78, 84, 94, 96, 127; cross-species, 27, 31, 35, 41, 45, 100, 120; interspecific, 36, 43; somaesthetic, 79, 84, 91; somatic, 92; transpecific, 30, 93

daimon life, 11, 139n34, 139n36, 139n41, 140n45, 141n68, 173n28
Dasein, 7–11, 13–14, 138n24, 140n45
Daseinsanalyse, 7, 9, 12, 14, 118, 139n43
death, 9, 13, 15, 80, 115, 160n32, 161n40; awareness of, 129; confrontation with, 128; "death as mine," 8
Del Caro, Adrian, 155n61, 155n67, 156n71, 156n76
deprivation, 10, 46, 145n13, 164n68
Derrida, Jacques, 7, 9, 101, 133, 138n28

embodiment, 6, 8, 14, 22, 36, 38, 40, 42, 44, 64, 68, 69
environmental ethic of, 165n84; hypertextualized, 22
empathy, 23, 26, 27–79, 82, 119, 135n3, 137n10, 144n96, 160n27, 166n93, 166n96; faculty of, 24; kinesthetic, 164n71, 154n77; interpersonal, 81
Evernden, Neil, 45, 132, 146n28, 148n56, 150n78, 169n41, 174n43